Policies and Initiatives for the Internationalization of Higher Education

Fatoş Silman
Cyprus International University, Cyprus

Fahriye Altinay Aksal
Near East University, Cyprus

Zehra Altinay Gazi
Near East University, Cyprus

A volume in the Advances in
Higher Education and Professional
Development (AHEPD) Book Series

Published in the United States of America by
    IGI Global
    Information Science Reference (an imprint of IGI Global)
    701 E. Chocolate Avenue
    Hershey PA, USA 17033
    Tel: 717-533-8845
    Fax: 717-533-8661
    E-mail: cust@igi-global.com
    Web site: http://www.igi-global.com

Library of Congress Cataloging-in-Publication Data

Names: Silman, Fatos, 1971- editor. | Altinay Aksal, Fahriye, 1982- editor. |
    Altinay Gazi, Zehra, 1982- editor.
Title: Policies and initiatives for the internationalization of higher
    education / Fatos Silman, Fahriye Altinay Aksal, and Zehra Altinay Gazi,
    editors.
Description: Hershey, PA : Information Science Reference, 2018. | Includes
    bibliographical references.
Identifiers: LCCN 2017037445| ISBN 9781522552314 (hardcover) | ISBN
    9781522552321 (ebook)
Subjects: LCSH: Education, Higher--Developing countries. | Education and
    globalization--Developing countries.
Classification: LCC LC2610 .P65 2018 | DDC 378.009172/4--dc23 LC record available at https://
lccn.loc.gov/2017037445

This book is published in the IGI Global book series Advances in Higher Education and Professional Development (AHEPD) (ISSN: 2327-6983; eISSN: 2327-6991)

British Cataloguing in Publication Data
A Cataloguing in Publication record for this book is available from the British Library.

For electronic access to this publication, please contact: eresources@igi-global.com.

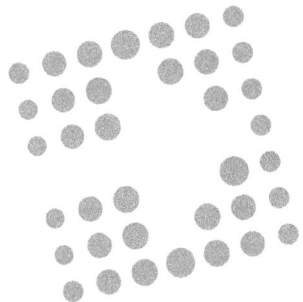

Advances in Higher Education and Professional Development (AHEPD) Book Series

ISSN:2327-6983
EISSN:2327-6991

Editor-in-Chief: Jared Keengwe, University of North Dakota, USA

MISSION

As world economies continue to shift and change in response to global financial situations, job markets have begun to demand a more highly-skilled workforce. In many industries a college degree is the minimum requirement and further educational development is expected to advance. With these current trends in mind, the **Advances in Higher Education & Professional Development (AHEPD) Book Series** provides an outlet for researchers and academics to publish their research in these areas and to distribute these works to practitioners and other researchers.

AHEPD encompasses all research dealing with higher education pedagogy, development, and curriculum design, as well as all areas of professional development, regardless of focus.

COVERAGE

- Adult Education
- Assessment in Higher Education
- Career Training
- Coaching and Mentoring
- Continuing Professional Development
- Governance in Higher Education
- Higher Education Policy
- Pedagogy of Teaching Higher Education
- Vocational Education

IGI Global is currently accepting manuscripts for publication within this series. To submit a proposal for a volume in this series, please contact our Acquisition Editors at Acquisitions@igi-global.com or visit: http://www.igi-global.com/publish/.

Titles in this Series

For a list of additional titles in this series, please visit:
https://www.igi-global.com/book-series/advances-higher-education-professional-development/73681

Handbook of Research on Media Literacy in Higher Education Environments
Jayne Cubbage (Bowie State University, USA)
Information Science Reference • ©2018 • 396pp • H/C (ISBN: 9781522540595) • US $255.00

Changing Urban Landscapes Through Public Higher Education
Anika Spratley Burtin (University of the District of Columbia, USA) Jeffery S. Fleming (University of the District of Columbia, USA) and Pamela Hampton-Garland (University of the District of Columbia, USA)
Information Science Reference • ©2018 • 301pp • H/C (ISBN: 9781522534549) • US $175.00

Preparing the Next Generation of Teachers for 21st Century Education
Siew Fun Tang (Curtin University, Malaysia) and Chee Leong Lim (Taylor's University, Malaysia)
Information Science Reference • ©2018 • 377pp • H/C (ISBN: 9781522540809) • US $210.00

Promoting Ethnic Diversity and Multiculturalism in Higher Education
Barbara Blummer (Center for Computing Sciences, USA) Jeffrey M. Kenton (Towson University, USA) and Michael Wiatrowski (Independent Researcher, USA)
Information Science Reference • ©2018 • 309pp • H/C (ISBN: 9781522540977) • US $185.00

Innovative Practices in Teacher Preparation and Graduate-Level Teacher Education Programs
Drew Polly (University of North Carolina - Charlotte, USA) Michael Putman (University of North Carolina - Charlotte, USA) Teresa M. Petty (University of North Carolina - Charlotte, USA) and Amy J. Good (University of North Carolina - Charlotte, USA)
Information Science Reference • ©2018 • 720pp • H/C (ISBN: 9781522530688) • US $275.00

Critical Assessment and Strategies for Increased Student Retention
Ruth Claire Black (Imperial College London, UK)
Information Science Reference • ©2018 • 352pp • H/C (ISBN: 9781522529989) • US $195.00

For an entire list of titles in this series, please visit:
https://www.igi-global.com/book-series/advances-higher-education-professional-development/73681

701 East Chocolate Avenue, Hershey, PA 17033, USA
Tel: 717-533-8845 x100 • Fax: 717-533-8661
E-Mail: cust@igi-global.com • www.igi-global.com

Editorial Advisory Board

Table of Contents

Detailed Table of Contents

Chapter 1

Şerife Gündüz, Near East University, Cyprus
Isam Fathi Laama, Near East University, Cyprus
Mirati Erdoğuş, Near East University, Cyprus

Libya, potentially with enormous landmass and environmental resources, has what it takes to spearhead the African continent and can equally stand as a sustainable nation. The authors have identified three broad areas that can electronically transform the government intentions into reality; these are an institutional framework, management, and public services for collaborative partners internally and externally, and infrastructural capacity building that will enhance government. This chapter has presented a theoretical concept for further research works that will help to reshape the e-government system which is an exemplary prototype of the procedures of obtaining the higher degree in tertiary institutions; thus, Libya must compete with the standards of other countries in university policies toward sustainable environmental practices. This is the higher aim of Libya state to acquire hi-tech skills as a fundamental step toward environmental issues prior to the implementation of e-learning systems and GIS aiming to control the investment of time, effort, and financial resources.

Chapter 2

Amna Hashim Hamdan Alzadjali, Near East University, Cyprus

This chapter studies the globalization of higher education in context of The Sultanate of Oman. It is a study on the understanding of internationalization of higher education which results in conclusions and recommendations on the enhancement of the future of internationalization of higher education in Oman. Internationalization of higher education is not new. In today's age of global knowledge and technology, an interconnected network and global awareness are increasingly viewed as major and sought-after assets. With the current labor market requiring graduates to have international, foreign language, and intercultural skills to be able to interact in a global setting, institutions such as World Trade Organization (WTO) and the General Agreement on Trade in Services (GATS) are placing more importance on internationalization. Complying with WTO and GATS agreements, Oman had to liberalize its HE, open the door for foreign universities to have campuses inside its borders, and encourage outbound and inflow of students.

Chapter 3

This chapter first describes UK HE from a systems theory perspective through reflection on the history of UK HE and the current system in relation to the criteria that are used to assess and audit universities. The current position of UK HE within the larger global HE system is then considered through analysis of the latest university rankings lists. Having identified the key elements of the current UK HE system and highlighted the centrality of international academic staff within that system, the rhetoric in the academic and political discourse and the printed media is then focused upon in order to highlight the potential impact of Brexit on how UK HE performs as an open system. A best case/worst case scenario narrative follows, resulting in the recommendation of fast action from the UK government to safeguard the retention and hiring of international faculty, a key element in the enviable current open system that is UK HE.

Chapter 4

In 1997, during the second ASEAN (Association of SouthEast Asian Nations) informal summit held in Kuala Lumpur, ASEAN Vision 2020 was adopted laying emphasis on integration of education and human capital development which was echoed in Hanoi Plan of Action (December 1997) and later on in Vientiane Action Programme (2004). During the first meeting of ASEAN Ministers of Education held at Singapore in 2006 the Cha-am Hua Declaration highlighted role of education in achieving enduring solidarity and unity among the nations and people of ASEAN.

Recently an ASEAN Socio-Cultural Community Blueprint 2025 was launched in 2016 recommending an innovative ASEAN approach to higher education with the purpose to promote greater people-to-people interaction and mobility within and outside ASEAN. This chapter discusses policies and practices for internationalization of higher education in South East Asia and how it is strengthening regional and global cooperation.

Chapter 5
    Umut Koldas, Near East University, Cyprus
    Mustafa Çıraklı, Near East University, Cyprus

Most of the challenges faced by the Palestinian higher education institutions (HEIs) towards internationalization stem from the problematic nature of bilateral relations of the Palestinian Authority (PA) in West Bank and Gaza Strip (WBGS) with Israel. Evaluating the geo-political, socio-economic, historical, and organizational barriers to internationalization of higher education in the WBGS, the chapter elaborates on the cumulative effects of the Israeli direct and indirect control over the WBGS on the development of universities, the impact of geo-political restraints of being a conflict zone, and logistical restrictions imposed on the movement of academics, visitors, and academic materials. Various domestic challenges including the political and ideological differences within the PA, the quality of national-level governance, and planning in higher education and financing are also highlighted throughout. Referring to the catalysts and obstacles, the chapter concludes with a reflection on the future challenges and prospects facing the Palestinian HEIs in a dynamic yet challenging context.

Chapter 6
    Behcet Öznacar, Near East University, Cyprus
    Gokmen Dagli, University of Kyrenia, Cyprus & Near East University,
        Cyprus

internationalization plays a great role to foster the quality in education systems. In this respect, leadership and risk managements are essential factors to disseminate the quality in education. Therefore, this chapter encapsulates the essence of risk management and leadership in order to enlighten the merits of internationalization context. In addition to this, a detailed examination on risk management and leadership in a school becomes a model for further implications for the internationalization. Qualitative research was conducted to set the criteria on risk management and leadership within a school.

Chapter 7

Mehmet Altınay, Near East University, Cyprus
Belal Shneikat, University of Kyrenia, Cyprus

Internationalization has become one of the hotly debated issues in higher education institutions due its role in competitive advantage. Countries around the world encourage their universities to engage in competition and cooperation on the local and global level, and this can't be achieved without internationalization. This chapter is proposed to shed light on a unique case study: internationalization of higher education in North Cyprus, which is a politically unrecognized country. To achieve the aim of this chapter, a survey from International Association of Universities (IAU) was adapted to evaluate the internationalization in the four largest and oldest universities in North Cyprus.

Chapter 8

Aylin Göztaş, Ege University, Turkey
Emel Kuşku Özdemir, Ege University, Turkey
Fusun Topsümer, Ege University, Turkey

The current study, based on the quantitative research approach, is structured on the basic question of whether participation in exchange programs and foreign language variables affect attitudes towards intercultural communication sensitivity. The research, which was conducted with the participation of university students from seven different geographical regions and from different educational fields, provides findings that support the existence of a relation between the contact with a foreign culture and language. Learning about different cultures and learning a foreign language in interaction with the culture reinforce individuals' language skills and improve their awareness about different cultures. Furthermore, it is remarked that the participants who acquired a foreign language through participating in an international exchange program are more confident and responsible in their interactions compared to the other group.

Chapter 9

Ainur Seitbattalovna Kenebayeva, University of International Business, Kazakhstan

This chapter highlights the internationalization of the higher education system in the Republic of Kazakhstan. It briefly discusses Kazakh national initiatives to enhance the country's global economic competitiveness through modernization and capacity-building in the field of higher education and science. National experience on integration to the international educational space by the consecutive implementation of Bologna principles is reflected. The importance of the Bolashak presidential scholarship program is addressed as a strategy for human capital development. This chapter also underlines trends, tendencies, and issues of internationalization of higher education in globalization. Key aspects of internationalization considered through the prism of the Kazakhstani experience include academic mobility, accreditation, university rankings, and research and development (R&D).

Preface

INTRODUCTION

Internationalization process involves policies and initiatives practiced by institutions and individuals in order to compete with the influences of globalization (Henard, Diamond, & Roseveare, 2012). The borderless world created by globalization gives importance to the diversity of cultures within countries, communities and institutions (Hassi & Storti, 2012), and allows better understanding of individuals or groups within various communities.

Over the past 25 years, internationalization has emerged as an important issue of higher education. Since economic globalization transformed knowledge into a commodity, higher education institutions have been encouraged to internationalize the recruitment of faculty and students in order to secure recognition for knowledge production (Mitchell & Nielsen, 2012). In a wider perspective, internationalization involves academic mobility, international perspectives in learning and teaching processes, recruitment of international academic staff and students, and having international partnerships with other higher education institutions (Knight, 2012).

The Bologna Declaration, which was signed in 1999, created a system of comparable degrees, supported student mobility and promoted European dimension in higher education. European countries as part of the Bologna process are assumed to fulfil the Bologna objectives and qualifications (Silman, Gokcekus, & Isman, 2012). However, the higher institutions of some countries (developing countries), which are not part of the Bologna process, may have difficulties in implementing the processes of internationalization due to political, economic, historical, and organizational barriers.

The basic aim of this book is to discuss the current situation of the internationalization processes in the higher education institutions. The authors are also expected to discuss the barriers and problems their countries may have in this process due to the above-mentioned limitations. The book will provide readers with the opportunity to compare how far different countries have achieved the processes required for internationalization in higher education institutions. The book also sheds some light on the "best practices" of the developed countries for the policy makers and stakeholders.

The authors framed their discussion of internationalization in relevance to some organizational theories such as New Institutionalism, Systems Theory, Globalization theories. Researchers, academicians, policy makers, officials of governmental education departments, graduate and undergraduate students, and education stakeholders can benefit from the book.

ORGANIZATION OF THE BOOK

The book is organized into nine chapters. A brief description of each of the chapters follows:

Chapter 1 provides detailed framework on the role of environment and internalization for the higher education system. The authors of this chapter contend that environment factor plays a great role to manage the higher education.

Chapter 2 presents an analysis of issues and concerns in higher education of Oman. The author underlines the policies and initiatives for the internationalization process in Oman.

Chapter 3 identifies the system theory view in higher education. The chapters examines the system theory related to the view of Brexit Brain Drain in British Higher Education.

Chapter 4 reviews the role of internalization. The authors discusses the situation of Southeast Asia with regard to higher education and internalization.

Chapter 5 analyses prospects and challenges of internalization. The chapter gives a comprehensive look into the regional and national margins of globalization for the internalization of Palestinian Higher Education.

Chapter 6 reviews factors for the internalization in higher education. The authors argue that risk management and leadership are crucial for the internalization in higher education.

Chapter 7 reviews the importance of internalization for higher education institutions. The authors gives examples on the practice of North Cyprus.

Chapter 8 discusses intercultural communication sensitivity in higher education. The authors shed light on the effects of internalization for intercultural communication sensitivity in higher education.

Chapter 9 takes the consideration of initiatives in higher education. The aim of the chapter is to give insights on expectations and experiences of Kazakh Higher Education System.

REFERENCES

Hassi, A., & Storti, G. (2012). *Globalization and Culture: The Three H Scenarios*. Retrieved from https://www.intechopen.com/books/globalization-approaches-to-diversity/globalization-and-culture-the-three-h-scenarios

Henard, F., Diamond, L., & Roseveare, D. (2012). *Approachers to Internationalisation and their Implications for Strategic Management and Institutional Practice: A Guide for Higher Education Institutions*. OECD Higher Education Programme IMHE. Retrieved from http://www.oecd.org/education/imhe/Approaches%20to%20internationalisation%20-%20final%20-%20web.pdf

Knight, J. (2012). Student mobility and internationalization: Trends and tribulations. *Research in Comparative and International Education*, *7*(1), 20–33. doi:10.2304/rcie.2012.7.1.20

Mitchell, D. E., & Nielsen, S. Y. (2012). *Internationalization and Globalization in Higher Education*. Retrieved from http://cdn.intechopen.com/pdfs-wm/38270.pdf

Silman, F., Gokcekus, H., & İsman, A. (2012). A study on quality assurance activities in higher education in North Cyprus. *International Online Journal of Educational Sciences*, *4*(1), 31–38.

Acknowledgment

We would like to thank our parents, friends, and colleagues who shared their moral support with us. Without their support and assistance, this book could not have been possible.

Chapter 1
The Significance of International Higher Education in Environmental Issues

Şerife Gündüz
Near East University, Cyprus

Isam Fathi Laama
Near East University, Cyprus

Mirati Erdoğuş
Near East University, Cyprus

ABSTRACT

Libya, potentially with enormous landmass and environmental resources, has what it takes to spearhead the African continent and can equally stand as a sustainable nation. The authors have identified three broad areas that can electronically transform the government intentions into reality; these are an institutional framework, management, and public services for collaborative partners internally and externally, and infrastructural capacity building that will enhance government. This chapter has presented a theoretical concept for further research works that will help to reshape the e-government system which is an exemplary prototype of the procedures of obtaining the higher degree in tertiary institutions; thus, Libya must compete with the standards of other countries in university policies toward sustainable environmental practices. This is the higher aim of Libya state to acquire hi-tech skills as a fundamental step toward environmental issues prior to the implementation of e-learning systems and GIS aiming to control the investment of time, effort, and financial resources.

DOI: 10.4018/978-1-5225-5231-4.ch001

INTRODUCTION

Libya as a country with other African countries is experiencing serious environmental transformation due to negative impacts of human activities that are prevailing much on its natural endowments. The environmental endowments have been degraded extensively and now being faced with severe environmental consequences such as climate change, desert encroachment, drought, erosion and flood. All these constituted the major environmental problems affecting Libya because of diverse forms of pollution from the petroleum industry, deforestation, overgrazing, poor system of farming, high rate of urbanization and inefficient water management system. Although, the global communities are equally being faced with ecological problems that are rapidly eating up our environmental endowments; in fact, the entire earth is diminishing with consistent loss of natural resources and without adequate plan for the utilization of renewable resources (Annan, 2000).

The major remedy to these aforementioned problems facing our world is the learning institutions that offer information and broaden the knowledge of people in every part of human endeavors with great opportunity for talents acquisition and training to further the advancement of the state as people develop communally, intellectually, materially, economically, technologically, politically and scientifically. Learning institutions are very crucial and fundamental in our present contemporary world because it gives room for communal growth, material enrichment, financial and governmental progress that eventually accelerates meaningful development (Jadhav et al., 2014). Tertiary institution of have the potential and the know-how to offer the right solutions to every challenge threatening the state and its immediate surrounding especially on natural resources and renewable advancement that may be critical on finance, commerce, civil related matters and nature endangering problems (Calder & Clugston, 2003). Actually, education have been conforming to several problems that are affecting many nations in the world, but it is pertinent at this age that academic communities should design its curriculum and activities toward ecological protection and renewability (Redman, 2013). This kind of learning enhance significantly to the developing and broadening of youth generation mental attitudes toward renewable advancement that provide remedies to every ecological problem that are confronting our global community (Toor, 2003).

In recent time, Libyan E- Government have been reinforcing all their efforts toward management restructuring, environmental evaluation and workable environmental practices by creating study institution according world environmental protection protocols and institutionalizing Geographical Information System that can be easily adopted by Libyan society. All these operations have been staged and implemented successfully with the sole objective of affiliating with foreign partners on environmental matters such as the United Nations Environmental Programme (UNEP) and United Nations Development Programme (UNDP); it was a collective collaboration that has Libyan society toward sustainable environmental initiatives and practices (Cassar & Bruch, 2003).

These initiatives also deal with the development of state program for preservation of ecosystem and bio-diversities, development of state workable programs or schemes in conjunction with corporate companies that connect nationwide with both grass root communities and global communities on environmental matters

Libyan legislative body designs the rules and regulations pertaining to l protection of natural resources that are provided by local communities and some are sourced from global communities. These regulations cover additionally environmental matters and institutions that include National Center for Standardization which works dwell on the verification and preparation exercises and giving testing and examination administrations to industry and business, and evaluation of natural resources standard.

The initiators have concurred on SWOT investigation and work on the evaluation of diverse indicators formerly to implement e-teaching scheme in various organizations that work along and promote environmental values and initiatives (Rimmon-Kenan, 2014)

As earlier asserted education is crucial for the training of the working forces of any given state so as to advance socially, economically, technologically and materially enriched and as well creating positive attitudes toward natural endowments. It indeed creates a collective responsible society as enshrined in the Constitutional Declaration of the year 1969 that education is a right and a duty for all Libyan citizens, it be freed and compulsory until the end of the preparatory level, while it is the nation responsibility constructing and organizing schools, institutes, universities and educational and cultural foundation (Singh, 2010)

THE SIGNIFICANCE OF HIGHER EDUCATION IN ENVIRONMENTAL ISSUES

Most importantly, higher institutions are the major forces behind enlightenment, exposure, searching of facts and accumulation of understanding through hi-tech devices and empirical facts finding for the larger societies that include the government, private sector, non-governmental institutions and as well as other research institution. It also trains young and older generations through all stages of academic institutions from primary institutions to various categories of tertiary institutions. In fact, tertiary institutions offer many courses in the field of environmental studies and sciences that are often related to diverse fields of science, social sciences, education and educational sciences like Biological sciences, Geography, education and environment and environmental education respectively. For instance, ecological renewability studies is gaining more popularity and relevance in our modern society because of the unrelenting moves and contributions of the tertiary toward the development of ecological and renewable studies; considering these considerations, all tertiary institution should then champion the campaign for the support and promotion for nature renewability in learning schemes, empirical study and public awareness (Beringer, 2006).

However, different categories of tertiary institutions are very dynamic and peculiar in the way they render educational services based on their customs, principles, practices and physical location considering the world at large. Tertiary institutions closely relate with the immediate environment, people, communities, government and other socio-economic components of the environment; thus, using the understanding of their immediate environment coupled with past research works to propound solutions to environmental challenges through interchanging or sharing of knowledge at various levels of our society. These enhanced regional friendliness and cooperation that help to keep our environment safe and secured; because of the privilege they have in identifying challenges and initiating the necessary means to work-out the solutions (Erdogan & Usak, 2009).

Ministry of higher education Must be actively instrumental by making strong decisions to establish activities and mead of research units thus, the establishment of international conferences to bringing some expertise from outside to joining with internal expertise to establishment of workshops for the swap new information at local and international levels as participation in the interchange of information through scientific messages in all disciplines. That will be a considerable outcome of establishing a valid base in this form we can reach to solution of environmental problems

Therefore, tertiary institution of learning should be ready to create and promote environmental viability as follows:

- Through learning and impartation schemes or curriculums. The academic working scheme should cover vital knowledge concerning ecological matters; learners must be familiar with all the knowledge and facts covering nature; the academic working schemes must be designed in such a way that will encourage the learners to be deeply involve, concern, knowledgeable, well informed and eager to find solutions to every ecological challenge affecting their domain (Yerkes & Haras, 1997).

- Through the promotion of empirical study by scholars in various areas of environmental studies and education. Empirical study is a very strong component of tertiary institution regardless of their programs, customs, vision and location. This aspect seems to be the utmost effective and efficient tools commonly used to advance ecological research so as to promote nature well-being, protection of exhaustible natural endowments and preservation of inexhaustible natural possessions for the value of human and the entire global communities (Ayeni, 2010).
- Through extended activities both within and outside of academic environment for collaboration, raising of human resources and public awareness initiatives that will provide practical way out and as well support learning capability of learners in our tertiary institutions (Kerr, 2001). These initiatives will impact the people in the society positively; creation of viable financial system, increment in capital per head and output per working force, total enrichment of the society in all works of life and learners will have the opportunity to acquire more skills toward viable growth of their states (Uhawenimana, 2012).

PROBLEMS CONFRONTING E- GOVERNMENT OPERATIONS IN LIBYA

It is of necessity and quite crucial especially in this modern age to establish E-Learning functioning system prior to the introduction of such scheme to users; nation like Libya where the desire for open legislature are high, state management of such initiative should be well structured to be able to achieve the expectations of the people and making use of such E-Learning idea for practical actualization is a strong aim that must be accomplished. State management on E-Learning should also be ready to reform the entire old which solely depend on the efficiency of the management system; management can achieve these by acquiring more information that are multi-functional to various theme search by users. Technocrats that are managing E-Learning must be flexible and opened to wide range of knowledge that are adaptable to any change of packages regarding the soft-wares and users demand (Rhema, 2013).

ASSESSMENT OF LIBYAN E-GOVERNMENT ACCORDING TO THE SWOT

Libyan E-Government system displayed standard or strength, weaknesses, advantages and threats (SWOTS-see details in Figure 1, 2 and 3) based on the evaluation of civil environment, capital constraints and government technological capability according to its human resources and physical facilities, government policies, societal rules and regulations, managerial know-how, system of government, capital, global prevailing matters, society safety, working conditions, income level, nature of information technology facilities, city structure, literacy level and existing facilities for evaluation (Rhema, 2013).

MATTERS AND TECHNIQUES RELATED TO ENVIRONMENTAL MANAGEMENT SYSTEM ANALYSIS IN LIBYA

Administration of Radioactive Waste in Libya

From the inception of crude oil inspection and discovery in the early 1950s till date, the state of Libya has been managing radioactive bases; Libya has more than one hundred and twenty-five bases of radioactive administrative centers nationwide in petroleum sector and research institutions. Libya acquired more nuclear facilities for the generation of 10 megawatt of electric power when Tajura Nuclear Institute was established in the year 1983. Radioactive elements are highly generated in Libya due to the activities of the petroleum companies; because of the safety of the environment and human health concern, rigorous research has been carried on the environmental implications of the emission of radioactive substances through efficient management institutional structure like the establishment of Libyan National Strategy for Radioactive Waste Materials using the concept of SWOT (see details in Figure 1, 2 and 3) in form of standard, weaknesses, opportunities and threats to evaluate the environmental impacts of radioactive elements (Elghawi & Shames, 2016).

Challenges and Opportunities

There are several challenges facing the management of waste materials from petroleum industry and radioactive power generation in Libya – which include capital constraints and poor management system due to lack of skilled personnel, technological know-how and require physical facilities (Karekezi et al., 2003)

MANAGEMENT STRUCTURE

This involves establishment of legally constituted management structure with the main function of securing human health, environmental safety, safety of all management centers and securing efficient coordination that will protect the entire Libya state from any pending dangers (Landesman, 2005).

GLOBAL AGREEMENTS AND PROTOCOLS

- The management framework and state regulations of Libyan nation on environmental matters are established according to the global agreements and protocols (International Atomic Energy Agency, 2005).
- Agreement on physical observation and protection of nuclear substances.
- Agreement on nuclear safety and environmental health.
- Agreement on quantity and capacity of nuclear enrichment.
- Agreement on immediate support and rescue in case of accidental mishap which accorded by Basel tradition and London Agreement in the counteractive action of water pollution.

Figure 1. The Procedure of SWOT and Mode of Operation
The Procedure and Operation of SWOT. (Riston, 2008)

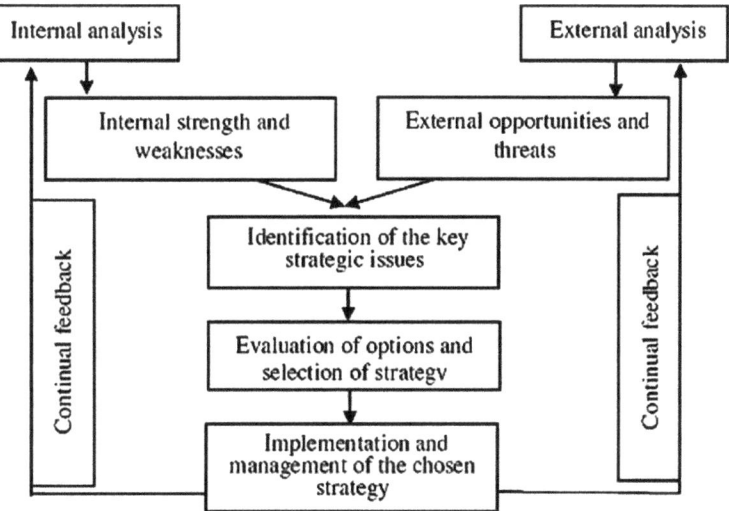

The state regulations that coordinate nuclear enrichment and usage are well stated in the Libyan national rules of: Act No. 2, 1982, with sole aim of controlling nuclear enrichment and prevention threat effects.

- The rules identified the conditions and methods for nuclear production and distribution for domestic and industrial and military purposes. It emphasizes the safety and protection of nuclear substances.
- The rules also emphasize on the need and techniques for the movement of unsecure nuclear substance on state main roads.
- Thus, dangerous nuclear substances are categorized into 8 according to the global agreements and protocols.
- The rules and regulations must also acknowledge the need and techniques for the protection of the environment from nuclear substances (Elghawi & Shames, 2016).

CONCLUSION

The state of Libya has been perceived and positioned to have what it takes with the enormous land and natural resources to direct all the African nations toward environmental sustainability through the 3 exemplary areas initiated to manage environmental system in Libya; these include management framework, management and opportunity for managerial partners, transparent and governmental supports for utmost environmental performance

This study revealed how E-Government could be redesigned in similitude upper academic grade – which implies that Libya ought to struggle with the rules and regulations of many countries according to the processes being observed in an educational system. The aim is to transform Libya into a teachable state in which communication technology is regarded as a valuable tool that can be used to address all ecological challenges using E-Learning structures, Geographic Information System to manage time in space, physical facilities, human and financial resources.

Lastly, to foster empirical research works with focus on major ecological challenges particularly on toxic substances while considering the management strength, weaknesses, opportunities and possible threats; all these be properly evaluated and compared at the local, state, national, regional and continental levels with the regards to the rules and regulations safeguarding the environmental resources and human health (El Fadel et al., 2013).

Table 1. Evaluation of the analysis of environmental management system in Libya

Challenges	Strength	Weakness
	1. The proliferation of digital technology. 2. The need to eliminate the administrative corruption aspects. 3. Libya has a strategic geographical location in Africa. 4. Available modern programmers and efficient management structures. 5. Treatment radioactive material that's affect to natural.	1. Lack of technological support and maintenance for the Lab tools and computers. 2. Mismanagement and corruption. 3. Post-war chaos that pervades all sectors of Libyan society. 4. Lack of awareness training courses will thus affect negative consequences on our communities. 5. Lack of technological support.
Opportunities 1. Create new business strategies to attract communities. 2. Gradual change of culture including more acceptances to of training systems. 3. Geographical position of Libya in Africa plays the successful strategic and necessary need of system of waste management.	**Opportunities:Strength Strategies** 1. Raise awareness of the major environmental challenges facing Libya through a national awareness campaign for Preserving Our Natural Environment. 2. Establish strict rules pertaining to pollution and strengthen enforcement mechanisms. 3. Enact a carbon tax to help curb carbon emissions to the atmosphere and protect the environment.	**Opportunities:Weakness Strategies** 1. Emergency construction waste management. 2. Emergency planning for disaster waste: a proposal based on the experience of the some countries.

Table 2. Evaluation of the environmental of the analysis of the environmental system in Libya

THREATS	THREAT-STRENGTH STRATEGIES	THREAT-WEAKNESS STRATEGIES
	1. Using of digital technology, it will affect to management structure in waste management and driving to strengths. In addition to that, the benefit of strategic geographical location to sort out the wastes and disposal it into saves area.	1. In this case for minimizing weaknesses and avoid threat in our opinion producing the new idea to the improvement of management and reduce Post-war chaos that pervades all sectors of Libyan society.
1. Lack of support from the government.		2. Furthermore, increasing awareness training courses will be affected benefit consequences to facing our communities. For that reason, focusing on technology support it will be helps to reduce the problems and the weaknesses in our community.
2. Numerous barriers related to collaborative learning processes stages.		
3. Increased migration of skills and intelligent people from Libya.		
4. Incoherent government policies to structure environmental legislation.		

REFERENCES

Annan, K. (2000). Secretary-general salutes international workshop on human security in Mongolia. *Two-Day Session in Ulaanbaatar*, 8-10.

Ayeni, M. A. (2010). Higher Education Research and Environmental Development. *European Journal of Educational Studies*, 2(3), 211–216.

Beringer, A. (2006). Campus sustainability audit research in Atlantic Canada: Pioneering the campus sustainability assessment framework. *International Journal of Sustainability in Higher Education*, 7(4), 437–455. doi:10.1108/14676370610702235

Calder, W., & Clugston, R. M. (2003). Progress toward sustainability in higher education. *Environmental Law Reporter News and Analysis*, 33(1), 10003–10022.

Cassar, A. Z., & Bruch, C. E. (2003). Transboundary environmental impact assessment in international watercourse management. *NYU Envtl. LJ*, 12, 169.

El Fadel, M., Rachid, G., El-Samra, R., Boutros, G. B., & Hashisho, J. (2013). Knowledge management mapping and gap analysis in renewable energy: Towards a sustainable framework in developing countries. *Renewable & Sustainable Energy Reviews*, 20, 576–584. doi:10.1016/j.rser.2012.11.071

Elghawi, U., & Shames, H. (2016). Management of Radioactive Waste in Libya: Case Study. *Journal of Hazardous, Toxic and Radioactive Waste*, 20(3), 04016003. doi:10.1061/(ASCE)HZ.2153-5515.0000314

Erdogan, M., & Usak, M. (2009). Curricular and extra-curricular activities to develop the environmental awareness of young students: A case from Turkey. *Educational Sciences. Odgojne Znanosti*, 11(1).

International Atomic Energy Agency. (2005). *INFCIRC/640: Multilateral Approaches to the Nuclear Fuel Cycle*. Vienna: International Atomic Energy Agency.

Jadhav, A. S., Jadhav, V. V., & Raut, P. D. (2014). Role of Higher Education Institutions in Environmental Conservation and Sustainable Development: A case study of Shivaji University, Maharashtra, India. *Journal of Environment and Earth Science*.

Karekezi, S., Kithyoma, W., & Initiative, E. (2003, June). Renewable energy development. In Workshop on African Energy Experts on Operationalizing the NEPAD Energy Initiative (pp. 2-4). Academic Press.

Kerr, C. (2001). *The uses of the university*. Harvard University Press.

Landesman, L. Y. (2005). *Public health management of disasters: the practice guide*. American public health association.

Redman, E. (2013). Advancing Educational Pedagogy for Sustainability: Developing and Implementing Programs to Transform Behaviors. *International Journal of Environmental and Science Education*, 8(1), 1–34.

Rhema, A. (2013). *An analysis of experiences and perceptions of technology-based learning in higher education institutions in Libya: informing the advancement of e-learning* (Doctoral dissertation). Victoria University.

Rimmon-Kenan, S. (2014). *Discourse in Psychoanalysis and Literature (Routledge Revivals)*. Routledge.

Singh, J. P. (2010). *United Nations Educational, Scientific, and Cultural Organization (UNESCO): creating norms for a complex world*. Routledge.

Toor, W. (2003). The Road Less Traveled: Sustainable Transportation for Campuses. *Planning for Higher Education*, 31(3), 131–141.

Uhawenimana, T. C. (2012, August 26). Higher education needs to engage in outreach-based research. *University World News*.

Yerkes, R., & Haras, K. (1997). *Outdoor education and environmental responsibility. Clearinghouse on Rural Education and Small Schools*. Appalachia Educational Laboratory.

Chapter 2
Policies and Initiatives for the Internationalization of Higher Education in Oman

Amna Hashim Hamdan Alzadjali
Near East University, Cyprus

ABSTRACT

This chapter studies the globalization of higher education in context of The Sultanate of Oman. It is a study on the understanding of internationalization of higher education which results in conclusions and recommendations on the enhancement of the future of internationalization of higher education in Oman. Internationalization of higher education is not new. In today's age of global knowledge and technology, an interconnected network and global awareness are increasingly viewed as major and sought-after assets. With the current labor market requiring graduates to have international, foreign language, and intercultural skills to be able to interact in a global setting, institutions such as World Trade Organization (WTO) and the General Agreement on Trade in Services (GATS) are placing more importance on internationalization. Complying with WTO and GATS agreements, Oman had to liberalize its HE, open the door for foreign universities to have campuses inside its borders, and encourage outbound and inflow of students.

DOI: 10.4018/978-1-5225-5231-4.ch002

INTRODUCTION

Globalization, a key reality in the 21st century, has already profoundly influenced higher education. (...) We define globalization as the reality shaped by an increasingly integrated world economy, new information and communications technology, the emergence of an international knowledge network, the role of the English language, and other forces beyond the control of academic institutions (...). Internationalization is defined as the variety of policies and programs that universities and governments implement to respond to globalization. (Altbach, Reisberg & Rumbley 2009, 7).

No higher education (HE) system across the world nowadays is not experiencing some form of what is called 'internationalisation'. Oman Higher Education adopted an international dimension to demarcate a position in the global arena. Decision-makers generated policies and executives inculcated procedures and inspired initiatives.

BACKGROUND OF HIGHER EDUCATION IN OMAN

Prior to 1970, there was no formal Higher Education in Oman; it was the stage of establishment of the schooling system. Public colleges (with an emphasis on vocational education and training, particularly in teaching and health) and Sultan Qaboos University were established around 1970s-1980s. First HE experience launched in 1985 with education institutes that produced teachers for schools. HE system was intended to serve the needs of Oman socio-economic development by preparing Omani youth with appropriate knowledge and skills. Sultan Qaboos University, the only state university, was founded in 1986. This university started with five colleges (Education, Engineering, Science, Medicine, and Agriculture) and 500 students. (11)

In the 1990s-present foreign programs were imported and delivered in through private HEPs (colleges and universities). This was an attempt to rapidly grow the sector in response to an identified need. A comprehensive higher education system launched in the new phase to bring about a more dynamic and ever-growing educational system. Oman has developed an independent system of higher education consisting of 62 HEIs and providing post-secondary diploma or degree programmes. Out of 62 HEIs, two-third is public institutions, operating through various ministries and agencies. (10)

According to OAAA, Omani HEIs are classified into three kinds of institutions which are Universities, University Colleges and Colleges of HE.

Oman started to import HE programs from the West. Currently, the HE system is undergoing a phase of "establishment of a comprehensive system of quality assurance and quality enhancement" (Carroll & Palermo, 2006, para. 9)

GLOBALISATION / INTERNATIONALISATION AND OMANI HE

The education systems around the globe have been affected by globalisation processes. Omani system of education - including HE- is no exception and obviously has been reformed to meet the challenges of globalization (Al'Abri, 2011).

Oman HE system is keeping track of current global trends where education systems are linked across the globe. To go contemporary Oman HE is using modern theories. Modern theories are based on the concept that the organization or institution is an adaptive system which has to suit and adjust to changes in its environment. To run its HE business, Oman had to meet the demands of Higher Education Systems around the globe.

System approach includes the socio-technical approach, the contingency or situational approach, etc…to mention a few. System approach is based on the fact that the organization or institution has a system that has to adapt to the dynamics of its environment for the sake to be effective. (Hicks & Gullet, 1975).

This is supported by Hicks and Gullet (1975) who say that an organization is defined as a designed and structured process in which individuals interact for goals and objectives. This system utilizes the contributions of several disciplines in solving problems. On Bertalanffy (1951) made a contribution by suggesting a component of general systems theory which is accepted as a basic premise of modern theory. System theory looks at an organization not as an entity by itself but as a component of other world systems (sub system). No organization operating by its own without connections with other organizations would be considered as effective and successful in running its business. Interconnectedness is a suitable recipe for an organization to achieve its intended goals and objectives. A system can be perceived as composed of some components, functions and processes (Albrecht, 1983).

There are variety of systems that are connected together in order to make other systems/ organizations work well…e.g. …Omani as a country does not live in isolation of other countries and as such educational policies of Omani should go hand in hand with what is happening in other countries in terms of systems theories.

Omani National Education policies are framed by new policy agents (international organizations) such as the United Nations Educational Scientific, and Cultural Organization (UNESCO), the World Bank, the United Nations Children's Fund (UNICEF).

Globalised education policy discourses have also appeared in the Omani education system and in policy rationales such as: life-long learning, knowledge economy, technology, and ESL.

INITIATIVES

Oman began its membership in the World Trade Organization (WTO) in 2000 and has worked hard to make certain commitments to HE that are proposed and prescribed by the WTO. (Al Harthy, 2011; Al Shemli, 2009; Donn & Al Manthri, 2010; Brandenburg, 2012).

The current practice of private higher education in Oman represents the model of affiliation or/and cooperation with foreign universities. (Al Harthy, 2011).

Oman is also a member of the General Agreement on Trade in Services (GATS). Under GATS, Oman has to liberalise its HE. (Brandenburg, 2012).

With liberalization, Oman is committed to opening the door for foreign universities to have campuses inside its borders, running alongside and competing with local institutions. Indeed, this will help to attract many foreign institutions to invest in the Omani HE system, offering further access, boosting participation, creating new programs and developing the infrastructure of the system. However, there are challenges resulting from these developments. This is globalisation bringing positive as well as negative effects (Brandenburg 2012).

The development of Human Resources and upgrading the skills of Omani nationals – as stated in the Human Development Report of 2003 by the Ministry of National Economy, contributes in keeping in touch with technological changes and meeting the demands of a knowledge-based economy and of increasing globalisation which is considered as a policy area of highest importance in Oman's developmental planning. (MONE, 2005, p. 19).

Hence, entering the global knowledge-economy requires fully skilled graduates who can compete in the global economy. Indeed, such demand for qualified Omani human resource creates pressure on HEIs.

The mission of the Omani HE system is to generate new policies and strategies that will help in supplying the labour market with the skilled graduates. According to Al Shmeli (2009), new programs and specializations need to be offered and standards must be increased to match the needs of the global knowledge economy.

HEIs have taken some steps toward achieving the production of qualified human resources. Baporikar and Shah (2012) mention some strategies such as,

- Imported curricula of western countries.
- Recruitment of native English teachers.
- Recruitment of qualified and experience faculty from all over the word in various disciplines.
- Provision of excellent infrastructure facilities to the students.
- Arrangements of one or two-year foundation courses by each HEI including English language, mathematics and IT to build students basis for advanced curricula at university level.

Globalisation and internationalisation has impacted the Omani HE system, provoking policy pressures from trade liberalisation and circulating certain policy discourses as shown in the table below:

HE POLICY DOMAINS AND SOURCES (cf: Khalaf Al'Abri, 2015)

Foreign Scholarships

Foreign scholarships refer to sending Omani students to study abroad for undergraduate and postgraduate studies and receive foreign students in Omani HE institutions. This enables the movement of Omani students to other countries to gain knowledge and experience through studying for a university degree. It is considered as a 'brain gain' investment. It is considered more rewarding and advantageous to have Omani academics study abroad in the best world universities. Those academics bring new global trends, ideas and experiences of international HEIs to Omani HEIs. It is argued that with many academics trained abroad, Omani HEIs are guaranteed to have diverse expertise. This is a capacity building exercise for the nation.

Affiliation

Academic affiliations between Omani HEIs and foreign universities is a significant impact of the interaction between the Omani and regional/global contexts with regard to HE policy. The Omani affiliation experience is a type of cross-border HE. Providing its background, affiliation as a policy in the Omani HE system

Table 1.

The uses of the term 'policy'	Explanation
Policy as a label for a field of activity	The usage here describes policy as fields of governmental activity and involvement. To illustrate, 'education policy' is considered a label for the government activity in regards to the field of education.
Policy as an expression of general purpose or a desired state of affairs	To indicate the intended purposes of a government in a specific field, as well as to describe the attained state of affairs following policy implementation. This might be seen as meta-policy.
Policy as a specific proposal	To refer to the specific actions in a policy field as opposed to general purposes, for example the introduction of fees on Australian universities.
Policy as a decision of government	Policy is here used to describe particular governmental decisions; here policy and decisions are synonyms.
Policy as a formal authorization	A policy by a government on a certain issue is often referenced in an Act of Parliament or statutory instrument which gives permission for such activity to be undertaken by the government. Authority carries the connotation of legitimacy.
Policy as a program	Policy is expressed here as a program applied by the government. Therefore, it is a specific activity that involves a particular package of regulations, resources and organizations.
Policy as output	To indicate what government really offers or achieves as opposed to its promises through legislation. Outputs mean the activities of governments at the point of delivery. These might not lead to the desired outcomes.
Policy as outcome	Policy can also be seen as what is actually achieved.
Policy as a theory or model	This suggests that policies engage some presuppositions regarding what governments can do and what the results of their actions are.
Policy as a process	Policy as a process refers to a series of steps in the policy cycle (e.g., development, implementation, evaluation).

started with the introduction of the private HEIs, pushing all private universities and colleges in Oman to be affiliated to an international HEI as a requirement for establishment and licensing.

With such affiliation policies, Oman Government has aimed to expand the HE system, but also to ensure quality, supported by imported programs and curricula from well-recognized international HEIs.

"The international affiliation policy in the Omani HE system is intended to work as a quality assurance mechanism". (Trevor-Roper, Razvi & Goodliffe, 2013).

"Links with foreign academic institutions were imposed by the government to ensure quality and to safeguard the interests of students and parents against low-quality programmes of education and unrecognized degrees and qualifications" (Wilkinson & Al Hajry, 2007 p.154).

Cooperation

It consists of creating a culture of collaboration and teamwork between HE policy makers as ministers, undersecretaries, HEIs rectors. Policy makers attend cooperation meetings and decide on policy, but these policies are not necessarily enforced in the Omani HE system. These cooperation meetings do not directly frame national Omani HE policy.

Policy Learning and Copying

HE policies take some account of what is happening in other states, Oman, for instance, and GCC countries have developed similar HE policies by learning and copying from each other. This is a clear example of convergence of HE policies, strategies and reforms in the GCC states, where policies are transferred from one state to another.

There is a significant degree of HE policy convergence in the GCC region 'driven' by globalisation. Examples of such policy learning and copying are massification of access, privatization of HE, creating accreditation and affiliation policies, and focusing on quality.

Competition

There is no doubt that countries in one region are most likely to have competitive relationships in various areas and fields. one of the impacts of the Gulf region on the Omani HE system was the heavy competition between the members trying to be more competitive and appealing by importing contemporary global reforms and policies.

The impact of this competition comes in various forms, such as efforts to improve the quality of HE, introducing international programs and HEIs, providing the best salary packages (mobility of staff) and attaining the best global ranking in the region.

Table 2. Omani HEIs with their international affiliates

Omani HEIs	Foreign HEI affiliate/ country	Medium of instruction
German University of Technology in Oman	RWTH Aachen University/ Germany	English
Sohar University	The University of Queensland/ Australia	English and Arabic
Dhofar University	American University of Beirut/ Lebenon	English and Arabic
Arab Open University	Open University/ UK	English
AL'Sharqiyah University	Oklahoma State university, Texas Tech University/ USA	English
University of Buraimi	Vienna University of Technology, Campus University of Vienna, The IMC University of Applied Sciences Krems/ Austria; University of Bradford/ UK	English
Majan College	University of Glasgow, University of Bedfordshire, University of Leeds/ UK	English
Caledonian College of Engineering	Glasgow Caledonian University/ UK; University Vellore Institute of Technology/ India	English
Middle East College	Coventry University/ UK	English
Modern College of Business and Science	University of Missouri, St Louis, Franklin University/ USA	English
MAZOON College	Missouri University of Science and Technology/ USA	English
Al Zahra College	Al Ahliyya Amman University/ Jordan	English and Arabic
Waljat College	Birla Institute of Technology/ India	English
Oman Dental College	AB Shetty Memorial Institute of Dental Sciences/ India	English
Scientific College of Design	Lebanese American University/ Lebanon; Arab Community College/ Gordan	English and Arabic
Oman Medical College	The University of West Virginia/ USA	English
Oman College of Management and Technology	Yarmuk University/ Jordan	English
Muscat College	University of Stirling, The Scottish Qualification Authority/ UK	English
International College of Engineering and Management	University of Central Lancashire/ UK	English
Oman Tourism College	International Institute of Tourism and management, University of Applied Management Sciences Kerms/ Austria	English
International Maritime College Oman	The STC-Group Rotterdam/ Netherlands	English
Gulf College	Staffordshire University, Hull University/ UK	English
Al Bayan College	Purdue University Calumet/ USA	English
Al Buraimi College	California State University Northridge/ USA; Ain Shams University/ Egypt	English
Sur University College	Bond University/ Australia; Administration and Information Technology American University in Cairo/ Egypt	English

(Khalaf Al'Abri,2015).

Establishment of Branch Campuses

Policy makers provide the opportunity for foreign institutions to establish subsidiaries jointly with Omani providers, and delivery is entirely by the foreign university, leading to a degree from Oman. There is only one Omani HEI with that model, which is The Open Arab University- Oman Branch.

Double/Joint Degree

The policy consists of providing a program that permits Omani students to pursue a program jointly offered by institutions in two countries. The qualification(s) can be either a degree that is jointly awarded or two separate degrees awarded by each partner institution.

Twinning (Localised)

For the sake of internationalization, policy makers in Oman HE instituted a policy which a variation on the twinning model with the part delivered in Oman developed for the local context and validated by the affiliate with articulation to the foreign institution program; the degree is awarded by the affiliate.

Franchised Program

The policies consist of delivering learning programs which are designed by the foreign provider (franchiser) in Omani HEIs (franchisee). The Omani students receive the qualification of the franchiser institution.

International Accreditation

The policies in this context assuring quality in the Omani HE system and gain the national accreditation through Oman's own National Accreditation Authority (OAAA): Oman Academic Accreditation Authority and then proceed to international accreditation for the sake of internationalization.

INTERVIEWS AND OUTCOMES

To support the previous points of polices and initiatives I conducted some interviews in the Ministry of HE and Sultan Qaboos University.

Ministry of HE

- **Dr. Halima Al-Badwawi** the Assistant Director General for Academic Affairs said that there is a program named (The Cooperative Education and Cultural Omani program) this program aimed to provide scholarship for international students. Also she added there is an exchange students program among Omani students with other countries students. Addition to that, the Ministry of HE has the recruitment of international academic staff and academic mobility.
- **Mr.Waleed Al-Ateeqi** the Assistant Director General For Licenses and Education Services has added that there is an international partnerships with other higher educational institutions. i.e. (Sohar University has an international partnerships with The University of Queensland/ Australia).
- **Dr. Zaid Ahmed Zabanoot** the Director General of planning and Development said that Colleges of Applied Sciences are reviewing their programs according to international standards as a whole for international perspectives in learning and teaching processes. The whole programs review takes place each four years.

Sultan Qaboos University

- **Mr.Adel Al-Mahrooqi** Head of Service Centers and University Hospitals Affairs Section said that there is specific office in the University itself for reviewing the a academic program named (Academic program Review Office) in this office, the international perspectives in learning and teaching processes are done by an outstanding experts.

SULTAN QABOOS UNIVERSITY STATISTICS DASHBOARD

Some data about the number of inflowing international students, number of foreign faculty members, number of staff scholarships is shown in the Tables 3-15 (SQU, 2015-2016):

CONCLUSION

From the research made it was noted that Omani Higher Education Policies keep trends of the current educational issues. It was clear from the interviews that Oman HE is going globally. A number of activities carried out in Oman HE show that it is not operating in isolation but with accordance with other

Table 3.

أعداد طلبة المقبولين حسب الكلية ، النوع ، والبلد في العام الأكاديمي ٢٠١٥-٢٠١٦م

Number of students Admitted in respective College according to Country group and Gender in the Academic Year 2015-2016

Country Group	الاجمالي العام Grand Total			دول أخرى Other Countries			دول عربية Arab Countries			دول مجلس التعاون الخليجي GCC Countries			عُمان Oman			الدول
College / Gender	الجملة Total	اناث Female	ذكور Male	الجملة Total	اناث Female	ذكور Male	الجملة Total	اناث Female	ذكور Male	الجملة Total	اناث Female	ذكور Male	الجملة Total	اناث Female	ذكور Male	الكلية / النوع
Agricultural & Marine Sciences	216	185	31	1	1	-	2	2		1	1	-	212	181	31	العلوم الزراعية والبحرية
Arts & Social Sciences	643	398	245	4	3	1	2	1	1	-	-	-	637	394	243	الاداب والعلوم الإجتماعية
Economics & Political Science	587	306	281	9	5	4	2	1	1	1	1	-	575	299	276	الإقتصاد والعلوم السياسية
Education	633	410	223	2	-	2	2	2		1		1	628	408	220	التربية
Engineering	554	140	414	9	4	5	17	8	9	3	3	-	525	125	400	الهندسة
Law	231	112	119	-	-	-	2	2		-	-	-	229	110	119	الحقوق
Medicine & Health Sciences	160	105	55	-	-	-	2	2		3	2	1	155	101	54	الطب والعلوم الصحية
Nursing	115	88	27	-	-	-	-	-	-	-	-	-	115	88	27	التمريض
Science	535	367	168	9	6	3	14	9	5	1	1	-	511	351	160	العلوم
Grand Total	3674	2111	1563	34	19	15	43	27	16	10	8	2	3587	2057	1530	الاجمالي العام

Table 4.

أعداد طلبة البكالوريوس المقبولين حسب الكلية ، النوع ، والبلد في العام الأكاديمي ٢٠١٥-٢٠١٦م

Number of students Admitted (Bachelor) in respective College according to Country group and Gender in the Academic Year 2015-2016

Country Group	الاجمالي العام Grand Total			دول أخرى Other Countries			دول عربية Arab Countries			دول مجلس التعاون الخليجي GCC Countries			عُمان Oman			الدول
College / Gender	الجملة Total	اناث Female	ذكور Male	الجملة Total	اناث Female	ذكور Male	الجملة Total	اناث Female	ذكور Male	الجملة Total	اناث Female	ذكور Male	الجملة Total	اناث Female	ذكور Male	الكلية / النوع
Agricultural & Marine Sciences	192	166	26	-	-	-	1	1	-	1	1	-	190	164	26	العلوم الزراعية والبحرية
Arts & Social Sciences	557	357	200	1	1	-	2	1	1	-	-	-	554	355	199	الاداب والعلوم الإجتماعية
Economics & Political Science	523	265	258	2	-	2	2	1	1	1	1	-	518	263	255	الإقتصاد والعلوم السياسية
Education	407	236	171	2	-	2	-	-	-	-	-	-	405	236	169	التربية
Engineering	484	99	385	2	-	2	2	1	1	3	3	-	477	95	382	الهندسة
Law	194	93	101	-	-	-	1	1	-	-	-	-	193	92	101	الحقوق
Medicine & Health Sciences	150	95	55	-	-	-	-	-	-	3	2	1	147	93	54	الطب والعلوم الصحية
Nursing	114	88	26	-	-	-	-	-	-	-	-	-	114	88	26	التمريض
Science	459	310	149	2	1	1	9	5	4	-	-	-	448	304	144	العلوم
Grand Total	3080	1709	1371	9	2	7	17	10	7	8	7	1	3046	1690	1356	الاجمالي العام

22

Table 5.

أعداد طلبة الماجستير المقبولين حسب الكلية ، النوع ، والبلد في العام الأكاديمي ٢٠١٥-٢٠١٦م

Number of students Admitted (Masters) in respective College according to Country group and Gender in the Academic Year 2015-2016

Country Group College / Gender	الاجمالي العام Grand Total			دول أخرى Other Countries			دول عربية Arab Countries			دول مجلس التعاون الخليجي GCC Countries			عُمان Oman			الدول الكلية / النوع
	Total	Female	Male	Total	Female	Male	Total	Female	Male	Total	Female	Male	Total	Female	Male	
Agricultural & Marine Sciences	22	17	5	-	-	-	-	-	-	-	-	-	22	17	5	العلوم الزراعية والبحرية
Arts & Social Sciences	71	36	35	2	1	1	-	-	-	-	-	-	69	35	34	الاداب والعلوم الاجتماعية
Economics & Political Science	64	41	23	7	5	2	-	-	-	-	-	-	57	36	21	الاقتصاد والعلوم السياسية
Education	115	84	31	-	-	-	2	2	-	1	-	1	112	82	30	التربية
Engineering	61	38	23	4	2	2	11	7	4	-	-	-	46	29	17	الهندسة
Law	37	19	18	-	-	-	1	1	-	-	-	-	36	18	18	الحقوق
Medicine & Health Sciences	8	8	-	-	-	-	1	1	-	-	-	-	7	7	-	الطب والعلوم الصحية
Science	1	-	1	-	-	-	-	-	-	-	-	-	1	-	1	العلوم
Nursing	61	46	15	3	2	1	4	3	1	-	-	-	54	41	13	التمريض
Grand Total	440	289	151	16	10	6	19	14	5	1	-	1	404	265	139	الاجمالي العام

Table 6.

أعداد طلبة الدكتوراه المقبولين حسب الكلية ، النوع ، والبلد في العام الأكاديمي ٢٠١٥-٢٠١٦م

Number of students Admitted (Doctorates) in respective College according to Country and Gender in the Academic Year 2015-2016

Country College / Gender	الاجمالي العام Grand Total	مجموع غير العمانيين Total Non-Omani	أذربيجان Azerbaijan	روسيا Russia	كندا Canada	بنجلاديش Bangladesh	ايران Iran	السودان Sudan	الهند India	سوريا Syria	تونس Tunisia	الامارات Emirates	عُمان Oman	البلد الكلية / النوع
Agricultural & marine Sciences	2	2	-	-	-	1	-	-	-	1	-	-	-	العلوم الزراعية والبحرية
Male	-	-	-	-	-	-	-	-	-	-	-	-	-	ذكور
Female	2	2	-	-	-	1	-	-	-	1	-	-	-	اناث
Arts and Social Sciences	10	1	1	-	-	-	-	-	-	-	-	-	9	الاداب والعلوم الاجتماعية
Male	6	-	-	-	-	-	-	-	-	-	-	-	6	ذكور
Female	4	1	1	-	-	-	-	-	-	-	-	-	3	اناث
Education	4	-	-	-	-	-	-	-	-	-	-	-	4	التربية
Male	-	-	-	-	-	-	-	-	-	-	-	-	-	ذكور
Female	4	-	-	-	-	-	-	-	-	-	-	-	4	اناث
Engineering	9	7	-	-	1	-	-	3	2	-	1	-	2	الهندسة
Male	6	5	-	-	-	-	-	3	1	-	1	-	1	ذكور
Female	3	2	-	-	1	-	-	-	1	-	-	-	1	اناث
Medicine & Health Sciences	2	1	-	-	-	-	-	1	-	-	-	-	1	الطب والعلوم الصحية
Male	-	-	-	-	-	-	-	-	-	-	-	-	-	ذكور
Female	2	1	-	-	-	-	-	1	-	-	-	-	1	اناث
Science	15	6	-	1	-	-	1	1	2	-	-	1	9	العلوم
Male	4	1	-	-	-	-	-	-	1	-	-	-	3	ذكور
Female	10	5	-	1	-	-	1	1	1	-	-	1	6	اناث
Grand Total	42	17	1	1	1	1	1	5	4	1	1	1	25	الاجمالي العام
Male	16	6	-	-	-	-	-	3	2	-	1	-	10	ذكور
Female	26	11	1	1	1	1	1	2	2	1	-	1	15	اناث

Table 7.

أعداد طلبة البكالوريوس المقيدين حسب الكلية ، النوع ، والبلد في العام الأكاديمي ٢٠١٥-٢٠١٦م

Number of students Registered (Bachelor) in respective College according to Country group and Gender in the Academic Year 2015-2016

Country Group	الاجمالي العام Grand Total			دول أخرى Other Countries			دول عربية Arab Countries			دول مجلس التعاون الخليجي GCC Countries			عُمان Oman			الدولة
College / Gender	الجملة Total	اناث Female	ذكور Male	الجملة Total	اناث Female	ذكور Male	الجملة Total	اناث Female	ذكور Male	الجملة Total	اناث Female	ذكور Male	الجملة Total	اناث Female	ذكور Male	الكلية / النوع
Agricultural & Marine Sciences	1417	865	552	11	7	4	3	1	2	3	3	-	1400	854	546	العلوم الزراعية والبحرية
Arts & Social Sciences	3094	2032	1062	4	3	1	11	9	2	3	3	-	3076	2017	1059	الاداب والعلوم الإجتماعية
Economics & Political Science	2756	1440	1316	11	6	5	12	8	4	4	1	3	2729	1425	1304	الاقتصاد والعلوم السياسية
Education	2177	1374	803	6	3	3	5	3	2	2	1	1	2164	1367	797	التربية
Engineering	2788	681	2107	25	9	16	55	29	26	3	3	-	2705	640	2065	الهندسة
Law	1103	542	561	1	1	-	2	2	-	-	-	-	1100	539	561	الحقوق
Medicine & Health Sciences	1120	725	395	4	4	-	7	4	3	10	7	3	1099	710	389	الطب والعلوم الصحية
Nursing	496	370	126	-	-	-	-	-	-	-	-	-	496	370	126	التمريض
Science	2735	1554	1181	29	17	12	21	16	5	2	1	1	2683	1520	1163	العلوم
Grand Total	17686	9583	8103	91	50	41	116	72	44	27	19	8	17452	9442	8010	الاجمالي العام

Table 8.

أعداد طلبة الماجستير المقيدين حسب الكلية ، النوع ، والبلد في العام الأكاديمي ٢٠١٥-٢٠١٦م

Number of students Registered (Masters) in respective College according to Country group and Gender in the Academic Year 2015-2016

Country Group	الاجمالي العام Grand Total			دول أخرى Other Countries			دول عربية Arab Countries			دول مجلس التعاون الخليجي GCC Countries			عُمان Oman			الدولة
College / Gender	الجملة Total	اناث Female	ذكور Male	الجملة Total	اناث Female	ذكور Male	الجملة Total	اناث Female	ذكور Male	الجملة Total	اناث Female	ذكور Male	الجملة Total	اناث Female	ذكور Male	الكلية / النوع
Agricultural & Marine Sciences	58	40	18	4	-	4	-	-	-	-	-	-	54	40	14	العلوم الزراعية والبحرية
Arts & Social Sciences	194	126	68	3	2	1	1	1	-	2	2	-	188	121	67	الاداب والعلوم الإجتماعية
Economics & Political Science	158	96	62	5	3	2	2	1	1	-	-	-	151	92	59	الاقتصاد والعلوم السياسية
Education	374	253	121	1	1		5	3	2	1	-	1	367	249	118	التربية
Engineering	140	80	60	12	5	7	21	11	10	-	-	-	107	64	43	الهندسة
Law	115	59	56	1	1	-	1	1	-	-	-	-	113	57	56	الحقوق
Medicine & Health Sciences	21	17	4	2	2	-	1	-	1	1	-	1	17	15	2	الطب والعلوم الصحية
Nursing	1	-	1	-	-	-	-	-	-	-	-	-	1	-	1	التمريض
Science	198	142	56	7	3	4	5	4	1	-	-	-	186	135	51	العلوم
Grand Total	1259	813	446	35	17	18	36	21	15	4	2	2	1184	773	411	الاجمالي العام

Table 9.

أعداد طلبة الدكتوراه المقيدين حسب الكلية ، النوع ، والبلد في العام الأكاديمي ٢٠١٥-٢٠١٦م

Number of students Registered (Doctorates) in respective College according to Country and Gender in the Academic Year 2015-2016

College / Gender	Grand Total	Total Non-Omani	Sudan	Russia	Nepal	Canada	Azerbaijan	Sri Lanka	Pakistan	Myanmar	Nigeria	Jordon	Tunisia	Iran	Emirates	India	Egypt	Bangladesh	Oman
Agricultural & Marine Sciences	24	8	·	·	·	·	·	1	2	·	1	·	1	·	3	·	·	·	16
Male	8	1	·	·	·	·	·	·	·	·	1	·	·	·	·	·	·	·	7
Female	16	7	·	·	·	·	·	1	2	·	·	·	1	·	3	·	·	·	9
Arts and Social Sciences	46	2	·	·	·	·	1	·	·	·	·	·	·	·	·	·	·	·	44
Male	27	1	·	·	·	·	·	·	·	·	·	1	·	·	·	·	·	·	26
Female	19	1	·	·	·	1	·	·	·	·	·	·	·	·	·	·	·	·	18
Education	11	·	·	·	·	·	·	·	·	·	·	·	·	·	·	·	·	·	11
Male	2	·	·	·	·	·	·	·	·	·	·	·	·	·	·	·	·	·	2
Female	9	·	·	·	·	·	·	·	·	·	·	·	·	·	·	·	·	·	9
Engineering	21	14	3	·	1	1	·	·	1	·	3	·	1	2	·	2	·	·	7
Male	15	10	3	·	·	·	·	·	1	·	3	·	·	2	·	1	·	·	5
Female	6	4	·	·	1	1	·	·	·	·	·	·	1	·	·	1	·	·	2
Medicine & Health Sciences	15	5	3	·	·	·	·	·	·	·	·	·	·	·	·	2	·	·	10
Male	4	2	2	·	·	·	·	·	·	·	·	·	·	·	·	·	·	·	2
Female	11	3	1	·	·	·	·	·	·	·	·	·	·	·	·	2	·	·	8
Science	62	22	1	1	·	·	·	1	1	·	·	1	·	2	1	12	1	1	40
Male	19	9	·	·	·	·	·	·	·	·	·	1	·	1	·	5	1	1	10
Female	43	13	1	1	·	·	·	1	1	·	·	·	·	1	1	7	·	·	30
Grand Total	**179**	**51**	**7**	**1**	**1**	**1**	**1**	**1**	**4**	**1**	**3**	**3**	**1**	**5**	**1**	**19**	**1**	**1**	**128**
Male	75	23	5	·	·	·	·	·	1	·	3	3	·	3	·	6	1	1	52
Female	104	28	2	1	1	1	1	1	3	1	·	·	1	2	1	13	·	·	76

Table 10.

أعداد الطلبة الخريجين حسب الكلية ، النوع ، والبلد في العام ٢٠١٥م

Number of students Graduated from respective College according to Country group and Gender in 2015

College / Gender	Grand Total			Other Countries			Arab Countries			GCC Countries			Oman		
	Total	Female	Male	Total	Female	Male	Total	Female	Male	Total	Female	Male	Total	Female	Male
Agricultural & Marine Sciences	201	123	78	2	2		1	·	1	·	·	·	198	121	77
Arts & Social Sciences	502	362	140	·	·	·	·	·	·	1	1	·	501	361	140
Economics & Political Science	470	265	205	1	1		1	1	·	·	·	·	468	263	205
Education	531	282	249	1	·	1	1	·	1	·	·	·	529	282	247
Engineering	510	145	365	10	1	9	5	2	3	·	·	·	495	142	353
Law	147	59	88	·	·	·	·	·	·	1	1	·	146	58	88
Medicine & Health Sciences	153	109	44	1	1	·	2	2	·	1	1	·	149	105	44
Nursing	72	63	9	·	·	·	·	·	·	·	·	·	72	63	9
Science	443	277	166	1	1	·	3	3	·	·	·	·	439	273	166
Grand Total	**3029**	**1685**	**1344**	**16**	**6**	**10**	**13**	**8**	**5**	**3**	**3**	**·**	**2997**	**1668**	**1329**

Table 11.

أعداد موظفي الجامعة* حسب الفئة في ٣١ ديسمبر ٢٠١٥م

Number of Staff in the University * by Category as on December 31, 2015

Category	المجموع Total	وافــد Expatriate	عُماني Omani	الفئـة
Academic Staff **	985	522	463	أعضاء هيئة التدريس **
Teaching Staff (Language Centre)	224	174	50	أعضاء الهيئة التدريسية (مركز اللغات)
Technical Staff	715	82	633	أعضاء الهيئة الفنية
Administrative Staff	1279	127	1152	أعضاء الهيئة الإدارية
Support Staff	238	25	213	خدمات مساعدة
Grand Total	**3441**	**930**	**2511**	**الاجمالي العام**

* Excludes Hospital Staff   * لا يشمل موظفي لمستشفى الجامعي

** Includes Ph D, Master and Bachelor holders in the case of Omani   ** يشمل حملة الدكتوراه، الماجستير، والبكالوريوس من العمانيين

Table 12.

عدد الموظفين (لا يشمل المستشفى الجامعي) حسب الفئة والبلد في ٣١ ديسمبر ٢٠١٥م

Number of Staff (excluding University Hospital) by Category & Country as on December 31, 2015

Country	% للأجمالي العام % to Grand Total	المجموع Total	خدمات مساعدة Support Staff	أعضاء الهيئة الإدارية Administrative Staff	أعضاء الهيئة الفنية Technical Staff	أعضاء الهيئة التدريسية (مركز اللغات) Teaching Staff (Language Centre)	أعضاء هيئة التدريس Academic Staff	البلد
Oman	72.97	2511	213	1152	633	50	463	عُمان
India	5.00	172	21	25	24	27	75	الهند
Egypt	3.34	115	-	31	7	3	74	مصر
U.S.A	1.98	68	-	3	-	41	24	أمريكا
Philippine	1.66	57	-	26	21	2	8	الفلبين
U.K.	1.48	51	-	1	1	30	19	بريطانيا
Jordan	1.48	51	-	5	3	2	41	الأردن
Canada	1.45	50	-	-	2	15	33	كندا
Sudan	1.37	47	-	5	3	4	35	السودان
Pakistan	1.08	37	1	1	6	4	25	باكستان
Tunisia	0.96	33	-	1	2	6	24	تونس
Australia	0.67	23	-	3	-	7	13	أستراليا
Iraq	0.64	22	-	1	-	-	21	العراق
Algeria	0.52	18	-	2	-	-	16	الجزائر
New Zealand	0.46	16	-	1	-	4	11	نيوزلندا
Russia	0.41	14	-	4	1	4	5	روسيا
Bangladesh	0.38	13	3	-	-	-	10	بنجلاديش
Sri Lanka	0.38	13	-	-	5	1	7	سريلانكا
Germany	0.35	12	-	1	1	-	10	المانيا
Iran	0.26	9	-	1	1	3	4	إيران

Table 13.

عدد الموظفين (لا يشمل المستشفى الجامعي) حسب الفئة والبلد في ٣١ ديسمبر ٢٠١٥م

Number of Staff (excluding University Hospital) by Category & Country as on December 31, 2015

Country	% to Grand Total	Total	Support Staff	Administrative Staff	Technical Staff	Teaching Staff (Language Centre)	Academic Staff	البلد
Uganda	0.26	9	-	-	-	-	9	أوغندا
Armenia	0.20	7	-	-	-	7	-	أرمينيا
Syria	0.17	6	-	-	-	-	6	سوريا
Libya	0.17	6	-	-	1	-	5	ليبيا
Turkey	0.15	5	-	1	-	-	4	تركيا
Azerbaijan	0.15	5	-	4	1	-	-	أذربيجان
Yemen	0.15	5	-	-	-	-	5	اليمن
Hungary	0.12	4	-	2	-	2	-	هنغاريا
France	0.12	4	-	-	-	-	4	فرنسا
Italy	0.12	4	-	-	1	-	3	إيطاليا
Nigeria	0.09	3	-	1	-	-	2	نيجيريا
South Africa	0.09	3	-	-	-	1	2	جنوب افريقيا
Ireland	0.09	3	-	-	-	3	-	إيرلندا
Malaysia	0.09	3	-	1	-	1	1	ماليزيا
Morocco	0.09	3	-	-	-	-	3	المغرب
Palestine	0.09	3	-	-	-	-	3	فلسطين
Bahrain	0.06	2	-	1	-	-	1	البحرين
Bulgaria	0.06	2	-	2	-	-	-	بلغاريا
Finland	0.06	2	-	-	-	-	2	فنلندا
Ukraine	0.06	2	-	-	-	1	1	أوكرانيا
Indonesia	0.06	2	-	-	-	-	2	اندونيسيا
Austria	0.06	2	-	-	-	-	2	النمسا
Greece	0.06	2	-	-	-	-	2	اليونان
Lebanon	0.06	2	-	1	-	-	1	لبنان

Table 14.

عدد الموظفين (لا يشمل المستشفى الجامعي) حسب الفئة والبلد في ٣١ ديسمبر ٢٠١٥م

Number of Staff (excluding University Hospital) by Category & Country as on December 31, 2015

Country	% to Grand Total	Total	Support Staff	Administrative Staff	Technical Staff	Teaching Staff (Language Centre)	Academic Staff	البلد
Korea	0.03	1	-	-	-	-	1	كوريا
Ethiopia	0.03	1	-	-	-	-	1	أثيوبيا
Belarus	0.03	1	-	-	-	1	-	بلاروسيا
Botswana	0.03	1	-	-	-	-	1	بوتسوانا
U A E	0.03	1	-	1	-	-	-	الامارات
Romania	0.03	1	-	-	-	1	-	رومانيا
Swaziland	0.03	1	-	-	-	-	1	سوازيلاند
Czech Republic	0.03	1	-	1	-	-	-	جمهورية التشيك
Tanzania	0.03	1	-	-	-	1	-	تنزانيا
Zimbabwe	0.03	1	-	-	-	1	-	زيمبابوي
Macedonia	0.03	1	-	-	-	1	-	مقدونيا
Spain	0.03	1	-	-	-	-	1	إسبانيا
China	0.03	1	-	-	1	-	-	الصين
Ghana	0.03	1	-	1	-	-	-	غانا
Norway	0.03	1	-	-	-	-	1	النرويج
Japan	0.03	1	-	-	-	-	1	اليابان
Belgium	0.03	1	-	-	-	-	1	بلجيكا
Myanmar	0.03	1	-	-	1	-	-	ميانمار
Nepal	0.03	1	-	-	-	-	1	نيبال
kuwait	0.03	1	-	-	-	-	1	الكويت
Grand Total	100	3441	238	1279	715	224	985	الإجمالي العام

Table 15.

أعداد الموظفين المبتعثين حسب المؤهل العلمي وبلد الدراسة في العام الأكاديمي ٢٠١٥-٢٠١٦م

Number of Staff Scholarship by Degree and Country of Study during 2015-2016

Country of Study	Total	Fellowships	Doctorates	Masters	Bachelor	المؤهل العلمي	بلد الدراسة
Spain	2	-	2	-	-		اسبانيا
Australia	12	3	4	4	1		استراليا
U.A.E	1	-	-	-	1		الامارات العربية المتحدة
Sweden	4	-	4	-	-		السويد
Germany	1	-	-	1	-		المانيا
Jordan	1	-	-	1	-		المملكة الاردنية الهاشمية
Saudi Arabia	1	1	-	-	-		المملكة العربية السعودية
United Kingdom	80	6	39	29	6		المملكة المتحدة
USA	26	1	13	9	3		الولايات المتحدة الأمريكية
Ireland	5	4	1	-	-		ايرلندا
Poland	1	-	-	1	-		بولندا
Tunisia	1	-	1	-	-		جمهورية تونس
Egypt	2	-	2	-	-		جمهورية مصر العربية
Oman	52	-	4	17	31		سلطنة عُمان
France	4	4	-	-	-		فرنسا
Canada	39	34	4	1	-		كندا
Malaysia	2	-	-	2	-		ماليزيا
Bahrain	1	-	-	1	-		مملكة البحرين
Grand Total	**235**	**53**	**74**	**66**	**42**		**الإجمالي العام**

Universities regionally and around the globe. Academic affiliations with other foreign universities over the world are a clear testimony that Oman HE shares a great deal with other universities across the globe. Programs such as cooperative Education and Cultural Omani program, Academic program Review done by outstanding experts, partnerships with other higher educational services, student exchange program between Omani students and other countries ' students is a clear evidence that Omani as a country in general and Ministry of Higher Education in particular are participating in the globally Higher Educational issues and that it has a close relation and interacts well with the outside world that's to say "Globalization".

ACKNOWLEDGMENT

My acknowledgment goes to the Ministry of Higher Education in Oman and Sultan Qaboos University for their kind support. I also want to appreciate the effort put by all the staffs of the department of Education administration control economy and planning Near east university.

REFERENCES

Al Abri, K. (2011). The impact of globalization on education policy of developing countries: Oman as an example. *Literacy Information and Computer Education Journal*, 2(4), 491–502. doi:10.20533/licej.2040.2589.2011.0068

Al Harthy, M. (2011). *Private higher education in the Sultanate of Oman: Rationales, development and challenges* (Doctoral dissertation). The University of Kassel, Hessen, Germany. Retrieved from http://d-nb.info/1013197429/34

Al Shmeli, S. (2009). *Higher education in the Sultanate of Oman: planning in the context of the globalization*. Paper presented at the IIEP Policy Forum: Tertiary Education in Small States: Planning in the context of globalization. Retrieved from http://www.iiep.unesco.org/fileadmin/user_upload/Policy_Forums/2009/Alshmeli_Oman.pdf

Albrecht, K. (1983). New systems view of the organization. In *Organization Development* (pp. 44–59). Englewood Cliffs, NJ: Prentice-Hall.

Altbach, P., Reisberg, L., & Rumbley, L. (2009). *Trends in Global Higher Education, Tracking an Academic Revolution*. Paris: UNESCO.

Baporikar, N., & Shah, I. (2012). Quality of higher education in 21st century – A case of Oman. *Journal of Educattional and Instructional Studies in the World*, 2(2), 9–18.

Brandenburg, T. (2012). *Bridging the knowledge gap: Internationalization and privatization of higher education in the State of Qatar and the Sultanate of Oman. (Doctoral dissertation), The Johannes Gutenberg University of Mainz*. Mainz: Rhineland Palatinate, Germany. Retrieved from http://scholar.google.com.au/scholar?q=Dissertation%2C+Bridging+the+Knowledge+Gap%3A+Internationalization+and+Privatization+of+Higher+Education+in+the+State+of+Qatar+and+the+Sultanate+of+Oman&btnG=&hl=en&as_sdt=0%2C5

Carroll, M., & Palermo, J. (2006). *Increasing national capability for quality higher education the case of the Sultanate of Oman*. Paper presented at the AAIR 2006: Community, Customers, Clients, Colleagues and Competitors: Defining relationships through institutional research, Coffs Harbour, Australia.

Donn, G., & Al Manthri, Y. (2010). *Globalisation and higher education in the Arab Gulf States*. Oxford, UK: *Symposium Books*. 10.15730/books.73

Hicks, G. H., & Gullet, C. R. (1975). *Organizations: Theory and Behaviour*. New York, NY: McGraw-Hill. See.

Hogwood, B. W., & Gunn, L. A. (1984). *Policy analysis for the real world. Oxford*. New York: Oxford University Press.

Khalaf Al'Abri, K.M. (2015). *Higher education policy architecture and policy-making in the Sultanate of Oman: Towards a critical understanding MA in Educational Studies: Leadership*. The University of Queensland in 2015 The School of Education.

Ministry of National Economy (MONE). (2005). *Oman: The development experience and investment climate* (5th ed.). Muscat, Oman: Ministry of National Economy.

Trevor-Roper, S., Razvi, S., & Goodliffe, T. (2013). *Academic affiliations between foreign and Omani higher education institutions: Learning from OAAA quality audits*. Paper presented at the INQAAHE Conference, Taipei, Taiwan. Retrieved from http://www.oaaa.gov.om/Conference/1paper_trevor-roper-razvi-goodliffe%20final2.pdf

Von Bertalanffy, L. (1951, December). General systems theory: a new approach to the unit of science. *Human Biology*.

Wilkinson, R., & Al Hajry, A. (2007). The global higher education market: The case of Oman. In M. Martin (Ed.), Cross-border higher education: Regulation quality assurance and impact. Chile, Oman, Philippines, South Africa. New Trends in Higher Education. Paris: International Institute for Educational Planning (IIEP) UNESCO.

KEY TERMS AND DEFINITIONS

ESL: A common abbreviation, it stands for "English as a second language." Used to describe the programs that educate students who are not native English speakers and for describing the ESL students themselves.

GATS: General agreement on trade in services.

Globalization: Considered by many to be the inevitable wave of the future.

HE: Higher education.

HEI: Higher education institutions.

HEP: Higher education private institutions.

Higher Education: An optional final stage of formal learning that occurs after completion of secondary education. Often delivered at universities, academies, colleges, seminaries, conservatories, and institutes of technology, higher education is also available through certain college-level institutions, including vocational colleges, and other career colleges that award academic degrees or professional certifications.

Internationalization: Refers to the increasing importance of international trade, international relations, treaties, alliances, etc.

OAAA: Oman Academic Accreditation Authority.

Policies: A policy is a statement of intent, and is implemented as a procedure or protocol. It is a deliberate system of principles to guide decisions and achieve rational outcomes.

UNESCO: United Nations Educational, Scientific, and Cultural Organization.

WTO: World Trade Organization.

Chapter 3

Reverse Internationalization?
Systems Theory, Brexit, and British Higher Education

Keith John Lay
Cyprus International University, Cyprus

ABSTRACT

This chapter first describes UK HE from a systems theory perspective through reflection on the history of UK HE and the current system in relation to the criteria that are used to assess and audit universities. The current position of UK HE within the larger global HE system is then considered through analysis of the latest university rankings lists. Having identified the key elements of the current UK HE system and highlighted the centrality of international academic staff within that system, the rhetoric in the academic and political discourse and the printed media is then focused upon in order to highlight the potential impact of Brexit on how UK HE performs as an open system. A best case/worst case scenario narrative follows, resulting in the recommendation of fast action from the UK government to safeguard the retention and hiring of international faculty, a key element in the enviable current open system that is UK HE.

DOI: 10.4018/978-1-5225-5231-4.ch003

INTRODUCTION

Brexit, the British Exit from the European Union (EU), scheduled for May, 2019, produces a number of questions that demand careful reflection. From a political perspective, this equates to questions such as: 'Is this a sign of a wider shift away from globalisation?', 'Will other EU member states follow the UK out the door?', 'Will the UK be able to return to having stronger economic and diplomatic ties with Commonwealth countries?', and 'How will Brexit impact upon the British economy in the short, medium, and long term?' While these issues are undoubtedly of great importance for the UK, the EU, and beyond, the discourse of many in the academic community has been dominated by the more specific matter of the effect of Brexit on higher education (HE) in the UK, with some of the key questions here being; 'Will non-UK EU students be subjected to the same fees and conditions as non-EU students?', 'Will there be a downturn in the number of non-UK students overall?, 'Will the conditions and status of EU academic staff change?', 'Will academic staff leave the UK?', and 'Will research opportunities and funding be adversely affected by Brexit?' When the issues at the heart of these questions are viewed from a Systems Theory perspective, the issue of academic staff appears to have the potential to greatly impact upon each of the elements within the UK HE system.

This chapter first describes UK HE from a Systems Theory perspective through reflection on the history of UK HE, and the current system in relation to the criteria that are used to assess and audit universities. The current position of UK HE within the larger global HE system is then considered through analysis of the latest university rankings lists. Having identified the key elements of the current UK HE system and highlighted the centrality of international academic staff within that system, the rhetoric in the academic and political discourse, and the printed media is then focused upon in order to highlight the potential impact of Brexit on how UK HE performs as an open system. A best case/worst case scenario narrative follows, resulting in the recommendation of fast action from the UK government to safeguard the retention and hiring of international faculty, the key element in the enviable current open system that is UK HE.

Systems Theory and UK HE

Systems Theory was developed largely as a reaction to the reductionism approach to describing systems. Rather than simply describing an organisation or system in terms of the parts that make up said entity, systems theory allows for the interaction between elements and the environment with the potential to change the system; "systems theory focuses on the arrangement of and relations between the parts which connect them into a whole (cf. holism)" (Heyligen & Joslyn, 1992). In terms of UK HE then, it is necessary to identify the elements within both the system and its environment and reflect upon how these interact with each other to result in an evolving system.

When applying Systems Theory to UK HE, the first thing to note is that it is an open system, as there are a great many factors in the environment in which UK HE exists that directly affect the system itself. These factors include, but are not limited to: research funding opportunities, the perceptions of potential students and academics in terms of quality, likelihood to be welcomed, employment opportunities and so on, the findings of rankings organizations such as Times Higher Education and Quacquarelli Symonds, the HE systems of other nations, the economy (locally and globally), political policies, and the needs of industry. Brexit then, is a factor from within the environment that the system of UK HE is located, the effect of which will likely change the structure of the input in the UK HE system to such an extent that there are substantial throughput and output consequences. In order to appreciate this potential change, it becomes necessary to establish the elements of the UK HE system which are most relevant.

One logical way to consider the elements of the UK HE system is to consult the criteria used by global higher education performance indicator organisations; namely the university rankings lists publishers Times Higher Education (THE) and Quacquarelli Symonds (QS). Although THE and QS jointly published world university rankings lists between 2004 and 2009, the two organisations have since published their own lists independently since then. As a result of their previous collaboration, many of the criteria are similar, as can be seen in the main categories they audit. THE identifies five areas for assessment; Teaching (30%), Research (30%), Citations (30%), International outlook (7.5%), and Industry income (2.5%). Here, research refers to volume, income, and reputation, and citations refers to research influence. The QS criteria are split into six areas; Academic reputation (40%), Employer reputation (10%), Faculty/student ratio (20%), Citations per faculty (20%), International faculty ratio (5%), and International student ratio (5%) (THE,2018; QS, 2018).

As is evident, differences in the philosophies and methods of the two organisations do exist, and it is therefore useful to delve a little further. While THE assign 30% to teaching, half of which is scored according to a survey, QS choose to highlight the faculty/student ratio as the key element in providing quality teaching. Nonetheless, however it is measured, teaching can be said to be one of the main elements of HE systems. In terms of academic reputation measurement, QS proudly boasts of their 70,000 participant annual survey of academics, allocating 40% of the scoring to this. THE assign 18% (from the 30% under the banner of research) to the same feature, measured through their own survey. In the next common category, THE assign a larger stake to citations (30% compared to the 20% QS assigns), with the justification being that the quality of research output can be understood best through citations. Both THE and QS implement normalisation strategies to balance up any potential unfair advantages of institutions that have larger proportions of subjects which perform better in citations. THE assigns 2.5% each to the international faculty ratio and international student ratio, whereas QS assigns 5% for each. So it can be seen that there are many areas of similarity in the criteria, with the common elements being teaching, academic reputation and research activity, quality of research output, and the degree of internationalisation of a university. These common areas account for 97.5% of the THE criteria and 90% of the QS criteria. (THE,2018; QS, 2018).

The remaining points are awarded by THE for the amount of income a university receives from industry, justified as an indicator of the valuing of a university by the marketplace. QS on the other hand, choose to conduct an employer survey to identify where employers consider their most valued workers graduate from, to which they assign 10% of the total assessment. These two areas can loosely be combined under the label of industry perspective for the description of the UK HE through Systems Theory, although the difference should be noted.

Having identified the elements of a successful university as: teaching, research activity, research output quality, the degree of internationalisation, and the value of the university from an industry perspective, applying Systems Theory to UK HE becomes possible. Teaching interacts with the other elements in various ways; academics involved in research activity must be, due to the very nature of research, continuously developing, students are more likely to put faith in teachers whose work has been cited by others in the scientific community, students and teachers alike benefit from the diversity of internationalisation in the classroom, and better teaching leads to better employees. In terms of research activity, the more funding a university wins, collaboration it has, and projects it contributes to, the more likely it is to produce quality research output that will be cited. The greater the amount of research activity, the greater the appeal to researchers and students alike, leading to more internationalisation. Furthermore, industry benefits from the findings of research in terms of problem solving and innovation. If an HE system produces high quality research output, it will again find internationalisation easier due to the increased appeal of the perceived excellence of the system. Finally, industry can benefit from having the pick of the best in the world owing to internationalisation, as opposed to hiring employees from a smaller field (and therefore having less choice), when only hiring domestically.

In order to accurately appreciate the impact of Brexit on the UK HE system as a whole, it is first necessary to consider the historical and current status of UK HE. The success of which rests on both its rich history and its impressive research output. In terms of the former, three main periods of relevance in the history of UK HE are distinguished here; 1096-1914; the period that saw the establishment of the early universities and the start of the widening of degree-granting capability in the period up to the first world war, 1945-1992; the post-war expansion which culminated in the 1992 wave of upgradings in status from polytechnics to universities, nearly doubling the number of UK universities, and 1993-2018; the subsequent period that has seen great collaboration and internationalisation through embracing students and faculty from a great many countries over the last quarter of a century. Applying Systems Theory, each of these periods can be said to have had their own incarnation of the UK HE system, with the evolution to the present day system evident through reflection of these earlier versions.

Historical Background

The University of Oxford and the University of Cambridge, known the world over, and ranking first and second respectively in the THE rankings for 2018, are central to the history of UK HE. Firstly, due to resistance from these two universities, attempts to open new universities in England were unsuccessful for several centuries. Although in Scotland the Universities of St Andrews, Glasgow, and Aberdeen were each established in the fifteenth century, and the University of Edinburgh in 1583 (British Council, 2018).

It was not until the nineteenth century that further universities in England were founded, followed by others in Northern Ireland and Wales. Also during the 19th century, many University colleges opened; preparing students for examinations by the University of London. Many of these went on to gain degree-awarding status and are currently universities in their own right (British Council, 2018). Later, in the period from 1900 to 1909, seven new non-collegiate, stand-alone universities were founded in England. In contrast, only one new university was founded, Reading University (in 1926), between 1909 and 1948 due to the first world war, great depression, and second world war. Thus, the system of the first period is defined by the long-standing dominance of Oxbridge, despite the establishment of four Scottish universities, followed by greater expansion from 1826 to 1909 through both new universities and collegiates.

During the period between 1948 and 1992 two government initiatives, The Robbins Report of 1963 and the Further and Higher Education Act of 1992, were to have a profound effect on the growth of UK HE. The Robbins Report recommended not only the expansion of the university system, but also, crucially, that places should be granted to all those of suitable ability (Robbins, 1963), which was in line with post-war entitlement policies, such as the right to benefit from national health, social security, and education for all. As a result of the report, the number of UK universities rose to 45 by 1970. This number rose to 84 as a result of the Further and Higher Education Act 1992, which allowed all polytechnics and central institutions functioning at the higher education level to change status and become universities. The UK HE system of the second period focused upon here was marked then by the move towards inclusivity and a four-fold increase in the number of universities through both the establishment of new universities and the granting of university status to degree awarding institutions (British Council, 2018). The system had therefore once again evolved.

The third period distinguished here (1993-2018) has seen the number of universities in the UK HE system rise to the current total of 132, with the number of students being around the 2.3 million mark each year between 2012 and 2017 (HESA, 2018a). However, what really sets this period apart is the strength of research activity and internationalisation.

CURRENT SYSTEM

Research

Research activity including collaboration, winning funding, and reputation (30% of the THE criteria and covered within the broader Academic Reputation category of QS which carries 40%), and the quality of output from those activities, measured by citations (30% of THE and 20% of QS criteria), constitute the major strength of the current UK HE system. Given the weighting allocated by the two rankings organizations, research is clearly the area of most importance in terms of achieving high rankings.

The good news here for the UK HE system is that it is arguably the top performer in terms of quality research output. Sir Steve Smith, vice-chancellor of Exeter University, held this argument by pointing out that while the UK has less than one percent of the world's population and only 3.2% of global research and development funding, UK HE produces 15.9% of the 'world's most highly-cited scientific research articles', placing the UK ahead of the US as world leader (Henley, 2015). This is underscored by Universities UK, who state their assertion that the UK 'ranks first among competitors by field-weighted citation impact' (UUK, 2018).

Sir Steve Smith puts the UK HE research success down to international collaborative research; only 48% of UK publications are from solely the UK (down from 84% in 1981), whereas the US figure is 67%, equating to less international collaboration (Henley, 2015). One of the factors in achieving high ratios of internationally collaborative research publications is having a high ratio of international faculty, as they bring with them not only connections, but also cultural and linguistic networking advantages. Having international academic staff then, is a key factor in the success of UK HE as an open system.

With approximately 15% of academic staff in UK HE being non-UK EU nationals (Cressey, 2016a), this group account for around half of all international faculty; the international make-up of the academic staff in UK HE had a ratio of around 30% non-UK in 2016-2017 (HESA, 2018b). However, the ratio of non-UK EU academic staff is not evenly spread, meaning some universities are more exposed to any potential adverse effects in this area (and, ergo, some are also less exposed). The figure is closer to 25% non-UK EU nationals in the academic staff of the University of Kent (Henley, 2015) and close to 20% in 'elite universities', according to Cressey (2016a).

The impact the non-UK EU faculty have on UK HE research success is formidable. "More than half the European Research Council's (ERC) prestigious mid-career grants in UK universities are held by researchers from other EU countries." - Henley, (2015). Winning research funding is a serious matter, with figures in the billions of euros; Horizon 2020, the current EU Framework Programme for research for the period 2014 to 2020 is the source of €1 billion per year in research funding for UK HE (Killwick & Cuddeford, 2016). Winning research funding is especially important for UK HE as the funding from the EU constitutes a larger proportion of UK research funding, 16% of UK university research money comes from the EU (Gannon, 2016), more than many other EU states, due to the UK investing less in its own research. Maria Nedera, in a panel discussion of the post-brexit reality at the University of Manchester in November, 2016, claimed that although the UK wins EU research grants, it is the German academic staff working in UK HE who are the best at winning the grants (Nedera, 2016).

Internationalisation

In terms of internationalisation, there are two criteria in the QS methodology, and three in the THE methodology; the ratio of international students and the ratio of international faculty in both sets of criteria, and international collaboration as the extra factor in the THE category for this area. In terms of student ratios, the number of non-UK students rose steadily from 424,815 in 2012/13 to 442,375 in 2016/17, representing 19% of all students studying in the UK in the 2016-2017 academic year (HESA). This accounts for around 10% of the global number of international students, a figure only surpassed by the USA, who have around 19%, and which nearly doubles the figures of the next two countries, Australia and France, which both claim around 6% (UUK, 2015). In the 2016/17 academic year, 134,835 students were non-UK EU nationals, meaning around 30% of international students in UK HE were non-UK EU students. So with around half of international academic staff being non-UK EU nationals (see above), almost a third of international students being from this category, and 52% of UK research output involving international collaboration (see above) with many of the other nations being EU states, the EU currently contributes well in the internationalisation of UK HE.

So where exactly does UK HE currently stand in the global HE system?

UK HE in the Rankings

All data in the following rankings analysis was taken from THE (2018) and QS (2018).

The status of UK HE within the global HE system can best be quantitatively understood in terms of the THE and QS university ranking lists. The 2018 lists provide a rank of the top 1000 and 959 universities respectively, and are therefore quite comparable in terms of overall figures. In order to reflect both excellence and strength in depth, it is useful to consider the rankings lists in more than one light. Consequently, the top 10, 100, and 500 of each list are analysed here.

The THE list has three UK universities in the top ten, including the first and second positions, with the remainder being US universities and one Swiss university tied for tenth. The QS top ten contains four UK universities, five from the US, and again one from Switzerland. So it can be said that, in terms of excellence, the UK is competing with the US for the top, and only Switzerland manages to claim any place in the top ten of either ranking list.

Expanding to the top 100, the THE list has 12 UK universities and the QS has 16. The US dominates both top 100s though, with 43 (THE) and 31 (QS) universities, although the former includes a tie for 100th between two US and one other university. In terms of other countries, the nearest percentages are attained by the following: THE – Germany 10%, Netherlands 7%, Australia 6%, QS – Australia 7%, China 6%, Hong Kong 5%, Japan 5%. So although both lists have the US very far clear and the UK second in the top 100, there is considerable variance in the next best performers. While the THE list has Germany in third, they did not perform so well in the QS list. Indeed, only Australia features with five or more universities in both lists (aside from the US and the UK). So in terms of quality, if the top ten shows excellence and the top 100 signals strength, a look beyond to the top 500 may better indicate depth. (THE, 2018; QS, 2018).

When the top 500 universities in the rankings are considered, some interesting patterns emerge. The dominance of the US stays intact, with the UK continuing to hold the second position. The aggregate of the US is 21.7% of the top 500, and for the UK it is 11.4%. Therefore, both countries experience a drop in the percentage, which could be indicative of the high number of universities already listed by the 100 mark, but could also signal greater competition at this point in the system as a whole. For instance, Italian universities do not feature at all in the top 100 of either list, yet by the 500 point mark, Italian universities take an overall aggregate position of 5th with 4.7%. Consequently, it could be argued that Italian HE has significant strength in depth despite having no particular institution that excels in the rankings. The third highest aggregate is claimed by Germany (7.6% of the top 500), and the fourth by Australia (5.2%). Although France (3.8%) and Canada (3.7%) come in 6th and 7th respectively, it should be noted that their combined figures still account for less than German universities. Indeed, the combined total of the aggregate percentages of just these first seven countries is 58.1%, leaving only 41.9% to the other 58 countries that make the lists (THE,2018; QS, 2018).

In terms of university ranking lists then, the UK is in a clear second place to the dominant US, although THE list supporters would of course point to the top two positions held by the universities of Oxford and Cambridge. In excellence, the top ten of both lists show the US-UK 'medal positions'. In strength, the top 100s show a clear gap to third and beyond again. Finally, in the top 500 of both lists a show of strength in depth comes from the place of the UK being firmly cemented behind the US and comfortably above its nearest rivals.

It has been shown that UK HE has a long and rich history which has allowed for growth periods and evolution of the system and its elements, and that this has resulted in a system which not only acts as a key performer in research activity, but also benefits from a high degree of internationalisation, leading to high ranking positions in the global market. Indeed, the performance of UK HE in recent decades has been outstanding when one considers the budget, population, and political support differences when comparing the UK to its competition.

With only the US HE system ahead in terms of rankings and the ability to attract international students, entering unknown territory with the risk of sliding down the performance continuum was not a popular choice among academics; in the lead up to the Brexit vote, of 907 active UK researchers polled by Nature journal, a staggering 83% declared a wish to 'remain' in the EU, while only 12% were in favour of 'leave', the other 5% being undecided (Cressey, 2016b). In a further sign of the academic opposition to Brexit, over 150 University of Cambridge researchers signed a letter, published in *The Times* newspaper on the 10th of March, 2016, which argued in favour of remaining in the EU for scientific benefit (Cressey, 2016b). However, the vote of June 23rd, 2016 produced the result many academics dreaded, a surprise result that even those who had campaigned for Brexit had not been confident of achieving. And so, Britain, and UK HE with it, entered the unknown.

Brexit Unknowns

In order to better reflect the active nature of the discourse, months are also given, where possible, in parantheses here.

One of the interesting and indeed worrying features of Brexit is that it is largely unknown how it will play out. This lack of clarity is due to the absence of any clear comparable example in the past. One term that has been much touted is 'hard brexit'; the loss of access to the single market in Europe by the UK as a reaction to the control of movement of people. Often described as a cliff-edge, there is also the prospect of 'no deal' at all. This would see the UK revert to World Trade Organization (WTO) rules and is seen as a disastrous prospect. Then there is the case for a 'soft brexit' in which many EU principles will stay intact, the UK will be allowed access to the single market, and the relationship will be amicable. The uncertainty surrounding Brexit and the position of the UK government (Theresa May, who opposed Brexit pre-referendum struck a particularly hard-line once elected as the Prime Minister, fueling the confusion) was a particularly common topic in the discourse following the referendum up until an announcement made in December, 2017; 'There is significant uncertainty about the UK's future relationship with the EU' (Macpherson, October, 2016, 2017), 'For EU academics working in the UK, the referendum brought uncertainty and confusion.' (Menendez Alvarez-Hevia & Zotzmann, August 2017), 'Prof Stuart Croft of Warwick University said…"the possibility of no deal being struck to exit the EU was "utterly bizarre", and that institutions needed certainty over residency rights by the end of the year to avoid seeing staff at all levels deciding to leave." (Adams, November, 2017b).

The reason for concern is clear; the case of Switzerland, who participate in European research as a non-EU member, is given as an example of what may happen. Switzerland saw research funding from the EU cut dramatically following a vote to restrict freedom of movement (Henley, 2015). Should a hard brexit take place the likelihood is the effect on UK HE would be equally, or perhaps more, severe as the EU may want to be seen to 'punish' the UK so as to deter other states from similar action. Should no deal take place, negotiating a potential new deal on buying in to the research programmes would be necessary, and would likely prove a hard sell to the voting public of the UK. Corbett & Gordon, in April 2017 during the height of uncertainty, argued that with reference to HE, the debate should not be whether to have a hard or soft Brexit, but to instead aim for an 'Intelligent Brexit' in which special conditions are made in cases related to HE, such as 'more generous visa regimes for international staff and students.' (Corbett & Gordon, April, 2017).

However, Arpita Dutt, a negotiator by profession, made it clear during a University of Manchester panel discussion on post-brexit reality, that 'There cannot be a blow by blow account.' of the Brexit negotiations (Dutt, November, 2016). Over twelve months later, a joint statement from the EU and the UK in December, 2017 provided some much needed indication of negotiation progress. The announcement focused on there having been enough progress in phase one of the talks to allow the commencement of the second phase of talks. Some of the points of agreement that came about from the first phase included the implementation of a transitional period from the exit in March 2019 until the end of 2020. This provides a cushion that to some extent softens the potential for damage from uncertainty.

Brexit Discourse and UK HE

Given the nature of the UK HE system and its elements, it is useful to reflect on the pre-referendum voices as well as those that have followed the vote in relation to the key areas identified earlier. This section should be read whilst bearing in mind the above-mentioned academic opposition to Brexit pre-referendum and the background of uncertainty and fears of a 'hard brexit' or 'no deal' situation in the period following the vote, up until the December 2017 announcement (although these fears still persist in a less panic stricken way). The system elements that are focused upon here are research and internationalisation as the two areas most affected by international academic staff ratios. This is followed by reflection of how the potential decrease in non-UK EU academic staff and indeed non-EU academic staff relates to the highlighted commentary.

Research Activity

The rhetoric pre-referendum in all areas of the discourse was strong and uncompromising. This tough talk was also seen in the discourse related to HE and Brexit, with research funding a hot topic. The *Guardian* cited leading academics as saying a British Exit would be 'catastrophic' and 'cost tens of millions of pounds in funding and leave the prestigious UK institutions struggling to compete on the world stage.' (Henley, 2015). Just five days before the vote, the Vice-chancellor of the University of Cambridge, Ross Anderson, stated that at the time of writing almost half of the income of Cambridge University was from research grants and contracts of which 15% came directly from the EU, and that even if the 'Remain' vote won 'we've all been damaged' (Anderson, May, 2016).

On the other hand, Angus Dalgleish, a medical researcher from the University of London and campaigner for Brexit, claimed that a post-Brexit UK would have much more money available for research funding as a result of the savings made from not making EU contributions (Cressey, February, 2016a) and that the not relying on the EU for funding would allow more freedoms from EU regulations in some areas of science (Cressey, March, 2016b). Justice minister Michael Gove also suggested that the shortfall could be made up through investing the money the UK currently gives to the EU.

Post-referendum, the issue of research funding certainly continued to be debated, although pro-Brexit voices are much less apparent in the discourse. The topic was mostly driven by the concerns over uncertainty described earlier, which continued until the December 2017 announcement. Frank Gannon, a voice from outside as an Australian researcher working in Australia, stated that in the worst case scenario Brexit will 'mean a loss for many laboratories and researchers' (Gannon, July, 2016). He went on to say 'a 16% cut will hurt', referring to the proportion of UK research funding that comes from the EU (Gannon, July, 2016).

Anecdotal evidence exists in the discourse of an immediate impact of the vote on funding activity; 'UK academics were either being removed from Horizon 2020 funding bids or asked to step down from the lead role in such bids' (Macpherson, October, 2016, 2017). Both of these scenarios would mean a net loss for UK funding as the lead role usually gets a higher percentage of the funds. Macpherson (October, 2016, 2017) also raised the concern that the UK would likely lose its influence in how research programmes make their fund-granting decisions, which is seen as vital to the success rate of UK bids as the UK has continually pushed for grants to be awarded on the basis of excellence, which has historically favoured UK bids (Macpherson, October, 2016, 2017).

Further evidence of British researchers, some from Oxbridge, being asked to leave projects due to them being seen as a financial liability was reported on soon after (Wilcock & Miller, November, 2016).

Despite a winter in which little tangible information flowed with regards to the Brexit negotiations, certainly in terms of HE, April 2017 saw commentary highlight an unexpected negative, which could be used as justification for the above-mentioned actions; the Department for Exiting the European Union admitted that there was 'no structure for dealing with research, education or universities and in the Department of Education there is no one dealing with leaving the EU' (Corbett & Gordon, April, 2017). This staggering disclosure can surely have given little or no respite to those in HE who were frustrated with the atmosphere of uncertainty. It comes as little surprise then that by November of 2017 commentators had become quite pessimistic; 'It is highly unlikely that UK universities will retain membership of the mainstream European research programs.' (Marginson, November, 2017).

However, there was a statement that did offer some relief to the academic research community in the UK. The chancellor, Philip Hammond, offered a guarantee that the British government would replace research funding that was underpinned by the EU (Adams, November, 2017b). This was soon followed, in December, 2017, by more good news in this area with the phase one agreement details. The announcement stated that the UK would stay in the Horizon 2020 programme for the duration and be able to participate in projects under that programme even if they are long term and continue after the transitional stage post-Brexit (UUK, December, 2017). Following these positive announcements, the discourse related to research funding for UK HE has quietened down considerably.

However, UUK point out that there are still serious issues to be resolved; 'Without the government taking action, there are risks that: ...access to key funding mechanisms to support research excellence are lost.' (UUK, March, 2018). They also call for action to secure some form of participation in the Framework Funding programme currently referred to as Framework Programme 9 (FP9), the research funding programme that will replace Horizon 2020 (UUK, March, 2018). In other words, while many seem to have been satisfied for now with the solution that covers the next few years, UUK have begun voicing the longer term research funding concern.

The discourse regarding research funding developed through three noticeable stages; from pre-referendum debate to post-referendum concern and uncertainty and finally to the current situation which perhaps may be best described as delaying the debate with the knowledge that things will not change too much over the coming few years. Although importantly, uncertainty remains in the longer term.

Longer term uncertainty may have a knock-on effect both to the international academics currently working in the UK who may feel it is safer to plan a longer term research future elsewhere, and with the same doubt this could affect UK HE's ability to attract research grant champions, those researchers who have already proven to be successful in winning research funding. The organic nature of the elements within the system become clearer when one considers that the potential for academics to relocate or choose not to go to the UK as a result of uncertainty regarding research funding in the longer term could also lead to a fall in the collaborative projects at which the UK has excelled in recent times. It could also mean a drop in international staff and students that will hurt the ranking of UK universities.

INTERNATIONALISATION

Attracting International Students

Not only is the potential loss of future research funding likely to hamper the recruitment of international students and staff alike, Marginson (2017) alludes to the possibility of changing the payment structure so the current EU students would pay the non-EU fees ('£12,000 to £20,000 a year') leading to a very swift drop in numbers, helping government net migration targets (Marginson, 2017, p9). This concern arises from the government's insistence on classifying international students as migrants in the figures (Corbett & Gordon, April, 2017). Considering Theresa May's ambition to cut annual net migration to 100,000 and the total number of international students being around 450,000, this is a clear worry. Marginson further postulates that the effect of such a drop in numbers would be particularly damaging to those universities 'lower down in the status order of higher education' (Marginson, 2017, p9). However, this could also hit the elite universities, as Ross Anderson, vice chancellor of the University of Cambridge points out (students)....."currently paying £9,000 a year will be put off if they have to pay the overseas rate of £17,000." (Anderson, 2016).

If the concern regarding attracting international students was doubted in any way, the statistics seemed to provide an answer. Noting a fall in non-UK EU student applications in 2017, it seemed that the pessimism was well founded (Corbett & Gordon, April, 2017). The *Telegraph* newspaper reported that fall as 4.4%, which came after five years of annual increases (Adams, November, 2017a) and culminated in the best figures on record in 2016. This fall was directly attributed to Brexit concerns by the chief executive of Universities UK, Alistair Jarvis (Adams, November, 2017a).

The 'Brain Drain' in the Discourse

Despite the doom and gloom of falling non-UK EU student numbers and the concerns of longer term research funding issues, the issue that is perhaps the most influential in the inter-related system of UK HE is that of international academic staff. The vice-chancellor of Cambridge University, Ross Anderson, when noting his concerns pre-referendum, concluded by identifying what he sees as the real problem for the future of UK; most new hires are foreign and America already prove strong competition in this area while Anderson worries about the image of the UK following a campaign that has had the potential to cause people to look on Britain as 'no longer the best place to send their kids, or to build research labs.' (Anderson, 2016). Other pre-referendum voices also expressed concern; *The Guardian* reported on the fears of scientists as early as November, 2015, claiming that a Brexit would cripple collaboration and stifle research, giving the analogy of Lionel Messi playing alone without his high-performing team mates (Henley, November, 2015). In the same article the vice-chancellor of Exeter University, Sir Steve Smith, is quoted as saying that working internationally is proven to be the best way to produce the best research (Henley, November, 2015). An EU researcher working in the UK and receiving funding from the ERC, Yvonne Peters, stated that she would find the UK less attractive were the regulations to change and require visas (Cressey, February, 2016a).

However, as with the discourse related to research, the number of voices increased following the referendum. Pointing out that requiring a visa and work permission will be restrictive, Gannon (July, 2016) shared his view that British science will lose out due to the reduced flow of talent (Gannon, July, 2016). Scotland clearly shared this view, with the Scottish Government and Universities Scotland calling for the 'recognition of attracting the best talent from across the world to deliver high quality teaching and research at Scottish HEIs' (Macpherson, October, 2016, 2017).

The fears soon became reality. QS echoed the concerns while referring to a considerable piece of evidence from a *Telegraph* poll from January, 2017; 'of over 1,000 lecturers and professors, three-quarters of continental EU academics in the UK said they are more likely to leave the country following the Brexit vote.' (Bridgestock, March, 2017). Corbett and Gordon (April, 2017), in their call for an intelligent Brexit that treats HE differently, claimed that universities were by that stage already facing challenges in recruiting EU staff due to 'public hostility towards immigrants and uncertainty about the future of collaborative research.' (Corbett & Gordon, April, 2017). The European Conference of Educational Research in August 2017 heard reports from a study of EU academics working in the UK; the findings stated that many were reacting to Brexit, and of these some were planning to leave the UK (Menendez Alvarez Hevia & Zotzman, August, 2017).

With the passing of nearly eighteen months between the referendum and the announcement of progression to phase two of negotiations in December, 2017, the discourse just prior to that event shows considerable frustration. The Russel Group, a powerhouse association of 24 of the top performing UK universities, had by November 2017 put the issue of non-UK EU nationals to the top of their priority list and were exerting considerable efforts to make progress with the government saying the EU staff 'urgently needed solid guarantees' (Adams, November, 2017b). Those guarantees came one month later, and the issue of academic staff leaving may have seemed to have been averted.

However, January 2018 saw the claim, in the *Independent*, that a 'Brexodus' of academic talent was underway. The article claimed that over 2,300 EU academics had already left UK HE, implying that this was as a result of Brexit concerns (Buchan, January, 2018). The University of Oxford was named as having lost the most (230), although they themselves stated that they had also hired a similar number (Buchan, January, 2018). The piece goes on to describe how a German academic stated some EU academics felt 'personally insulted' at the speed it took to guarantee their rights (eighteen months as mentioned above), and that he expects a delayed departure of academics as many are waiting to make a decision and that it takes time to secure new employment on the continent (Buchan, January, 2018).

The recommendations of Universities UK published in March, 2018, show a continued focus on trying to pressure the government into being more positive towards UK HE and in particular to non-UK EU staff working therein. Welcoming the December 2017 announcement that guarantees the rights of those employees, UUK call for the government to enshrine these guarantees into UK law (UUK, March, 2018). It is not difficult to understand why UUK would want the government to 'cross the Ts', so to speak, on that particular issue considering the turmoil the Conservative party has seemingly gone through over the past few years. They also call for an immigration system that is amiable for potential academic staff, and for regulatory standards that safeguard collaborative research (UUK, March, 2018).

Best Case/Worst Case Brexit Scenarios for UK HE

Given the uncertainty that still surrounds the details of Brexit, aside from those covered by the progression to phase two announcement in December, 2017, there have been many predictions as to the impact on the various elements of the system. As an open system, UK HE is exposed to a great many variations in the possibilities for change; such as immigration policies and measures, research funding programme agreements, government funding levels, legislation related to tuition fees, and industry support to name but a few. As the elements of the system, in order to function at the most efficient and effective level, rely on the input of international faculty (to aid research, win funding, facilitate collaboration, bring about internationalisation, teach, and gain the support of industry), when making predictions about the future of the system it is necessary to consider the best and worst case scenarios and their implications for the evolution of the UK HE system.

The best case scenario with regards to international academic staff and students (barring a reversal of the entire Brexit referendum) would involve some sort of special deal for UK HE in the new legislation. Indeed this is exactly what Corbett and Gordon (April, 2017) and UUK (March, 2018) have been calling for with their recommendations of an 'Intelligent Brexit' (Corbett & Brown, April, 2017) and 'an immigration system that supports universities' ability to attract global talent' (UUK, March, 2018). One of the first changes of a best case scenario immigration system would be to cease the practice of including students in immigration figures (and therefore targets). If the path for international students and staff was clear and unhindered, UK HE would benefit greatly. There could be a reversal in the recent trend of non-UK academic staff leaving and non-UK EU student application figures falling. However, as Ross Anderson pointed out just prior to the vote, a lot of damage was done by the way that the debate evolved (Anderson, June, 2016) and many may feel that even in a best case scenario of no extra hurdles being in place in terms of immigration relating to UK HE, the UK is no longer a destination in which they feel welcome.

Considering the best case scenario then, the likely effects on UK HE from a Systems Theory perspective would still be considerable in the short, medium, and long-term. In the short-term, until such a system was announced, ratified and had come into force, the uncertainty could still lead to adverse effects on the retention and hiring of academic staff. The knock on effect to the other elements of the system mean; that there could be less collaboration as networks are lost and new connections are not gained, the ability of UK HE to compete for research funding will be weakened as expertise and experience declines, new research projects may have a lower citation impact for the same reasons, innovation and originality may be affected by the reduction in the collaborative international nature of the environment, and the overall status of UK HE could decrease as universities lose places in the rankings lists as a result of these auditable changes. In the medium-term (for example in the five years following the Brexit date), following the announcement, ratification, and application of such a system, the best case scenario would see a return of lost staff and the return to pre-referendum levels of talent applying for UK academic positions. However, given the short-term effects predicted above, even with the removal of the issue there would be a delay in the return to status of UK HE (in the best case scenario). In this case, in the long-term and still thinking in a best case scenario way, UK HE could recover lost ground and further develop and grow as the beneficiary of new improved trade and political links elsewhere, such as in the Commonwealth.

The worst case scenario is bleak. If there is a change in the progress of the negotiations it is still possible that no deal will be struck, despite the 2017 announcement. The UK could fall off the cliff edge with very little cushioning in place should the worst happen. In the short-term, here being up to the end of the transitional period of 2020, academic staff would at least have time to try and find new positions elsewhere. However, the most likely scenario in the event of strong immigration policies and no deal or a hard brexit would be an exodus of academic staff and a huge drop in international student applications. If students are to be counted as immigrants and immigration targets are set low (the home secretary Amber Rudd resigned today over the issue of immigration targets), universities will find themselves firmly out of pocket. With no access to EU research funding and dropping student numbers, the atmosphere could feel like abandoning a sinking ship to the non-UK EU academic staff in UK HE. Even with guarantees of their right to stay in place, they may well decide enough is enough. Clearly, the knock on effect to the other elements of the system would be catastrophic. In the worst case scenario, the status of UK HE would drop significantly in the rankings in the medium-term and this would act like a vicious cycle to further propel UK universities down the rankings lists. In a time of enhanced globalisation and with the rise of the East in HE already taking place, the worst case scenario is indeed worrying.

This chapter has attempted to describe UK HE from a Systems Theory perspective with reference to the British Exit from the EU and its potential to change the current dynamic open system through the loss of international academic staff. Having reflected on the past incarnations of the UK HE system throughout history and reflected on the elements of the system as identified using the audit criteria of THE and QS, the discourse surrounding Brexit was then described with an emphasis on research and internationalisation as the key factors of the system and the most susceptible academic staff changes. A best case/worst case scenario narrative then postulated the potential for change in the UK HE system. As even in the best case scenario it seems that UK HE is heading towards a period of decline, it would seem logical that the UK government acts fast to minimize the damage done by adhering to the calls for a special system for HE that side steps the political hurdles of the Brexit negotiations.

REFERENCES

Adams, C. (2017a). Universities blame Brexit for fall in foreign students. *The Telegraph*. Retrieved February 17th, 2018 at https://www.telegraph.co.uk/news/2017/11/27/universities-blame-brexit-fall-foreign-students/

Adams, R. (2017b). UK universities 'face disaster within weeks' without clear Brexit plan. *The Guardian*. Retrieved April 3rd, 2018 at https://www.theguardian.com/education/2017/nov/22/uk-universities-disaster-weeks-brexit-plan-eu-citizens

Anderson, R. (2016). Report of the Council on the financial position and budget of the University, recommending allocations from the Chest for 2016–17. *Reporter*. Retrieved March 14th, 2018, at http://www.admin.cam.ac.uk/reporter/2015-16/weekly/6426/section6.shtml

Bolton, P. (2012). Education: historical statistics. *House of Commons Library, 27*.

Bridgestock, L. (2017). What Does Brexit Mean for Students? *QS Top Universities*. Retrieved February 16th, 2018 at https://www.topuniversities.com/student-info/university-news/what-does-brexit-mean-students

Buchan, L. (2018). Brexit: more than 2,300 EU academics resign amid warning over UK university 'Brexodus'. *The Independent*. Retrieved on April 12th at https://www.independent.co.uk/news/uk/politics/brexit-latest-news-uk-university-eu-academics-resign-immigration-brexodus-citizens-europe-a8143796.html

Corbett, A., & Gordon, C. (2015). *The university challenge: what type of Brexit would work for Higher Education?* British Politics and Policy at LSE.

Cressey, D. (2016a). Academics across Europe join 'Brexit'debate. *Nature*, *530*(7588), 15. doi:10.1038/530015a PMID:26842034

Cressey, D. (2016b). Scientists say 'no'to UK exit from Europe in Nature poll. *Nature*, *531*(7596), 559–559. doi:10.1038/531559a PMID:27029257

Dutt, A. (2016). *University of Manchester: Post-Brexit Reality*. Panel Discussion Brodacast Live. Retrieved on February 19th, 2018 at https://www.youtube.com/watch?v=xFBsbQEYd-g&t=3390s

Gannon, F. (2016). Brexit and research: Goodbye EU money and colleagues? *EMBO Reports*. PMID:27466322

Henley, J. (2015). Leaving EU would be a 'disaster', British universities warn. *The Guardian*. Retrieved on March 18th, 2018 at https://www.theguardian.com/ politics/2015/nov/11/leaving-eu-would-be-a-disaster-british-universities-warn

HESA. (2018a). *Higher Education Student Statistics: UK, 2016/17 - Where students come from and go to study*. Retrieved April 10th, 2018 at https://www. hesa.ac.uk/news/11-01-2018/sfr247-higher-education-student-statistics/location

HESA. (2018b). *Staff numbers and characteristics*. Retrieved April 10th, 2018 at https://www.hesa.ac.uk/data-and-analysis/staff

Heylighen, F., & Joslyn, C. (1992). What is Systems Theory. In F. Heylighen, C. Joslyn, & V. Turchin (Eds.), *Principia Cybernetica Web*. Retrieved March 18th, 2018, at URL: http://cleamc11.vub.ac.be/SYSTHEOR.html

Killwick, C. A. P., & Cuddeford, V. (2016). *How Universities can continue to attract the best minds post Brexit*. Academic Press.

Macpherson, S. (2017). *Brexit: Higher Education in Scotland*. Scottish Parliament Information Centre (SPICe).

Marginson, S. (2017). Brexit: Challenges for Universities in Hard Times. *International Higher Education*, (88), 8-10.

Menendez Alvarez Hevia, D., & Zotzman, K. (2017). *Brexit and the Internationalisation of UK Universities: The Experiences of Academic Staff from EU Member States*. Academic Press.

Mitchell, N. (2018). Some UK universities are shaking off the Brexit blues. *University World News*. Retrieved March 20th, 2018 at http://www. universityworldnews.com/article.php?story=20180119062806710

Nedera, M. (2016). *University of Manchester: Post-Brexit Reality*. Panel Discussion Brodacast Live. Retrieved on February 19th, 2018 at https://www. youtube.com/watch?v=xFBsbQEYd-g&t=3390s

QS. (2018). *QS World University Rankings*. Retrieved January-April, 2018 at https://www.topuniversities.com/university-rankings/world-university-rankings/2018

Robbins, L. R. B. (1963). *Higher Education: Report of the Committee appointed by the Prime Minister under the chairmanship of Lord Robbins, 1961-63* (No. 2). HM Stationery Office. Accessed at http://www.educationengland.org.uk/documents/robbins/robbins1963.html

Times Higher Education (THE). (2018). *World University Rankings*. Retrieved from https://www.timeshighereducation.com/world-university-rankings

UUK. (2015). *International Undergraduate Students: The UK's Competitive Advantage*. Retrieved April 12th, 2018 http://www.universitiesuk.ac.uk/policy-and-analysis/reports/Documents/International/international-undergraduate-students-uk-competitive-advantage.pdf

UUK. (2017). *Brexit FAQS*. Retrieved March 18th, 2018 at http://www.universitiesuk.ac.uk/policy-and-analysis/brexit/Pages/brexit-faqs.aspx

UUK. (2018). *How Can the Government Ensure Universities are Best Placed to Maximise Their Contribution to a Successful and Global UK Post-EU Exit?* Retrieved April 6th, 2018 at http://www.universitiesuk.ac.uk/policy-and-analysis/reports/Documents/2018/brexit-briefing-march-18.pdf

Wilcock, J., & Miller, A. (2016). The truth and consequences of Brexit: Could a catastrophe for academia be an opportunity for publishers? *Insights*, *29*(3), 216–223. doi:10.1629/uksg.328

KEY TERMS AND DEFINITIONS

Academic Staff: The personnel employed for research and teaching by higher education institutions.

Brexodus: A portmanteau of British exodus which refers to large numbers of non-UK EU national academic staff leaving the UK.

British Exit: The act of the UK leaving the European Union. Britain is used interchangeably with UK although technically does not include Northern Ireland.

EU: The European Union, the political shared sovereignty of 27 member states of Europe.

Internationalization: The mixing of people of different nationalities within a system.

QS: The Quacquarelli Symonds organization that is one of the two leading auditors of universities for the preparation of rankings lists.

THE: The Times Higher Education organization that is one of the two leading auditors of universities for the preparation of rankings lists.

UK: The United Kingdom of England, Scotland, Wales, and Northern Ireland.

University Rankings: The lists prepared as performance indicators by specialist organizations.

Chapter 4
Internationalization of Higher Education in Southeast Asia

Ramesh Chander Sharma
Wawasan Open University, Malaysia

M. Rajesh
Indira Gandhi National Open University, India

ABSTRACT

In 1997, during the second ASEAN (Association of SouthEast Asian Nations) informal summit held in Kuala Lumpur, ASEAN Vision 2020 was adopted laying emphasis on integration of education and human capital development which was echoed in Hanoi Plan of Action (December 1997) and later on in Vientiane Action Programme (2004). During the first meeting of ASEAN Ministers of Education held at Singapore in 2006 the Cha-am Hua Declaration highlighted role of education in achieving enduring solidarity and unity among the nations and people of ASEAN. Recently an ASEAN Socio-Cultural Community Blueprint 2025 was launched in 2016 recommending an innovative ASEAN approach to higher education with the purpose to promote greater people-to-people interaction and mobility within and outside ASEAN. This chapter discusses policies and practices for internationalization of higher education in South East Asia and how it is strengthening regional and global cooperation.

DOI: 10.4018/978-1-5225-5231-4.ch004

INTRODUCTION

Educational systems all over the world have some challenges: of quality, of numbers, of access, of equity and of equality etc. ICT plays an important role in meeting these challenges by bridging the knowledge gap, increasing access to educational opportunities, faster delivery of knowledge products, massification of education and enhancing student-centered learning (ADB, 2009). In educational institutions, ICT is integrated into various systems, not only to assist in teaching and learning, but also for administration and management purposes like student enrolment, course schedules, student grading, staff evaluation etc. (UNESCO, 2011). Not only in universities, ICT is used in TVET institutions for creating a skilled, ICT-capable workforce (ADB, 2009). If we examine the adoption and integration of ICT into educational systems, we note some disparity, some take full advantage while some lack those. Possible reasons are lack of support from management, shortage of trained staff, uncoordinated planning and implementation, ambiguity in roles and responsibilities, staff resistance to training and reluctance for re-training and inadequate finances for developing, purchasing and implementing ICT (UNESCO, 2011).

In recent times, Massive Open Online Courses (MOOCs) have been a wave of disruptive technology with many universities, governments and other institutions developing and offering MOOCs. MOOCs were reported to be next big thing in the technology development of higher education (NMC, 2012) and then the Year 2012 being declared as the Year of the MOOC by the New York Times. As in open and distance education system, MOOCs also reflect the move towards openness in learning. A team of scholars at United Kingdom Open University (UKOU) examines the pedagogical trends affecting higher education sector. The 2016 report examined new science of learning drawing from the research outcomes from neuroscience, cognitive sciences, educational and social sciences to understand the dynamics of how we learn. In this report (Sharples et al., 2016) some of the innovative technologies and pedagogies identified to have transformed education were: Learning through social media (Using social media to offer long-term learning opportunities); Learning through video games (Making learning fun, interactive and stimulating); Formative analytics (Developing analytics that help learners to reflect and improve); Trans-languaging (Enriching learning through the use of multiple languages); and Blockchain for learning (Storing, validating and trading educational reputation). The 2017 edition of the similar report from UKOU, the focus has been on online world where 'learners are faced with fake news, pseudo-science, 'post truth' and increasing tensions between some communities' (Ferguson et al., 2017, p.6). Some of the important innovative pedagogies as per this report are: Open textbooks (Adapting openly licensed textbooks); Immersive learning (Intensifying learning by experiencing new situations); Student-led analytics (Using data to help learners set and achieve their own goals); and Big-data inquiry: thinking with data (Understanding the world by working with large sets of data). These developments have a significant bearing upon the ODL world. Before we examine the impact of these developments to our focused institution, let's have a brief look at distance education in South East Asia.

Brief on Southeast Asia

Southeast Asia (SA) (extending for around 4000 miles roughly from northwest to southeast and comprises of around 13,000,000 square kilometers of land and sea) is a very interesting region as it comprises of many cultures and ecologies. It is situated east of Indian subcontinent and south of China, has two dissimilar portions: a continental projection (indicated as mainland Southeast Asia) and Insular Southeast Asia (consisting of many archipelagos to the south and east of the mainland (Britannica Online Encyclopaedia, 2017). The region falls into tropical and subtropical climatic zones and observes regular monsoon. Geographically the region is marked with mountains, plains and plateaus. The countries of Cambodia, Laos, Myanmar, Thailand, Vietnam and Singapore are at the southern tip of the Malay Peninsula. Malaysia is both mainland and insular. The ten member countries constitute ASEAN (Association of Southeast Asian Nations): Brunei, Cambodia, Indonesia, Laos, Malaysia, Myanmar, the Philippines, Singapore, Thailand, Vietnam. Southeast Asia comprises many cultures and ecologies. These represent a rich diversity in economy, geography, polity and education.

ASEAN Approach to Higher Education

In the year 2017, ASEAN completed its 50 years of establishment and during these past five decades member states have worked on achieving the 'One Vision, One Identity, One Community' motto. In 1997 during the Second ASEAN Informal Summit held in Kuala Lumpur 'ASEAN Vision 2020' was adopted laying emphasis on integration of education and human capital development which was echoed in Hanoi Plan of Action (December 1997) and later on in Vientiane Action Programme (2004). During the first meeting of ASEAN Ministers of Education held at Singapore in 2006 the Cha-am Hua Declaration highlighted role of education in achieving enduring solidarity and unity among the nations and people of ASEAN.

Table 1. Key facts on ASEAN

	HEI	Population	GER (%)	Size (Sq Km)	GDP (USD in Billion)	GNI (USD)	HDI (Rank)
Brunei	4	417400	32	5,765	17.10	37,320	31
Cambodia	37	15.3 m	16*	181,035	16.78	1,020	143
Indonesia	546	254.5 m	31+	1,910,931	888.5	3,630	110
Lao PDR	11	6.6 m	17	236,800	12.00	1,660	141
Malaysia	51	29.90 m	39	330,290	338.1	11,120	62
Myanmar	99	53.44 m	14!	676,577	64.33	1,270	148
Philippines	1346	99.14 m	36	300,000	284.8	3,500	115
Singapore	8	5.47 m	-	716	307.9	55,150	11
Thailand	150	67.73 m	51	513,120	404.8	5,780	93
Vietnam	70	90.73 m	30	331,212	186.2	1,890	116

Sources: Higher Education Institutions: WHED, 2016; Population: World Bank, 2014; GER, = Gross enrolment Ratio, tertiary, both sexes, 2014 (* = 2011; † = 2013; ! = 2012); Encyclopaedia Britannia: 2016; World Bank, 2014; World Bank, 2014; Human Development Index (HDI): 2015 [as produced in IAU (2016). Higher Education in ASEAN. (page 8)]

Recently an ASEAN Socio-Cultural Community Blueprint 2025 was launched in 2016 recommending an innovative ASEAN approach to higher education with the purpose to promote greater people-to-people interaction and mobility within and outside ASEAN with the objective to promote "free flow of ideas, knowledge, expertise and skills to inject dynamics within the region".

Owing to the diverse geography and cultural settings, it is important to learn something about higher education in Southeast Asia. This has been echoed well in the UNESCO Bangkok and SEAMEO RIHED (2006) Report "Higher Education in Southeast Asia" that, "For constructive and productive cooperation, policy makers and practitioners must be well-informed about higher education development and trends in other countries so that they can convert such information into useful policies and practices within the confines of their national needs and circumstances" (p.1). The ASEAN Socio-Cultural Community Blueprint 2025 lays emphasis on co-operation on human and social development in relation to among other areas, education and ICT use. For education, it specifies, "The ASEAN Work Plan on Education 2016-2020, which was adopted at the Ninth ASEAN Education Ministers meeting in Kuala Lumpur in May 2016, covers co-operation in areas including regional history and culture, education access, ICT in education, Technical and Vocational Education and Training (TVET) and lifelong learning, education for sustainable development, quality assurance, university-industry partnerships and capacity building in the education sector. Improving accessibility is a particular emphasis of the ASEAN Declaration on Strengthening Education for Out-of-School Children and Youth, adopted at the ASEAN Summit in September 2016." (OECD 2017, p. 124)

Higher Open and Distance Education System

Literature is abundant to prove that open and distance education system is a very successful model to serve educational needs of masses. Distance education is an effective medium to solve the problem of accessibility of higher education when it comes to social issues and working hours etc, in addition to increasing learning efficiency (Vasilevska et al., 2017). Calderon (2012) estimated that by 2030, globally higher education sector will observe 414.2 million enrolments, an increase of 314 per cent from worldwide enrolment in 2000. By 2035, student enrolment in higher education worldwide is expected to exceed 520 million. On these lines, MOOCs have been tried in SA region too. The National Institute of Education (NIE), Singapore offered a MOOC on management and school leadership in 2015. National University of Singapore and Nanyang Technological University also experimented with MOOCs (Teng, 2015). Malaysia also launched MOOCs on OpenLearning.com platform in 2013 and currently many of the universities not only in Malaysia but other countries too use OpenLearning. com platform to offer MOOCs.

The establishment of UNESCO Bangkok Asia Pacific Bureau in 1961 and creation of Southeast Asian Ministers of Education Organisation (SEAMEO) in 1965 were important milestone for boosting regional cooperation in education, science and culture. This was soon followed by launch of ASEAN in 1967 (Chou & Ravinet, 2017). The seriousness of the governments to higher education provisions can be noticed as ASEAM members established an ASEAN University Network (AUN) in 1992 to manage various discipline-based collaborative initiatives, projects, networks and associated mobility scholarships among 30 flagship higher education institutions (Chou & Ravinet, 2017, p. 151). Southeast Asian Ministers of Education Organisation's Regional Centre for Higher Education and Development (SEAMEO RIHED) also plays a great role in higher education cooperation in ASEAN region. There are around 12 million post-secondary students studying in 6500 higher educational institutions (Morrison, 2016). The region is characterised with student and programme mobility and observes innovative forms of managing and regulating transnational education, however there is no inter-regional regulatory framework for tertiary education, credit transfer or quality assurance (Morrison, 2016, p.3).

Ramkhamhaeng University of Thailand (established in 1971) is considered to be the first open admissions university in Southeast Asia (Jung & Latchem, 2007). Its purpose was to provide a platform to large number of school leaving students to get university education because other Thai Universities were not able to accommodate large admissions. Gradually almost all countries in the region established open universities to provide an alternate mechanism for tertiary education. This became so popular that some of them acquired the status of 'super mega universities' (Ali, 2012). Indonesia started an Open Junior Secondary School in 1979 initially in 5 locations in 5 provinces, later on spread to whole country to provide basic and secondary education to school age children who were not able to attend formal schooling due to geographic, socio-economic and cultural reasons (Sadiman, 2006). Open Universities were established in Thailand, Indonesia, Philippines, Myanmar, Vietnam and Malaysia etc, to cater to not only primary, secondary and tertiary education but also teacher education. In addition, ICT has been prominently used in the region, for example, radio broadcasts were provided for primary school teachers since 1970s. Thailand started using TV broadcast way back in 1964 and then Radio for distance education programmes from primary to pre-university level in 1978 (Sadiman, 2006). Some of the countries adopted ICT policy (e.g., Thailand and Malaysia). This promoted use of e-learning or online education greatly in the region. Philippines has been using ICT for Basic Education for a long time for areas like infrastructure development, technical support, teacher training on the design, production and use of ICT-based instructional materials, research and development, technology integration in the curriculum, use of innovative technologies in education and training, and fund generation (UNESCO, 2003). Not only this, there is a policy focus on reforming higher education to deliver better quality and cost effectiveness of tertiary education in the region. For example, higher education is expanding in Myanmar with 32 institutions in 1988 to 163 in 2012 (OECD, 2017, p. 237). While expanding access to university education in Myanmar, the Govt need to focus on technical and vocational education and training (TVET) because it will create more jobs. Thus a Comprehensive Education Sector Review (CESR) was started in 2012 as a SWOT analysis and one of the recommendation was "assigning dedicated staff to teach and manage distance-education courses" (CESR Office, 2014).

Academic Mobility

Tan (2018) reported that more Southeast Asian students are choosing China for higher education, for example in case of students from Myanmar opting for

China, reasons cited were joint ventures between two countries, and more job opportunities due to experience in China when they get back home. Highest number of students studying at higher education institutions in China come from ASEAN, followed by South Koreans (Tan, 2018). QS Digital Marketing (2018) in the Asian perspective, in addition to China and India, other countries like Vietnam, Indonesia, Nepal, and Bangladesh are also reporting improved economic development and thus would be some of the prime recruitment zones within the next few decades. Take the case of Vietnam, its economy is steadily growing and thus people are able to afford better and overseas education. According to Ashwill (2016) out of around 1.2 million international students enrolled in bachelor, masters or doctoral programmes in USA, 77% are from Asia. There was an increase of 13.3% in the number of active international students in 2016 as compared to 2015 studying in USA. From Southeast Asia, students going from Vietnam to USA have increased 18.9% from July to November 2015. The reasons for this increase of students' mobility from Vietnam are various: its robust economic growth, increase in ultra high net worth individuals, liking towards branded goods and merchandise and the over living cost in USA getting affordable by Vietnamese.

Rastogi et al. (2013) predicted that the number of middle-class and affluent consumers (MACs) in Indonesia is going to be double from 74 million to approximately 141 million by 2020. Use and adoption of digital technology is also on the increase and supermarkets and hypermarkets are mushrooming all over the country. With these economic developments in sight, Indonesia is one of the 20 largest economies in the world and by 2030 it will enter the league of top ten (ICEF Monitor, 2015). With the number of graduates the country needs, student mobility to other destinations can be noticed already.

AS what the Erasmus programme did to the success of mobility programme in Europe (European Union, 2014), ASEAN too launched a scheme in 2010 with collaborating Ministry of Education Malaysia; the Directorate General of Higher Education, Ministry of Education and Culture, Indonesia; and Office of Higher Education Commission, Ministry of Education, Thailand; and the Southeast Asian Ministers of Education Organization-Regional Centre for Higher Education and Development (SEAMEO RIHED) as the ASEAN International Mobility for Students (AIMS) Programme. Initially launched as a Malaysia-Indonesia-Thailand and SEAMEO RIHED (M-I-T) Student Mobility Pilot Project, its scope was expanded later on. With participating countries like Brunei Darussalam, Indonesia, Malaysia, the Philippines, Thailand, Vietnam, Japan and Republic of Korea, the mobility Programme offers students to enrol in the region for various undergraduate study programmes, like Hospitality and Tourism, Agriculture,

Table 2. Secondary education: Percentage of teachers in secondary education who are qualified, both sexes (%)

	2013	2014	2015	2016	2017
Brunei Darussalam		86.52734	95.71722	91.60248	
Indonesia				74.77849	
Laos	76.34388	79.22581	79.90643	80.32819	
Malaysia				100	
Myanmar					93.25925
Philippines	100		99.40958		
Thailand		100	100		

Indicators 4.c.1-4.c.4 and 4.c.6
Source: UNESCO Institute for Statistics, 2011

Language and Culture, International Business, Food Science and Technology, Engineering, Economics, Environmental Management and Science, Biodiversity and Marine Science.

International Perspectives in Learning and Teaching Processes

According to SDGs, by 2030, there shall be a substantially increase in the supply of qualified teachers, including through international cooperation for teacher training in developing countries, especially least developed countries and small island developing states. Table 2 shows the percentage of qualified secondary teachers in the countries of Southeast Asia, the trends indicate a rise over the years.

CONCLUSION

There is a rising demand for higher education in Southeast Asia due to its young population, steadily growing economies and effective social changes. There are voices seeking institutional autonomy and corporatization of public universities in Southeast Asia. One of the reason is the decline of government funding of public universities. These are expected to be self-financing. Thailand's Office of Higher Education Commission (OHEC) launched a Thailand Qualification Framework (TQF) for approving autonomy status for public universities. Joint collaborations are being signed among institutions.

REFERENCES

ADB. (2009). *Good practice in information and communication technology for education. Mandaluyong City.* Asian Development Bank.

Ali, A. (2012). *Surviving the 21st century in Southeast Asia: open and distance learning for human capital development.* SEAMEO SEAMOLEC and HOU international seminar on open and distance learning: Southeast Asian open and distance learning in the 21st century, Danang City, Vietnam.

Ashwill, M. (2016). Vietnamese student numbers growing in the US. *Web News.* Accessed at http://www.universityworldnews.com/article. php?story=2016011313585113

UNESCO Bangkok and SEAMEO. (2006). *Higher education in Southeast Asia.* Bangkok: UNESCO Asia and Pacific Regional Bureau for Education.

Britannica online Encyclopedia. (2017). *Southeast Asia.* Retrieved from https:// www.britannica.com/print/article/556489

Calderon, A. (2012, September 2). *Massification continues to transform higher education.* Retrieved from University World News: http://www. universityworldnews.com/article.php?story=20120831155341147

CESR Office. (2014). *Comprehensive Education Sector Review Phase (2) Report (Draft): Consultation Meeting for Development Partners (presentation).* Yangon: Comprehensive Education Sector Review Office.

Chou, M., & Ravinet, P. (2017). Higher education regionalism in Europe and Southeast Asia: Comparing policy ideas. *Policy and Society, 36*(1), 143–159. doi:10.1080/14494035.2017.1278874

Digital Marketing, Q. S. (2018). Emerging Student Markets in South and South East Asia. *Web News.* accessed from http://www.qs.com/emerging-student-markets-in-south-and-south-east-asia/

European Union. (2014). *The Erasmus Impact Study: Effects of mobility on the skills and employability of students and the internationalisation of higher education institutions.* Accessed from http://ec.europa.eu/dgs/education_culture/ repository/education/library/study/2014/erasmus-impact_en.pdf

Ferguson, R., Barzilai, S., Ben-Zvi, D., Chinn, C. A., Herodotou, C., Hod, Y., ... Whitelock, D. (2017). *Innovating Pedagogy 2017: Open University Innovation Report 6.* Milton Keynes, UK: The Open University.

IAU. (2016). *Higher Education in ASEAN*. The International Association of Universities. Accessed from https://www.iau-aiu.net/IMG/pdf/iau_higher_education_in_asean-2.pdf

ICEF Monitor. (2015). Indonesia looks to education to help drive growth. *Webnews*. Accessed from http://monitor.icef.com/2015/05/indonesia-looks-to-education-to-help-drive-growth/

Jung, I. S., & Latchem, C. (2007). Assuring quality in Asian open and distance learning. *Open Learning*, *22*(3), 235–250. doi:10.1080/02680510701619885

Morrison, K. (2016). *A rough guide to Southeast Asia for BC Institutions*. Available online http://bccie.bc.ca/wp-content/uploads/2016/06/ascendance-of-southeast-asia.pdf

NMC Horizon Report, . (2012). *2012 Higher Education Edition*. Austin, TX: The New Media Consortium.

OECD. (2017). *Economic Outlook for Southeast Asia, China and India 2017: Addressing Energy Challenges*. Paris: OECD Publishing.

Rastogi, V., Tamboto, E., Tong, D., & Sinburimsit, T. (2013). Indonesia's Rising Middle-Class and Affluent Consumers: Asia's Next Big Opportunity. *Webnews*. Accessed from https://www.bcg.com/publications/2013/center-consumer-customer-insight-consumer-products-indonesias-rising-middle-class-affluent-consumers.aspx

Sadiman, A. S. (2006). *Challenges in education in Southeast Asia*. Paper presented at the International Seminar on "Towards Cross Border Cooperation between South and Southeast Asia: The Importance of India's North East Playing Bridge and Buffer Role", Kaziranga, India. Available online at http://www.seameo.org/vl/library/dlwelcome/publications/paper/india0

Sharples, M., de Roock, R., Ferguson, R., Gaved, M., Herodotou, C., Koh, E., ... Wong, L. H. (2016). *Innovating Pedagogy 2016: Open University Innovation Report 5*. Milton Keynes, UK: The Open University.

Tan, V. (2018). Why more Southeast Asian students are choosing China for higher education. *Web News*. Accessed at https://www.channelnewsasia.com/news/asia/why-more-southeast-asian-students-are-choosing-china-for-higher-10042118

Teng, A. (2015, November 12). *NIE to offer courses on open online platform*. Retrieved from Straits Times: http://www.straitstimes.com/singapore/education/nie-to-offer-courses-on-open-online-platform

UNESCO. (2003). *Synthesis of Country Case Studies, South East Asian ICT Advocacy and Planning Workshop for Policy Makers*. Bangkok: UNESCO Asia and Pacific Regional Bureau of Education.

UNESCO. (2011). *ICT in higher education: Case studies from Asia and the Pacific*. Bangkok: UNESCO Bangkok.

Vasilevska, D., Rivza, B., Alekneviciene, B., & Parlinska, A. (2017). Analysis of the Demand for Distance Education at Eastern and Central European Higher Education Institutions. *Journal of Teacher Education for Sustainability*, *19*(1), 106–116. doi:10.1515/jtes-2017-0007

Chapter 5
National Prospects and Regional Challenges for Internationalization of the Palestinian Higher Education:
On the Margins of Globalization

Umut Koldas
Near East University, Cyprus

Mustafa Çıraklı
Near East University, Cyprus

ABSTRACT

Most of the challenges faced by the Palestinian higher education institutions (HEIs) towards internationalization stem from the problematic nature of bilateral relations of the Palestinian Authority (PA) in West Bank and Gaza Strip (WBGS) with Israel. Evaluating the geo-political, socio-economic, historical, and organizational barriers to internationalization of higher education in the WBGS, the chapter elaborates on the cumulative effects of the Israeli direct and indirect control over the WBGS on the development of universities, the impact of geo-political restraints of being a conflict zone, and logistical restrictions imposed on the movement of academics, visitors, and academic materials. Various domestic challenges including the political and ideological differences within the PA, the quality of national-level governance, and planning in higher education and financing are also highlighted throughout. Referring to the catalysts and obstacles, the chapter concludes with a reflection on the future challenges and prospects facing the Palestinian HEIs in a dynamic yet challenging context.

DOI: 10.4018/978-1-5225-5231-4.ch005

INTRODUCTION

Internationalization of higher education has been one of the primary concerns of the Palestinian National Authority for its development in the field of education. The Palestinian higher education community has not considered internationalization simply as a process of adopting the international means for development. Internationalization has rather been perceived as a driving force for economic, political and societal recognition by the international society as well as by Israel. Indeed, from the very early phases of their establishment, activities of the Palestinian higher education institutions toward internationalization have been mediated by the perplexing context of Israeli control over the education system, Palestinian struggle for national independence, socio-political turmoil and economic development (Zelkovitz, 2014). In this respect, Palestinian universities have been the dynamic forces of human empowerment (Bruhn, 2006) and national development under the most troubled social, political, and economic circumstances (Abu Lughod, 2000) especially until the end of the Israeli control over Palestinian territories in West Bank and Gaza Strip (WBGS) in the early 1990s. With the end of the Israeli rule over the WBGS territories and the establishment of the Palestinian National Authority in 1994, the higher education was restructured and initial efforts toward internationalization begun under the auspices of the Ministry of Education and Higher Education. These efforts gained momentum with further developments generated by the emerging necessity of adapting to the new processes of globalization and internationalization in the higher education field globally from the late 1990s onwards.

The bourgeoning literature on the Palestinian higher education and its various aspects including the organizational effectiveness of Palestinian higher education institutions and programs (Abushawish et al., 2013), challenges (Gerner & Schrodt, 1999) and prospects of research and development in the Palestinian higher education (Qumsiyeh & Isaac, 2012) strategic impact and the socio-economic outcomes of higher education (Alfoqahaa, 2015), compatibility of Palestinian higher education with the local labour market (Abu Hilal, 1998) and the readiness of Palestinian higher education for e-learning (Shraim, 2012) have all been invaluable in shedding much-needed light onto the current situation with regards to the internationalization of the Palestinian higher education.

These works have also underlined, in one way or another, the fact that Palestinian Higher education continues to be widely framed by the efforts towards global recognition and overcoming the obstacles emanating from the intra-regional tensions. In a fluid context marked by conflict and instability, there is nonetheless a persistent need to place the abovementioned debates and discussions about the existing structure of the Palestinian higher education system into a socio-political context in order to adequately account for the changes and continuities in the structural factors that mediate the efforts in relation to internationalization in the field of higher education. This chapter focuses on the dynamics and processes of internationalization of the Palestinian higher education by with particular reference to both catalysts of and challenges to internationalization. Reflecting on the catalysts for internationalization, the chapter examines the extent to which the key benchmarks in internationalization have been met. To this end, participation of the Palestinian higher education institutions in the internationally coordinated/funded programs such as *Tempus* and Erasmus through collaborative projects (Hammond, 2012) internationalized curricula, quality assurance (Dagga & Alyan, 2014); recruitment policies of international academic staff and students (Robinson, 2010) are evaluated with specific attention to the attainment of desired internationalisation outcomes.

Most of the challenges faced by the Palestinian higher education institutions towards internationalization stem from the problematic nature of bilateral relations of the Palestinian Authority in West Bank and Gaza with Israel. Evaluating the geo-political, socio-economic, historical and organizational barriers to internationalization of higher education in the West Bank and the Gaza Strip, the chapter elaborates on the cumulative effects of the Israeli direct and indirect control over the WBGS on the development of universities (Moughrabi, 2004), the impact of geo-political restraints of being a conflict zone for internationalization of higher education (Ben Tsur, 2009) and logistical restrictions imposed on the movement of academics, visitors and academic materials (Atshan, 2015). Various domestic challenges including the political and ideological differences between Hamas and Fatah (Saleh el-Namey, 2016), the quality of national-level governance and planning in higher education and financing are also highlighted throughout. Referring to the abovementioned catalysts and obstacles the chapter concludes with a reflection on the future challenges and prospects facing the Palestinian Higher Education institutions in a dynamic yet challenging context.

CONCEPTUAL FRAMEWORK AND METHODOLOGY

The globalization of higher education is a compelling, multifaceted process which entails several characteristics including but not limited to: the multinational and cross-border market-driven activities of the higher education institutions

(Varghese, 2008); growing academic capitalism (Davidovitch *et al.,* 2012); significant commercialization of higher education activities; increasing flow of students, academics and knowledge; commodification of knowledge and trans-boundary expansion of knowledge economy; growing challenges to control of state over the inter-institutional activities in higher education; growing interconnectedness between the higher education institutions and the global economic networks (i.e. global labour markets, multinational companies, global entrepreneurs, corporate entities, cross-border educational agents of supply and demand).

Within a globalized context of education moreover, cross-border education has become an important constituent of the internationalization processes with regard to increasing academic mobility of students and academic staff, adopting international and multicultural outlook in learning and teaching programs, recruiting international academic staff and students, developing international collaboration with trans-border higher educational institutions, obtaining international accreditations, and adapting to international norms and standards of higher education.

In a global context, directions of flow of students' academics and knowledge are increasingly influenced by the cost and quality of higher education and less so by the political, ideological and geographical considerations (unlike the earlier historical periods of colonization and Cold War). With higher education being rendered an intercultural commercial activity, which is traded globally through attracting capital investments and generating billions of dollars in world economy, the objectives and organization of the higher education have also evolved from serving merely ideological purposes toward a market-oriented approach shaped by a socio-cultural and economic rationale. Referring to the abovementioned ties between the internationalization processes of higher education and globalization, the chapter will draw on a selection of globalization theories and internationalization approaches in its evaluation of the Palestinian higher education system. Within the conceptual framework adopted here, rationales and imperatives (Knight & De Wit, 1997; de Wit, 1999; Scott, 1994) as well as elements (Scott, 1992; Francis, 1993; Knight, 1994) of internationalization of higher education are assessed with reference to the comparative internationalization approaches (Qiang, 2003) and globalization theories of higher education (Held et al., 2000; Bloom, 2006; Horta 2009; Jones & de Wit, 2012).

Knight and de Wit (1997) distinguish between the political and economic rationales (including economic growth and investment) and educational and cultural rationales (the developing an international dimension to research and teaching, quality improvement etc.). Scott highlights seven reasons or "imperatives" which relate to economic competitiveness, labour market, national security and mutual understanding. A number of elements (different types of activities including student/faculty exchanges, curriculum, recruiting international students etc.) are then identified which play an important role in the internationalization process (Francis, 1993; Knight, 1994). In the analysis below, such *indicators* of internationalization (participation in the internationally coordinated/funded programs such as *Tempus* and Erasmus +, internationalized curricula, quality assurance and international recruiting) are assessed with particular reference to the imperatives and elements outlined in the literature. In empirical terms, the discussion is based on the statistics and reports of the Palestinian Ministry of Education and Higher Education, numbers of incoming and outgoing students, academic exchanges from/to Palestine, trends in employment of foreign academic staff in Palestinian universities, number of countries that accredits the Palestinian higher education institutions, number of joint academic programs and joint research projects.

The empirical assessment of the selected internationalization indicators is then pegged onto the discussion on the challenges that emanate largely from the international context and the troubled relationship with Israel in particular. In the approach developed by Qiang (2003) moreover, specific attention is called for the interplay of various international and national forces and actors. In his comparative research of the ETH Zurich and IST Lisbon, Horta also found that internationalization cannot be withdrawn from its national and local socio-economic contexts as well as the international context (Horta, 2009). Within this framework, the cumulative effects of the Israeli control, the impact of the conflict and logistical restrictions imposed on the movement of students and academics will be assessed in tandem with the domestic challenges including the political contestation between Hamas and Fatah, inadequate policy coordination at the national level as well as the issues relating to financing.

INTERNATIONALIZATION OF THE PALESTINIAN HIGHER EDUCATION: KEY INDICATORS AND CHALLENGES

Within Palestine, there are currently 50 accredited higher education institutions consisting of universities, university colleges, polytechnics and community colleges. In the West Bank, out of 33 higher education institutions, there are nine "traditional universities" (2 governmental, 6 public, 1 private). In Gaza, there are institutions which include 5 "traditional" universities (1 governmental, 2 public and 2 private). In 2015-2016 academic year, the total number of students registered at the Palestinian universities was around 216,028 with 132,348 registered at the 'traditional' universities (Tempus, 2012). It is estimated that the gross enrolment rate for the age group of 18- 24 year olds is more than 25.8% — a relatively high figure by international standards, and when compared to other countries in the region (World Bank, 2007). The higher education sector is overseen by the Ministry for Education and Higher Education (MOHE) while the responsibility for policy formulation rests with the Council for Higher Education formed under the Accreditation and Quality Assurance Commission (AQAC) which oversees the quality of Palestinian higher education institutions and their academic programmes (Tempus, 2012). In terms of funding, the Palestinian National Authority runs and finances the governmental higher education institutions in the West Bank (Palestine Technical University-Khadoorie) and the Gaza Strip (Al Aqsa University) which are under the direct supervision of the Palestinian Ministry of Education and Higher Education. Most higher education institutions ("traditional universities" in particular) were set up mostly during the period of Israeli occupation of the West Bank and the Gaza Strip. The majority are non-profit and originally created and owned by local charity associations and NGOs. They depend on fundraising and receive partial government funding. Administrators at Al-Quds University, for instance, indicated the institution receives just 12 percent of its funding from the PA, while tuition fees make up 62 percent and private donations account for the rest (cited in Robinson, 2010). This has meant that while being overseen by the Council and the AQAC, higher education institutions still enjoy a good degree of autonomy and self-management in terms of admissions, recruitment of staff, assessment of students, granting of degrees and diplomas and the development of facilities (Bekhradnia, 2009).

The theme of internationalization has been first introduced and consolidated into the Palestinian Higher Education system through the membership of the Tempus Programme in 2001 and currently through Erasmus+. The Tempus Programme was initiated in 1990 as a response to the fall of the Berlin Wall in 1989 and the prospect of certain Eastern European countries (the first three eligible countries for Tempus funding were Poland, Hungary, and Czechoslovakia) joining the EU. The Programme was extended into the Mediterranean region, including Palestine, in 2001 with an aim to contribute to the modernisation of universities in non-EU partner countries through academic co-operation structured around projects that focus on academic subjects identified as being priorities by the partner countries concerned. This was done through the EU funded programmes, previously known Erasmus Mundus and Tempus. The Erasmus+ (Erasmus Plus) was introduced in 2014 to combine all the EU's schemes for education, training, youth and sport (Erasmus, Leonardo da Vinci, Comenius, Grundtvig), Youth in Action and five international co-operation programmes (Erasmus Mundus, Tempus, Alfa, Edulink and the programme for co-operation with industrialised countries) (European Commission, 2017). The EU Programmes such as Tempus and now the E+ mechanism have opened invaluable channels for mobility not only for students but also for Palestinian HEIs. A number of universities like An-Najah and Birzeit universities have established strong partnerships with the European HEIs where a number of students and staff have benefitted from the exchange programmes. For its part, the Palestinian authorities passed a law in 2016 that for the first time accredits joint master programs and diplomas obtained in Europe and elsewhere.

International Collaboration

16 universities in Palestine currently have bilateral agreements for partnerships and cooperation with universities in the Arab world, Europe, USA, Australia, China, Japan, Canada and other countries in the region. In this respect, France has been a particularly important partner for Palestine in fostering partnerships and twinning for the Palestinian HEIs. In multilateral terms, the tailor-made PEACE (Palestinian European Academic Co-operation in Education) Programme has 64 members: 52 European and 12 Palestinian universities. An office of the Programme was established at UNESCO, in Paris in 1995. The PEACE Programme helps to implement activities in this area within the framework of action launched by UNESCO, mainly through strengthening existing networks and establishing new ones between Palestinian higher education institutions and universities all over the world. More specifically, its activities in terms of fostering collaboration are chiefly concerned with maintaining consortia of universities which support one or several Palestinian universities in developing programmes in particular academic fields (e.g., the Law Studies Centre at Birzeit University, supported by seven European universities, the MA Programme in Applied Mathematics in Economics, developed by five French universities, etc.), or international chairs, sponsored jointly by UNESCO, under its UNITWIN/UNESCO Chairs Programme, the European Union, and other organisations, foundations, and bodies (Chitoran, 2010). Moreover, with the participation of the Occupied Palestinian Territories in the Tempus programme between 2002 and 2006 and then from July 2007 until 2014, the Palestinian institutions have been able to access different networks,

Table 1. Participation of Palestinian universities in Tempus projects (2008-12)*

Institution	Total
Birzeit University	8
An Najah University	7
Al Quds University	5
Palestine Polytechnic	5
Islamic University	3
Hebron University	2

*(Tempus, 2012)

not least those set up for the participating institutions of the Tempus projects (Table 1). Under the Tempus Programme, Palestine was awarded 22 projects in which 11 Palestinian HEIs were involved as partners.

In other fora too, the Palestinian universities have been able to collaborate with other HEIs in a number of different ways. Birzeit University's Institute of Women's Studies, for example, has established links with the sociology department at the London Schools of Economics (LSE). A joint project was also set up between Birzeit and the University of Warwick on 'Reconceptualising Gender: Transnational Perspectives', funded by the British Academy (Sowula, 2015). Birzeit has also benefitted from the British Council's 'HESPAL' scholarship scheme, a fund set up to support junior Palestinian academics to study in the UK. During 2012-2015, 69 scholars gained degrees in the UK (Sowula, 2015).

Mobility nonetheless is a significant issue as Palestinian academics and students experience serious obstacles — most notably in terms of obtaining visas — which have hindered their ability to study abroad or take part in various scholarship/exchange programmes. These challenges are elaborated further below.

Recruitment

Although student mobility within the Palestinian territories is very difficult due to the existing isolation of different cities imposed by the Israeli control, enrolment in higher education has increased significantly since the 1990s. From less than 40,000 students in 1993-1994, the number of students enrolled in HEIs exceeded 180,000 students in 2008/2009. Currently, the number of students enrolled in Palestinian HEIs stands at 216,000 (Ministry of Education, 2016).

Table 2. Flow of Tertiary Level Students (Top 10) – 2016*

Outbound (Palestinian Students)	Country
Jordan	10960
United Arab Emirates	4180
Saudi Arabia	4174
Turkey	976
Qatar	942
Malaysia	760
Germany	616
Egypt	575
United States	421
Ukraine	351

*(UNESCO, 2017b)

Table 3. Palestinian students studying abroad, all countries, both sexes (2010-2016) *

2010	2011	2012	2013	2014	2015	2016
15410	16678	19128	20861	24015	26278	26279

*(UNESCO, 2017a)

In addition, there are a number of multilateral as well as bilateral scholarship and academic exchange programmes, particularly at Bachelor and Master Level which has enabled Palestinian students to study abroad (Table 2). The PEACE (Palestinian European Academic Co-operation in Education) Programme, established in 1992 offers a scholarship scheme which supports Palestinian postgraduate students and young academics to pursue post-graduate studies abroad. By 2012, some 170 students had benefited from the scheme and many of them are now teaching at Palestinian universities. Such scholarships and exchange programmes have experienced a strong development during the last few academic years, contributing significantly to the numbers of Palestinian students studying abroad which has increased from 15,410 in 2010 to 26,279 in 2015 (UNESCO, 2017a).

More recently, Palestine was awarded 495 mobility places for students and staff (272 outbound to EU and 53 incoming from the EU) under the Erasmus Plus Credit Mobility Action. However, such cooperation has remained one-

Table 4. Erasmus + Mobility Statistics*

Year	Outgoing (to the EU)	Incoming (from the EU)
2015	270	51
2016	359	136

*(National Erasmus Office, 2017a)

sided as it has tended to be the Palestinian students usually going abroad, while international students have been discouraged not least by the significant problems encountered in obtaining visas. Although international students are allowed to enrol and study in Palestinian universities, their numbers remain extremely low due to the difficulty of obtaining visas from the Israeli authorities.

In this context, some Palestinian higher education institutions have devised innovative programmes in efforts to attract foreign students. The Palestine and Arab Studies (PAS) Programme offered by the University of Birzeit is a case in point. Offered as Arabic language courses with an option to enrol on a number of elective social science modules and regular university classes, the Programme entails 24 weekly contact hours over a 3-month period (Birzeit, 2017). More remarkably, the program's duration is set in consideration of the political situation and the difficulty of obtaining visas. As one participant has explained: "After students have been denied entry to Israel after stating their plans to study, especially when aiming for their second tourist visa, the university decided on a program fitting into the three month stay of one tourist visa [...]" (Yen, 2015).

The professional development of staff members is similarly restricted due to similar problems in obtaining visas. According to one Palestinian academic: "The Islamic University of Gaza (IUG) is currently a partner in four Erasmus Mundus exchange projects and about 50 students and staff members have won full scholarships to join about 30 universities in 14 European countries including the UK, Italy, France, Spain, Germany, Portugal, Greece, Sweden, Finland, Poland, Cyprus, Belgium, Austria and Czech Republic. All these grant holders were supposed to get visas in July and join their orientation and study programs in August or September, but it seems this is not going to happen" (Al-Masri, 2014).

According to an academic who took part in a rare faculty exchange: "despite the new buildings and dedicated activity, however, faculty at all the universities we visited reported a feeling of isolation—not only was travel for Palestinian academics restricted and expensive, but faculty exchanges were also difficult to arrange [...] visiting international academics could rarely get permission to stay beyond two or three months, which made teaching a class for a semester or long-term academic partnerships virtually impossible" (Visweswaran, 2015).

The recruitment of foreign academics too is frustrated not only by low salaries but also by the tight restrictions placed on their entry. Israeli authorities refuse issuing work visas to foreigners travelling to the West Bank; those who wish to enter the West Bank are granted a 3-month tourist visa instead. Temporary entry into Gaza is forbidden, unless for exceptional humanitarian reasons as determined by Israeli authorities (Robinson, 2010). When making international appointments, one of the most pressing problems facing universities is that they cannot be certain that the appointees will be allowed to enter the country by the Israelis.

Curriculum and Quality Assurance

The Tertiary Education Project which was funded by the World Bank and the European Commission and concluded in 2012 represents the largest intervention in the Palestinian higher education in terms of financing (World Bank, 2017). Within the Project's framework 21.6 m/USD was spent on the strengthening the policy-making role of the Ministry of Education and Higher Education and its relevant bodies (most notably the AQAC and the Education Council), increasing the efficacy and quality of the higher education institutions and in setting up a student aid program. One of the most notable outcomes of the project was the creation of a framework for accreditation in line with the international standards which played a major role in increasing the connection between the Palestinian HEIs and their counterparts around the world.

In a similar vein, the earlier Tempus programme also contributed significantly to the development of existing curricula by supporting a number of projects which focused on curriculum development. Within the project's framework moreover, new postgraduate courses were created collaboratively with partners from the Middle East and Europe (National Erasmus Office, 2017b). Another important progress in this respect was the establishing of a management information system and later the accreditation of the European Credit Transfer and Accumulation System (ECTS). The Tempus-funded RecoNow project has since enabled the Palestinian HEIs to accredit international student credentials with greater ease and in line with international standards. While making national systems more compatible, the ECTS is also a crucial tool in internationalization efforts by facilitating greater student mobility and recruitment through the recognition of the study period abroad as well as easier collaboration in developing joint programmes with other institutions (European Commission, 2014).

Such impressive progress has been overshadowed in recent years by domestic quarrels and the ongoing strife between the main Palestinian political factions, Hamas and Fatah. The bitter dispute between the two parties effectively means that universities in the West Bank and those in Gaza are run separately. Although academic staff co-operate with each other, there is no co-operation between the systems. The roots of the conflict affecting higher education is traced back to 2015 when the two factions begun fighting for control of the Al Aqsa University following the resignation of its chairman, Ali Abu Zuhri in August. Hamas, which controls the Gaza Strip then appointed Mohammed Radwan as acting chairman of the university without clearing the decision with the Fatah-controlled Palestinian Authority (El-Namey, 2016). The Palestinian Authority represented by Fatah responded by cutting the salaries of 11 pro-Hamas academics from the university (El-Namey, 2016). At its lowest point, in 2016 the Palestinian Ministry of Higher Education declared that it would no longer recognize new degrees from Al Aqsa University, the Gaza Strip's largest academic institution (Lieber, 2016). The political crisis has been compounded by an economic crisis largely as a result of Israel's decision to withhold taxes it collects from Palestinians. According to the World Bank: "The Government of Israel's decision to suspend the transfer of clearance revenue, which accounts for over 60 percent of the PA's revenues, has made it virtually impossible to achieve the objective of sustainable fiscal management." With the fiscal crisis and inadequate public funding for higher education, universities have been hit hard. Recent efforts nonetheless to politically reunite the two factions may eventually lead to the establishment of a unity government under which such problems can be overcome (Al-Mughrabi & Sawafta, 2017).

CONCLUSION

The cumulative effects of the Israeli military control and the impact of the conflict, not least through the logistical restrictions imposed on the movement of students and academics, are real obstacles to progress in higher education in general and internationalization in particular. Yet, the Palestinian HEIs have pursued with determination an agenda of internationalization despite the impeding dynamics of conflict and against the odds. Palestine's universities have trustees, the funding body is not part of the Government and the Quality Assurance Agency is independent of both. Most HEIs have also actively sought to maintain an international presence evident in their level of participation in various multilateral programmes and bilateral agreements. In this context, most universities have established strong partnerships with the European HEIs where a number of students and staff have benefitted from the exchange programmes. Such collaborative action is a key element of internationalisation. ECTS is also a crucial tool in internationalization efforts by facilitating greater student mobility and recruitment through the recognition of the study period abroad as well as easier collaboration in developing joint programmes with other institutions. The Palestine case shows that while conflict is certainly detrimental to progress in higher education, other factors including an enabling international environment and an active interest in the internationalization agenda can nonetheless drive it forward.

REFERENCES

Abou-dagga, S., & El-Holy, A. (2014). Enhancement of Quality in Palestinian Higher Education Institutions: The Case of Islamic University of Gaza (IUG). *The Online Journal of Quality Higher Education*, *1*(2), 53–59.

Abu-Lughod, I. (2000). Palestinian Higher Education: National identity, liberation and globalization. *Boundary 2*, *27*(1), 75–95. doi:10.1215/01903659-27-1-75

Abushawish, H. F., Ali, A. J. B., & Jamil, H. B. (2013). Key predictors of organizational effectiveness in Palestinian higher education: What matters for outcome. *Journal of Education Policy, Planning and Administration*, *2*(2), 55–80.

Al-Masri, N. (2014). Imagine you are a Palestinian academic or student. *Mondoweiss*. Available online at: http://mondoweiss.net/2014/08/palestinian-academic-student/

Al-Mughrabi, N., & Sawafta, A. (2017). Fatah, Hamas to discuss security in Gaza under unity deal. *Reuters*. Available online at: https://www.reuters.com/article/us-palestinians-reconciliation/fatah-hamas-to-discuss-security-in-gaza-under-unity-deal-idUSKBN1CE17Q

Alfoqahaa, S. (2015). Economics of Higher Education under Occupation: The Case of Palestine. *Journal of Arts and Humanities*, *4*(10), 25–43.

Atshan, S. (2015). Introduction. In *Impediments to education in the occupied Palestinian territories*. AURDIP. Available online at http://aurdip.fr/les-entraves-a-l-education-dans.html?lang=en

Bekhradnia, B. (2009). Battered but unbowed. *Times Higher Education*. Available online at: https://www.timeshighereducation.com/features/battered-but-unbowed/409752.article

Ben-Tsur, D. (2009). The impact of conflict on international student mobility: A case study of international students studying in Israel. *International Studies in Sociology of Education*, 19(2), 135–149. doi:10.1080/09620210903257257

Birzeit University. (2017). *About the PAS Programme*. Available online at: http://sites.birzeit.edu/pas/about

Bloom, D. E. (2006). Education in a globalized world. *Globalization and Education, Political Academy of Sciences, Extra Series 28*. Available online at http://www.pas.va/content/dam/accademia/pdf/es28/es28-bloom.pdf

Bruhn, C. (2006). Higher Education as Empowerment: The Case of Palestinian Universities. *The American Behavioral Scientist*, 48(8), 1125–1142. doi:10.1177/0002764205284722

Chitoran, D. (2010). *The Peace Programme: A Unique Interuniversity cooperation network*. Global University Network for Innovation. Retrieved from http://www.guninetwork.org/articles/peace-programme-unique-interuniversity-cooperation-network

Davidovitch, N. (2012). Academic Capitalism in Higher Education – A Cross Cultural Perspective: CIS – Israel. *International Journal of Academic Research in Progressive Education and Development*, 1(4), 326–339.

De Wit, H. (1999). Changing Rationales for the Internationalization of Higher Education. *International Higher Education*, 15.

El-Namey, S. (2016, October 14). Hamas-Fatah feud stalls Gaza higher education. *The Electronic Intifada*.

European Commission. (2014). *ECTS and diploma supplement label holders 2011 & 2012: Internationalisation in Europe's universities*. EU Publications. Retrieved from https://publications.europa.eu/en/publication-detail/-/publication/a3713d20-71dd-4b06-b19f-796972dd86e9

Francis, A. (1993). *Facing the future: the internationalization of post-secondary institutions in British Colombi*. Vancouver: Centre for International Education.

Gerner, D. J., & Schrodt, P. A. (1999). Into the New Millennium: Challenges facing Palestinian higher education in the Twenty First Century. *Arab Studies Quarterly*, *21*(4), 17–33.

Hammond, K. (2012). Lifelong learning in Palestine. *Journal of Holy Land and Palestine Studies*, *11*(1), 79–85. doi:10.3366/hls.2012.0031

Held, D. (2000). Global Transformations: Politics, Economics and Culture. In C. Pierson & S. Tormey (Eds.), *Politics at the Edge, Political Studies Association Yearbook Series*. London: Palgrave Macmillan. doi:10.1057/9780333981689_2

Hilal, M. A. (1998). *The compatibility of higher education with the local labor market: Analytical study. Palestinian Ministry of Finance, No.9*. Nablus.

Horta, H. (2009). Global and national prominent universities: Internationalization, competitiveness and the role of the state. *Higher Education*, *58*(3), 387–405. doi:10.100710734-009-9201-5

International Network for Cooperation with Palestinian Universities. (1999). *Peace Programme: Palestinian/European/American Cooperation in Education*. Retrieved from: http://unesdoc.unesco.org/images/0011/001176/117620Eo.pdf

Jones, E., & de Wit, H. (2012). Globalization of Internationalization: Thematic and regional reflections on a traditional concept. *The International Journal of Higher Education and Democracy*, *3*, 35–54.

Knight, J., & de Wit, H. (1997). *Internationalisation of Higher Education in Asia Pacific Countries*. Amsterdam: European Association for International Education.

Lieber, D. (2016, August). Ramallah invalidates new degrees from top Gaza university. *Times of Israel*, *10*. Retrieved from http://www.timesofisrael.com/ramallah-invalidates-new-degrees-from-top-gaza-university/

Moughrabi, F. (2004). Palestinian Universities Under Siege. *International Higher Education*, *36*, 9-10.

National Erasmus Office. (2017b). *Project Summaries (2008-2012)*. Retrieved from http://www.erasmusplus.ps/page-577-en.html

National Erasmus Office Palestine. (2017a). *2015-2016 Statistics on Key Action 1*. Retrieved from: http://www.erasmusplus.ps/page-703-en.html

Qiang, Z. (2003). Internationalization of Higher Education: Towards a conceptual framework. *Policy Futures in Education*, *1*(2), 248–270. doi:10.2304/pfie.2003.1.2.5

Qumsiyeh, M., & Jad, I. (2012). Research and Development in the Occupied Palestinian Territories: Challenges and opportunities. *Arab Studies Quarterly*, *34*(3), 158–172.

Robinson, D. (2010). The Status of Higher Education Teaching Personnel in Israel, the West Bank and Gaza. *Education International*. Retrieved from www.ei-ie.org

Scott, R. A. (1992). *Campus developments in response to the challenges of internationalization: The case of Ramapo College of New Jersey*. Springfield: CBIS Federal.

Shraim, K., & Khlaif, Z. (2012). An e-learning approach to secondary education in Palestine: Opportunities and challenges. *Information Technology for Development*, *16*(3), 159–173. doi:10.1080/02681102.2010.501782

Sowula, T. (2015). Why Palestinian Universities are looking abroad. *The British Council*. Retrieved from: https://www.britishcouncil.org/voices-magazine/why-palestinian-universities-are-looking-abroad

TEMPUS. (2012). *Higher Education in the Occupied Palestinian Territories*. Retrieved from: http://eacea.ec.europa.eu/tempus/participating_countries/overview/oPt.pdf

UNESCO. (2017). *Outbound internationally mobile students by host region*. Retrieved from: http://data.uis.unesco.org/Index.aspx?queryid=172

Varghese, N. V. (2008). *Globalization of higher education and cross-border student mobility*. IIEP Research Papers. Retrieved from http://www.iiep.unesco.org/en

Visweswaran, K. (2015, September). Palestinian universities and everyday life under occupation. *American Association of University Professors Academe*.

World Bank. (2007). *West Bank and Gaza Public Expenditure Review. Vol. 1: From Crisis to Greater Fiscal Independence*. Report No. 38207-WBG. Retrieved from: http://unispal.un.org/pdfs/38207WBGVol1.pdf

World Bank. (2017). *Tertiary Education Project*. Retrieved from: http://projects.worldbank.org/P083767/wbg-tertiary-education-project?lang=en

Yen, E. (2015). Internationals at Birzeit University. *Palestine-Israel Journal of Politics, Economics and Culture*. Retrieved from: http://www.pij.org/details.php?blog=1&id=329

Zelkowitz, I. (2014). Education, Revolution and evolution: The Palestinian universities as initiators of national struggle 1972-1995. *Journal of the History of Education Society*, *43*(3), 387–407. doi:10.1080/0046760X.2014.889226

Chapter 6
Risk Management and Internationalization in Education Institutions

Behcet Öznacar
Near East University, Cyprus

Gokmen Dagli
University of Kyrenia, Cyprus & Near East University, Cyprus

ABSTRACT

internationalization plays a great role to foster the quality in education systems. In this respect, leadership and risk managements are essential factors to disseminate the quality in education. Therefore, this chapter encapsulates the essence of risk management and leadership in order to enlighten the merits of internationalization context. In addition to this, a detailed examination on risk management and leadership in a school becomes a model for further implications for the internationalization. Qualitative research was conducted to set the criteria on risk management and leadership within a school.

DOI: 10.4018/978-1-5225-5231-4.ch006

INTRODUCTION

Risk Management is a scientific approach that explains the matter of using the management approach in a specific situation or what the institution could do when facing possible risks. Risk management emerging from the insurance management is to determine the risks in facing any situation, to create options for those risks and to inspect the application process of the most proper option to the situation. Risk Management is applied by taking rapid actions upon fast decision making, and by developing a plan for strategies for resolution, assessment and control within the framework of risks (Dayan, 2006). Behaviors of the related institutions appear as the primary factor that influences both the nation itself and overseas. Decisions in providing resources for overseas activities is based on the experiential power of the company, and they pay attention to what alternatives are developed and how they are selected. This is an indicator stating that economies of the world depend on each other now. Higher education tends to be disrupted disproportionately by the government budget determinants. Even though the states and educational conditions are facing hard time, it is believed that everything will recover when risk determinants are used correctly (Knight, 2006).

Uppsala model has been placed in the frame of analytic formula which is handled on the risk factor basis as a mechanism that nationalizes the international problems and their solutions, making decision and determining risks. Risk management under educational process is a training unit which is prescribed with regard to how to prevent an argument that may arise among stakeholders. In a general sense, risk management which detects the risks of the organization is embraced as an academic attitude regarding what conditions should be protected or realized. Besides, it is a system which takes precautions for the problems, reduces problems and contains plans. In this context, previously developed risk management, namely the notification of strategy becomes effective in revealing the factors that will endanger the institutions in terms of the related vision, mission and values in order to boost the success and target regarding education management (Derici, Tüysüz & Sarı, 2008).

In literature science, the risk management characterizing the risks to which the institution would be subject as an academic attitude regarding in which conditions to protect or realizing the meaning of administration or management in a particular field, in fact, it has been brought forth from the insurance management and it is the inspection of the procedure by determining the risks in a possible individual case on condition that the alternatives are put into practise for handling the risks (Aras, 2007).

It is an inspection that helps to fix the negative factors which can form instability and uncertainty in risk management. It is a preliminary factor that has a retention capacity before problems emerge. It is a system that includes the plans that take precautions and minimize the damage by identifying the risks before problems emerge and create danger (Güzel, 2007). It can be seen that there are many internationalizations of higher education put forth by Jane Knight and Stephen Wilkins. Among them there are exchange programs, online programs that are marketed globally, matching agreements, joint evaluation programs, opening work centers and installation of in-branch campus areas (Knight, 2006; Wilkins, 2011). Each of these internationalization activities states the potential of generating income for a new institution. However, physical welfare of a faculty and personnel provides ways in stratifying of risk levels related to international operations in respect of the brand and reputation of an institution in each profit gaining. The risks for academic quality and institutional resources as well as academic activities provide institutions with many options in order that they could better adapt to their mission and culture. Thus, they can be associated through the factors that may be used to understand whether there is coherence with risk scale, which may be expected from the application of professional activities in relation to risk and nationalization at higher education (Beecher & Streitwieser, 2017).

All risks that are determined in a quality manner regarding the institution are conducted over precise basic conditions. These basic conditions should be predetermined; these are mission, vision and values. The risks should be determined by handling the goals and targets of the institution. In this way, in the context of the mentioned vision, mission and values in advance notification of strategy, it will be possible to reveal the factors that will endanger the institution to achieve its goal or to raise its success. The mission, vision and values are the main building stones of the strategic management and due to the fact that these concepts need to take place in notification of strategies of the institutions that use the strategic management, it will be necessary to take into consideration the current definitions instead of remaking the definitions of these terms when risks are detected (Derici, Tüysüz & Sarı, 2008).

Risk management is among the most comprehensive solutions of the contemporary management theory. The reason is that risk management creates an administrative mentality by having a scale role among the yield, capital and risk relations (Çolak & Yiğidim, 2001).In a study of Whitfield (2003), it was shown that the risk management models that have an entrepreneur spirit brought forth in business sector could also be applied to higher education. Furthermore, according to Abraham (1999), the risk management in educational institutions is to handle the occurring risks in the most effective and predictive manner during the application of the educational and research technics but not to eliminate the risk. It is a scientific approach that foresees the situation and minimizes the damage and prepares and apply policies for them in order to prevent the possible damages in case of any risk (Alkın, Tuğrul & Akman, 2001).

The risk management is under responsibility of the employer or manager. This task is provided by forming risk management or risk team in some institutions. The risk management team is offered by trained people on this matter in order to manage certain risks (Çelik & Kaplan, 2005). For instance, we can show the example of an administrator in an educational institution playing the role of training director of the institution. For this reason, the administrator may be regarded as responsible for undertaking the risks that are formed as a result of violating the rules with regard to operation of the educational institutions and even for the situation regarding the improvement of the structure of institution.

Risk management ensures the companies to continue their activities in a profitable manner, so it maintains the earning power of the institution by protecting the properties and persons; this process reduces the loss to a minimum level in case of any loss that is possible to emerge and takes the source and activity planning into the management and control of the organization (Emhan, 2009).

A branch of the risk management is the institution with its modern use. The matters that the institution deals with during a usual activity are to resolve, to minimize and to insure the risks that are faced. For instance, the subjects that a risk administrator deals with comprise preventing accidents, ensure the security of the building and facilities, credit management and take out the most appropriate policy (Seyidoğlu, 1999).

Even if there are differences among the definition of the risk management, there can be seen certain aspects in common. Internal controls and their independencies are among the leading principles. The main goal is that the persons who will make the assessment of decisions and activities of the risk persons and decision makers to assess in a different aspect to be different persons. Separating the risk types is a principle that is generally accepted and the fact that the risk is put into numeric data helps to facilitate the risk management (Phillips, 2009).

Profitability risk detects the income sources of an institution management; it is a capability of directing the activities to the profit-making areas. In order to increase the profit rate, it is the main object of the risk management to meet the increasing obligatory demands of the market by making compatible the capital, yield and risk (Aydın, 2010). It can be seen that there are many internationalizations of higher education put forth by Jane Knight and Stephen Wilkins. Among them there are exchange programs, online programs that are marketed globally, matching agreements, joint evaluation programs, opening work centres and installation of in-branch campus areas (Knight, 2006; Wilkins, 2011). Each of these internationalization activities states the potential of generating income for a new institution. However, physical welfare of faculty and personnel provides ways in stratifying of risk levels related to international operations in respect of the brand and reputation of an institution in each profit gaining. The risks for academic quality and institutional resources as well as academic activities provide institutions with many options in order that they could better adapt to their mission and culture. Thus, they can be associated through the factors that may be used to understand whether there is coherence with risk scale, which may be expected from the application of professional activities in relation to risk and nationalization at higher education (Beecher & Streitwieser, 2017).

The disadvantages that the institution will meet will be able to be decreased to minimum level in terms of quality and quantity with help of a proper risk management. It is only possible with a successful risk management that the possibility of negative condition is minimized (Lokumcu, 2009).

In order to detect and prevent the risks, the internal inspections that will be carried out by those skilled in risk management and controlling the educational institutions will be beneficial in minimizing the risks.

In the process of organizing, using, reporting and examining the inspections, the inspection standards forming a stakeholder point are the norms which are guiding minimally and binding to the person who carries out the inspection in accordance with the management of the inspection activities.

Risk management is important for educational institutions in two aspects. The first is that the educational institutions are established during decision and continue their functionality and are subject to some problems during this period. The reason for this, every decision that is made has the possibility of being wrong just like it would be right (Erdoğan, 2000), that is why training administrator is regarded to have accepted in advance the possible risks in case that the decision is wrong. When this situation is taken as basis, it can be understood that the training administrator is always subject to the risks which have the possibility of influencing the objectives of the school negatively. The second is that the cost of educational activities is high due to the fact that the key element of the educational institutions is human.

According to the research that is made by Huber (2011), it is indicated 8 major risk groups in education. Those risks are grouped as follows;

1. Prestige Status of Educational Institution in the Sector
2. Research
3. Learning and Teaching
4. Knowledge Transfer
5. Strategic Partnership
6. Human Resources
7. Infrastructure Possibilities of Educational Institution
8. Financial Problems of Educational Institution.

It has been notified that there is no difference in the order of importance of the risks consisting of eight articles and they all have the same importance level.

The sources of the risk, mitigating factors and early warning mechanisms should be assessed as a whole in order that the risk management could be applied efficiently besides indicating those risks. So, risk is just like two faces of a medal generally; correspondingly, we can face risk and ambiguities in every field. In relation to the risk and internationalization that are provided at higher education, Hleslood and Jong (2006) state in their study that risk cannot be taken entirely in social security; the risks such as theft, sexual abuse and violence are perceived as risk only, yet no solution is sought for and just like more radical institutions, only very few institutions perceive the threats like extremism and terrorism as a counter risk to some extent.

North Cyprus has the potential to transform the educational system into a successful sector. It has most of the necessary preconditions for the success. There is high demand for education, well-educated teachers, a sufficient number of schools and a significant amount of budget allocated to this sector.

The structure of the educational system of North Cyprus consists of; kindergarten, primary school of five years, secondary education of six years and higher education and non-formal education. The compulsory education comprises the primary and secondary schools. Within this period, the students are selected to the private academic schools and programs through an examination after the fifth degree of the primary school. In this examination, approximately a rate of 10% of the students is selected to the private academic colleges preparing for superior, secondary and higher education. The language of education in those schools is English. In this case, those schools are regarded as preparation schools for foreign universities. Furthermore, nearly 10% of the students go to private schools.

The secondary school is divided into two as general and vocational education. There is no significant difference between them. Principally in two systems, the graduates have the right to apply to higher education. However, vocational schools are the second option for Cypriot youth and their families.

There are some factors that can help the educational services to improve in North Cyprus: The first is that North Cyprus allows the direct interventions in the field instead of being based on a multi-level strategy due to the fact that it has limited number of schools and teachers. The second is that all age groups give great value to education. This situation has shown that the participation in all educational levels is high and has directed an increasing number of adults to the education after the secondary education. Thirdly, the teaching occupation draws heavy attention among young people, because the social rights and fees of teachers are quite higher when compared to other countries. The number and percentage of the students who go to schools according to their educational levels in North Cyprus are given in table 1.

Table 1. Table of schooling rate according to educational level (Ministry of Education)

Educational Level	Number of Students				Total Student Percentage			
	1990	2000	2005	2010/11	1990	2000	2005	2010/11
Pre-school	3,174	2,085	3,507	4,254	7.2	3.5	4.9	4.9
Primary Education	16,514	15,493	15,102	19,886	37.5	26.2	21.0	22.8
Secondary Education	19,525	17,702	14,416	18,718	44.3	30.0	20.0	21.5
Higher Education	4,812	23,791	38,912	43,476	10.9	40.3	54.1	49.9
Total	**44,025**	**59,071**	**71,937**	**87,080**	**100.0**	**100.0**	**100.0**	**100.0**

Table 2. Table of size of the educational system (Ministry of Education)

Educational Level	Student	Teacher	Institution	Rate of Student-Teacher 2010/11
Kindergarten	1,489	92	15	16.2
Primary School	18,189	1,537	88	11.8
Secondary School	6,208	610	14	10.2
High School	9,430	1,054	18	8.9
Vocational High School	3,080	554	11	5.6
Special Education	208	35	6	5.9
Total	**38,60**	**3,882**	**152**	**9.8**

As the statistics do not always have correct data on the migrating population, it is very difficult to detect how many children of these immigrants have never went to school or have not attended regularly. There are schools where the children of the citizens of Turkish Republic that come to the island temporarily among the students in Nicosia.

The size of the school network with regard to infrastructure is sufficient. There are 15 training institutions. 3,882 teachers have been employed in these schools for 38,604 students. The teacher-student rates are as follows; 1 to 16,2 in kindergartens, 1 to 11,8 in primary schools, 1 to 10,2 in secondary schools and 1 to 8,9 in high schools. This rate is 5,6 in vocational high schools. This situation is an indicator that vocational schools have been designed quite badly for the service to the current needs. For example, the fields and branches of the vocational high schools in Nicosia are relatively close to each other and most of them are insufficient in terms of physical infrastructure. Yet, the administrative staff is much greater than it should be in those schools. However, they do not have enough students to execute the programs of vocational schools efficiently in other districts. The figures that show the condition of the size of educational system in North Cyprus are given in Table 2.

The kindergarten is provided to all for free and the compulsory education is given as full public service. The special education is given by the trained specialists in 6 private educational institution and schools. The private schools

Table 3. Table of working hours of secondary school teachers

Country	Week	Training Day	Net Study Period (Hours)
TRNC	31	155	415 (Greek Cypriot 840)
Australia	38	184	622
Denmark	42	200	640
England	38	190	-
Finland	38	190	599
Germany	40	189	735
Hungary	37	185	555
Italia	33	165	594
Korea	37	220	560
Turkey	38	180	600
USA	36	180	1127
OECD Average	**38**	**186**	**701**

have smaller rate of teacher-student, better equipped classrooms, sports facilities, workshops and their own business budgets in order to finance their development activities during academic period. For this reason, the parents prefer the private schools in an increasing way for the education of their children.

The working hours of the teachers are determined on weekly basis. The working hours limitation is 20 courses in secondary school, 25 courses in the primary school and 30 courses in the kindergarten. The duration of every course is 40 minutes. The school year is 31 weeks. The working hours are normally between 08.00 and 13.00. Yet, it lasts until 16:15 on Mondays. The work load of the teachers is compared to OECD and EU countries in Table 3.

The teachers have two syndicates. One of them is for primary school teachers and the other is for secondary school teachers. The rate of syndication among teachers is quite high. Almost all of the teachers are members of their own syndicate. These two teacher syndicates are active in national policies and they have obtained quite favourable conditions for their own members.

Teachers and other public sector employee are wholly assigned as permanent staff by the "Public Service Commission". For this reason, the Ministry of Education has no right to recruit or discharge the teachers in continuous cadre or the school principals.

The students go to school 443 days (more than 2.5 years school period) less than their average peers in EU in the obligatory educational system of North Cyprus. The average school period is 187 days in Europe (this is 212 days in Southern Cyprus) and 155 days in North Cyprus.

The rate of 85% of the secondary education completion is high. However, the 27% of the students who go to high school prefer vocational high schools. Today occupational and technical education are regarded as option two or option three by the families and young people on account of their low quality with regard to further education or future employment possibilities.

In 1989, there were 3 universities having 3,443 students in North Cyprus. This rate became 5 universities and 38,900 students in 2005, and 6 universities and 43,476 students in 2010-2011.

In North Cyprus, the number of Cypriot university students was 790 in 1989, 9,862 students in 2005 and 11,038 students in 2010-2011 (State Planning Organization).

65% of the whole foreign students coming to North Cyprus come from Turkey. The decline of this number has influenced the financial status of the universities negatively. 32,438 foreign students that are coming from Turkey and other countries receive education in the 2010-2011 academic year. The students not only pay the tuition fees, but they also stay in the island for a 10 month period. According to official estimations, it is equal to 1,3 million of tourist visit in terms of economy that the students enter the country. The higher education is the biggest economic sector in North Cyprus. An increase in the number of higher education students between 1979 and 2013 can be seen below.

In the educational system, there are school-induced risk factors to the family, individual, society and environment. Although there was no research or study conducted with risk analysis and management in educational institutions in North Cyprus, a pilot questionnaire study has been conducted in order to bring to light the situation in the current educational system and the problems. Because this study that was reported in 2009 by Beyond Standards Limited was not published officially, a license was obtained regarding the use of the obtained information.

This pilot questionnaire study has been concluded in the direction of the views and observations of the students of Güzelyurt Vocational High School. 194 students participated in the questionnaire. The students answered the question about health and preservation against accidents that could emerge from bad habits as insufficient 21% and a little bit sufficient 22%.

The following results have emerged in another question asked to the students about the adequacy of the sports and social activity places that are under the risk that the students cannot maintain their education due to school and environmental factors.

The insufficiency in the infrastructure of the technological tools and information technologies creates risk for maintaining the education quality which contributes to the improvement of student education and as it is indicated in the previous studies. In this context, the answers of the question asked to the students are as follows:

Table 4. The sufficiency of the safety precautions inside the school

Very good	Good	Moderate	A little bit sufficient	Insufficient	I have no idea
11%	18%	17%	19%	33%	2%

Table 5. Adequacy of preservation against accidents that could emerge from bad habits and health

Very good	Good	Moderate	A little bit sufficient	Insufficient	I have no idea
14%	18%	24%	22%	21%	1%

Table 6. The efficiency of the social activity areas

Very good	Good	Moderate	A little bit sufficient	Insufficient	I have no idea
8%	19%	30%	19%	23%	1%

Table 7. The efficiency of the sports activity areas

Very good	Good	Moderate	A little bit sufficient	Insufficient	I have no idea
10%	17%	23%	24%	24%	2%

Table 8. The efficiency of technological tools and information technologies

Very good	Good	Moderate	A little bit sufficient	Insufficient	I have no idea
6%	14%	27%	28%	24%	1%

Table 9. Are the views of the students consulted in selecting the elective courses?

Very good	Good	Moderate	A little bit sufficient	Insufficient	I have no idea
18%	19%	23%	18%	16%	6%

Table 10. The adequacy of school guard services

Very good	Good	Moderate	A little bit sufficient	Insufficient	I have no idea
14%	15%	20%	18%	26%	7%

Table 11. The adequacy of briefing on higher education or the work that the students will find after graduation

Very good	Good	Moderate	A little bit sufficient	Insufficient	I have no idea
23%	23%	20%	14%	11%	9%

Table 12. The adequacy of the activities for the introduction of the school

Very good	Good	Moderate	A little bit sufficient	Insufficient	I have no idea
11%	24%	24%	21%	16%	4%

Table 13. The adequacy on ensuring the participation of the parent to the process that the student directing operations are carried out

Very good	Good	Moderate	A little bit sufficient	Insufficient	I have no idea
9%	19%	28%	21%	17%	6%

Table 14. The adequacy of the student informing about preventing the violence and the fight against harmful habits

Very good	Good	Moderate	A little bit sufficient	Insufficient	I have no idea
23%	22%	18%	17%	15%	5%

Table 15. the sufficiency of the students on ensuring the local, national and international activities

Very good	Good	Moderate	A little bit sufficient	Insufficient	I have no idea
16%	20%	25%	12%	20%	7%

It is necessary for maintaining the importance that the students give for education to have motivation and individual goal. The fact that these important subjects are disappear in individual level emerges the risk for the student not to maintain his education. Taking into consideration this subject, the following pattern has come to light upon the question of preparing the asked elective course educational subjects by considering the views of students.

The adequacy of the guard duty was questioned in another question in order to bring to light the safety risk situation which is another risk in the field of education.

The prestige has sustainability risk as it is indicated in the literature for an educational institution. In this context, respectively the adequacy of informing with regard to finding jobs after school and the adequacy of the activities about school presentation were questioned:

The role of the relation between the student and family during education has been indicated in literature. In this context, the adequacy of the parent participation in student directing operations and guidance was questioned.

Another question was asked to the students about bad habits indicated as risks that affect the sustainability of individual motivation in education. The results of the question whether the necessary studies were conducted or not for preventing the bad habits are as follows:

In the interrogation conducted for the definitions put forward as environmental and social risk factors, the sufficiency of the students on ensuring the local, national and international activities was questioned. The resulting situation upon the answers that the students have given is as follows:

If we should summarize as main headings the findings emerging in the report that was prepared by Beyond Standards Limited (2009) where the results regarding the subject are used, the matters posing risk can be shown as follows:

1. **The Health and Safety of the Students and Workers:** There are empty fire extinguishers in the sections which is said to be maintenance in some points of the building. It has come forth that the fire drills have not been exercised and the employee is not trained on how to evacuate the building in case of a possible fire. The lack of fire alarm poses a major problem for the risk factor which has a high impact value.

2. **Attendance of Students:** It has been observed in the conducted study that attendance of students was recorded to the registries, but this information has not been analysed. According to the information obtained from the school, the 35% of the students were absent from school as 10+ days of unauthorized absence in addition to the holidays. The causes of this data that are the indicator of individual motivation deficiency can be investigated in the future studies too. Possible suggestions have been made regarding the reduction of risks and development of the education sector with regard to the subject in the discussion part.

3. **Attendance of Workers:** The fact that the courses are cancelled because teachers do not complete the courses of each other and so the students are not given a chance to make up for the missing lessons pose risk for the educational institution.

4.   **Insufficient Infrastructure:** The lack of computers in classes; old tables and chairs and the presence of sports equipment for little children but not for those who are 14-19 years old; workshops equipped at the minimum level; missing showers for sports activities; Weak and inaccessible library; form insufficient and unsuitable infrastructure for vocational school.

As Beyond Standards Limited pointed out in the report that was published in 2009, observing the absenteeism of the employee commonly shows that there is a great insufficiency in this educational system.

It was pointed out in the conducted research that there is no sanction system to control the absenteeism of students or teachers. As a result of this, inevitable and serious problems arise in the educational system. It poses risk for the sustainable structure of the educational system which is important for the development of the country and it causes the loss of prestige.

The findings of this pilot research which is concluded in four main substances pose a risk for the sustainability of the educational system of the high school where the research is conducted.

Internationalization is a key solution to reach out the merits of strategic development within education institutions. In this respect, considering the importance of risk management leadership in the practice of education is essential (Öznacar & Dagli, 2016). Technology becomes a solution to overcome obstacles and problems in leadership (Öznacar & Dericioglu, 2017).

REFERENCES

Abraham, J. M. (1999). Identifying and Managing Risk. *New Directions for Higher Education, 1999*(107), 83–89.

Alkın, E., Tuğrul, S., & Akman, V. (2001). *Entering Risk Management in Banks.* İstanbul: Çetin Typography.

Altbach, P. G. (2005). Globalization and the University: Myths and Realities in an Unequal World. *The NEA 2005 Almanac of Higher Education.* Retrieved from http://www.nea.org/assets/ img/PubAlmanac/ALM_05_06.pdf

Aras, G. (2007). Relations between Institutional Management and Internal Inspection. *Internal Inspection Magazine, 19*, 90-95.

Aydın, A. (2010). *The Usage of Derivative Financial Tools in Risk Management Within the Banking Sector and Entering it in Accounts at International Accounting Standards* (Unpublished Post-graduate Thesis). Gazi Uni. Institution of Social Sciences, Business Majors, Accounting Sciences, Ankara, Turkey.

Beecher, B.& Streitwieser, T. B. (2017). A Risk Management Approach for the Internationalization of Higher Education. *Journal of the Knowledge Economy.*

Çelik, T., & Kaplan, M. (2005). *Competition in the Turkish Insurance Sector:2002-2004.* İstanbul: Aves Publications.

Childress, L. K. (2009). Internationalization Plans for Higher Education Institutions. *Journal of Studies in International Education, 13*(3), 289–309. doi:10.1177/1028315308329804

Çolak, Ö. F., & Yiğidim, A. (2001). *Crisis in Turkish Banking.* Ankara: Nobel Publication Distribution.

Dayan, V. (2006). *Developments in the Field of Risk Management in the Exchange Market for Forward Transaction and Option, Basel II Standards and Application Examples* (Unpublished post-graduate thesis). Celal Bayar University Institution of Social Sciences Business Majors, Manisa.

Derici, O., Tüysüz, Z., & Sarı, A. (2008). Institutional Risk Management and Audit Office Application. *Audit Office Magazine, 65*, 70.

Emhan, A. (2009). Risk Management Process and Techniques used in Managing. *Atatürk University Economics and Administrative Sciences Magazine, Volume, 23*(3), 209–220.

Erdoğan, M. (2000). *Business*. Eskişehir: Anadolu University Publications.

Güzel, V. (2007). *Numerical Methods Used When Determining Financial Risk Values: ISE applications with ARCH/GARCH Models* (Unpublished post-graduate thesis). Marmara University Institution of Social Sciences Business Majors Branch Financial Markets and Investment Management Science Branch, İstanbul, Turkey.

Knight, J. (2006). Cross-border education: Conceptual confusion and data deficits. *Perspectives in Education, 24*(4), 15–27.

Lokumcu, S. (2009). *Financial Risk Management* (Post-graduate Thesis). Yıldız Technical Universitesi Institution of Science and Technology, İstanbul, Turkey.

Öznacar, B., & Dagli, G. (2016). Evaluation of Risks for School Directors in Education in Developed/Developing Countries. *The Anthropologist, 23*(1-2), 1-10.

Öznacar, B., & Dericioglu, S. (2017). The role of school administrators in the use of technology. Eurasia Journal of Mathematics. *Science & Technology Education, 13*, 1.

Phillps, J. (2009). *Project Management Professional Study Guide* (3rd ed.). McGraw-Hill.

Seyidoğlu, S. (1999). Activities in the Financial Market of Financial Risk and Risk Management. Economic Approach org.

UNESCO Institute for Statistics (UIS). (2016). *Global Flow of Tertiary-Level Students*. Retrieved from http://uis.unesco.org/ en/uis-student-flow

Whitfield, R. N. (2003). *Managing İnstitutional Risks: A Framework. EdD*. University of Pennsylvania.

Wilkins, S. (2011). Who benefits from foreign universities in the Arab Gulf States? *Australian Universities Review, 53*(1), 73–83.

Chapter 7
Internationalization of Higher Education Institutions in North Cyprus

Mehmet Altınay
Near East University, Cyprus

Belal Shneikat
University of Kyrenia, Cyprus

ABSTRACT

Internationalization has become one of the hotly debated issues in higher education institutions due its role in competitive advantage. Countries around the world encourage their universities to engage in competition and cooperation on the local and global level, and this can't be achieved without internationalization. This chapter is proposed to shed light on a unique case study: internationalization of higher education in North Cyprus, which is a politically unrecognized country. To achieve the aim of this chapter, a survey from International Association of Universities (IAU) was adapted to evaluate the internationalization in the four largest and oldest universities in North Cyprus.

DOI: 10.4018/978-1-5225-5231-4.ch007

INTRODUCTION

The intense of competition among universities and colleges can be attributed to globalization; universities and colleges compete with each other not only on the local level but internationally (Alpenidze, 2015). Moreover, systems and policies in higher education institutions (HEIs)are being transformed by globalization (Márquez, Torres, & Bondar, 2011). Because of this, universities started adopting strategies for internationalization. Therefore, the theme of internationalization in higher education started gaining attention by scholars and policy makers in the last decades of twentieth century (de Wit, 2011; Knight, 2013). At the moment, Internationalization is considered to be one of the major aspects to be dealt with higher education institutions (Pohl, 2015).

Knight (2004) defined internationalization in higher education as "the process of merging global, international, or intercultural dimensions into the objective or delivery of post-secondary education". This definition is widely accepted (Yemini & Sagie,2016). This broad acceptance might be related to a fact that is in this current era of global technologies and knowledge, markets and companies recruit university graduates who have the international knowledge, awareness, intercultural relations, and who can speak foreign languages (Chokheli & Alpenidze, 2015). University graduates can't have these characteristics without studying at international universities.

De Wit (1995) and Knight (1997) stated that internationalization of HEIs needs two strategies to sustain and improve the international dimensions of HEIs functions, these strategies are, organizational and program strategies. Organizational strategies include initiatives for the organizational level to institutionalize and facilitate global dimensions at HEIs through operating systems and management (Márquez, Torres, & Bondar, 2011). Program strategies include Research, university services, and academic initiatives (Márquez, Torres, & Bondar, 2011). Although that these strategies are necessary for internationalization, but they are not enough if there is a lack of support from the state.

The governments throughout the world can play a vital role in internationalization. Governments hope to have universities that can cooperate and compete on the global level (Márquez, Torres, & Bondar, 2011). Thus, governments can intervene to stimulate internationalization through funding (offering scholarships for international students as it is in the case of North Cyprus). However, OECD (2009) posited that continuing reforms in the national systems work as a first condition for the responses of institution and systems to globalization, the second condition are the reforms in the HEIs' managements themselves. Van der Wende (2007) stated that HEIs have become robust in the foreign educational markets as a result of lowering tuition fees and this has resulted in using more and new tools in public management. These tools include accountability and autonomy, financial incentives, and deregulation (Márquez, Torres, & Bondar, 2011). Nevertheless, Castells (2000) suggested that globalization can lead to both development and underdevelopment, and the need to curb some imbalances require HEIs to go beyond profitability by broadening their internationalization's mission.

RATIONALE FOR INTERNATIONALIZATION

It is vital for us to distinguish between why we internationalize higher education and what does internationalization mean? (De Wit, 2011). Many studies don't define the why when they mention internationalization (De Wit, 2011). Rationale for internationalization is usually used as a definition for the concept and as a result, rationales and meanings of internationalization are often muddled (De Wit, 2011).

De Wit (1999) stated that there were some changes that have happened to the rationales for internationalization of higher education; for example in European Medieval University and even in the Arab University earlier, the rationales for internationalization was to gain more knowledge and comprehend other cultures " social and cultural rationales" (De Wit, 1999). The same scholar suggested four traditional types of rationales: academic, social/cultural, political, and economic. Academic rationales include supplying a global dimension to teaching and research, enhancing the academic horizons, quality, international academic standards, profile status, institution building (De Wit, 2002, p. 85). Social/ cultural rationales include respecting cultural diversity, and it involves the role of the country's own language and culture (Jeptoo & Razia, 2012). Political rationales include technical assistance, foreign policy, national identity, national security, regional identity, peace and mutual understanding (De Wit, 2002, p. 85). Economic rationales for internationalization of higher education include financial incentives for domestic organizations and governments, economic growth and competitiveness, demand on the national education, and the local labor market (De Wit, 2002, p. 85). It is notable here that these types of rationales don't work independently; in fact, they work together and they are interdependent.

De Wit, (2000, 2002); van Vught, van der Wende, and Westerheijden, (2002) have written much about the changes in the rationales for internationalization. Knight (2004, 2012) proposed four new rationales and called them national level rationales. They are: Human Resource Development (HRD), Strategic Alliances, Commercial Trade, Nation Building, and Social/Cultural Development. These rationales were added because the scholars couldn't place them in one of the traditional rationales (Knight, 2004). HRD refers to the depending on international education initiatives to recruit and develop brain power or human capital and preparing students to be more knowledgeable about global issues (Knight, 2004, 2012). Strategic alliances are represented in the mobility of international academic staff and students. In addition to that, the joint initiatives of education and researches have been considered as fruitful methods to develop strong economic nexuses and geopolitical bonds (Knight, 2004). Commercial trade represents the opportunity to generate money from cross border education (Knight, 2004). Nation building refers to importing institutional and educational programs to achieve nation building objectives (Knight, 2004). Social/cultural development as suggested by Knight (2004) should be given equal importance as the economic/political rationales.

INTERNATIONALIZATION AT HOME AND CROSS-BORDER

Internationalization can be divided into two types: Local Internationalization "Internationalization at home" and External internationalization "Cross border education" (Knight, 2012). The two pillars are interdependent although they are split (Beelen & Jones, 2015). Knight (2006) suggested that internationalization at home is one of two ways in internationalization which she considers as intertwined rather than separate. She confirms that internationalization abroad is made up of all forms of across borders education, mobility of projects, curriculum, programs, courses, academics, and students. Cross border education also called offshore, borderless and/or transnational education, so they are considered as interchangeable terms (Knight, 2012). Knight (2012) stated that there are three generations of offshore education: The first generation is the mobility of students and people, the second one is provider and program mobility, and lastly education hubs where some countries started attracting international academic staff, students, researchers, programs, research and development companies and providers for education and knowledge production. Internationalization at home, on the other hand includes activities that assist students to improve their intercultural skills and global understanding. Beelen and Jones (2015) stated that this is a doubtful distinction, clearly proposing, for example, that cross border education does not improve intercultural skills and international understanding, and that curricula are not instantly involved in internationalization at home.

LEVELS OF INTERNATIONALIZATION

Internationalization as a process can be divided into two modes: top down and bottom up. Top down mode is a process that is oriented from the national state to the HEIs. Bottom up is a process that is oriented from HEIs to the national state (HEIDA, 2017). Practically, these modes are intertwined because the process of internationalization happens usually at different levels as stated by Knight (2004) and not only at different orientations. However, it is necessary to comprehend all sides of policy orientation in both " top down" and "bottom up" and how to implement at different levels (Sanderson, 2007 as cited by HEIDA). Sanderson (2007, p 280 as cited by HEIDA) proposed this figure for the dimensions of the reach of internationalization.

Figure 1.
Origin: Sanderson (2007, p280)

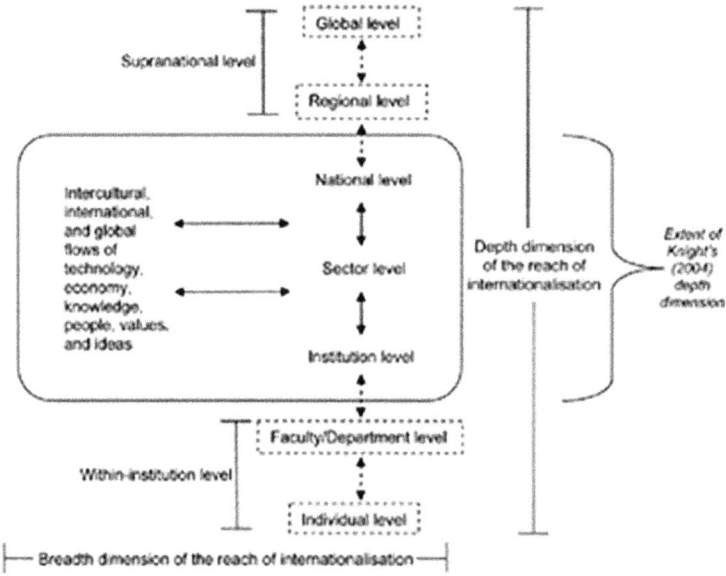

PERSPECTIVES OF INTERNATIONALIZATION

Four generic perspectives were identified under which internationalization can be understood: like an activity, like competencies, like ethos, and like a process. Activity approach interprets internationalization in terms of some activities such as students and staff exchange, joint programs, branch campuses, international students and technical assistance (Knight, 2005, p.30-31). The competency approach explains internationalization as developing new skills, knowledge, and values by students and staff. So, in competency approach the emphasis is not on the academic activities, it is on the human dimension (Knight & de Wit, 1995). Ethos approach focuses on the designing international initiatives and culture. The process approach depends on the integration of intercultural/international dimensions by using different procedures, policies, and activities.

However, these approaches were amended by Knight (2005). Competency approach was renamed to become outcome approach. Also, she defined new two approaches that are internationalization at home and cross border education. Internationalization at home considers the climate and culture that backs and promotes intercultural/international comprehending at home institutions. Cross border education is the internationalizing of education abroad and this type of education can be achieved through different methods of mobility such as branch campuses (establishing new branches abroad), twinning programs and franchise conventions.

WHY MEASURING INTERNATIONALIZATION?

Internationalization has become a significant aspect of higher education and is going to be the center of the academic institutions' interests which focus more on quality rather than quantity (Green, 2012). Many reasons have emerged to measure internationalization such as considering internationalization as a part of comprehensive institutional performance, to evaluate the effectiveness of internationalization strategies or their components inside a certain institution, to compare with other HEIs, and to improve practices and programs of internationalization (Green, 2012). Improvement considered the key type of measuring internationalization, and thus, the process should include a specific articulation of goals and agreed-upon indicators should be carefully chosen (Green, 2012). The fierce competition between HEIs requires institutions to distinguish themselves and create their profile or brand. Some performance indicators such as having Noble prize winners among academic staff or graduation rates can be used as solid markers for success (Green, 2012). Some HEIs usually use the number of international students as an indicator of success.

Institutional Data Management and Data-driven Decision Making in Higher Education

Institutional data management in higher education is very important because HEIs live in a changing environment and have become more complex with different business/academic functions. It involves the practices and policies by which HEIs efficiently and effectively gather, keep, and utilize information to achieve business and academic goals (Yanosky, 2009, p.12). Five aspects of data management were defined: content & records management, data stewardship & security, research data management, analytics, and data integrity & quality (Yanosky, 2009, p.7).

Data-driven decision making involves administrators, teachers, and principles which are collecting and analyzing different kinds of data in a systematic way (Marsh, Pane & Hamilton, 2006, p.1). This data will help decision makers to improve the success of HEIs. However, the five factors that affect the use of data by decision makers were identified: quality of data, data timeliness, data accessibility, motives to use data, lack of time, staff support & capacity, organizational leadership & culture, passing pressures of curriculum, history of state accountability (Marsh, Pane & Hamilton, 2006, p.8-9).

TOOLS AND INDICATORS FOR THE INTERNATIONALIZATION

Some tools such as Questionnaires /surveys, checklist, benchmarking, accreditation/certification, Audit/Review (internal and external evaluation), performance indicators (outcomes based) can be used to assess internationalization (de Witt & Knight, 1999). Some scholars argue that a certain tool is right or perfect tool, but the fact is no one right tool or perfect approach to assess internationalization and actually it depends on the scope and purpose of the evaluation and the HEI.

There are different tools that are used in different countries to assess internationalization. e.g. IQRP (Internationalization Quality Review Process) is used in OECD, IEC (Internationalization Evaluation Criteria) in Japan, International Checklist in the USA, Mapping internationalization in the

Netherlands, and Erasmus Mobility Quality Tools in Europe and it should be mentioned here that this tool is just for staff and students mobility (de Witt & Knight, 1999). International Association of Universities (IAU) developed a survey that covers all issues related to internationalization from institutionalization perspective.

INTERNATIONALIZATION OF HIGHER EDUCATION IN NORTH CYPRUS

Introduction

The world started witnessing a new phenomenon called international education since 1950s. During that period, the number of students who were travelling abroad to study increased significantly. Many reasons pushed international students to seek education in other countries, one of the most important reasons is job prospects (Abubakar, Shneikat & Odai, 2014). Due to importance of recruiting international students at local universities, most of the countries in the world have strategies, plans, and policies to internationalize their universities in order to recruit more students, since more international students mean more revenues for local governments and communities. As an example on that, the USA stated in 2016 that they have 1 million international students (Zong & Batalova, 2016). The USA still keen to recruit more international students although the recent changes in the political system in the USA and electing Mr. Donald Trump is said to affect the image of the USA as a preferred educational destination for international students as some experts mentioned (Slater, 2017).

Not just the large countries in the world such as the USA, Australia, China and India are eager to internationalize their universities to have more international students, some small countries such as Malta, Singapore, Mauritius, and Qatar have their strategies to internationalize their HEIs and hosting international campuses for some universities from the USA and UK mainly (Aktas, 2013).

North Cyprus is considered to be a special and unique case in terms of internationalization of HEIs. Although the country has no political recognition from any country in the world except Turkey, what they have achieved in internationalization of HEIs is remarkable and even large countries with enormous human and financial resources haven't achieved what North Cyprus have gained in terms of internationalization. Till academic year 2015/2016, the number of international students including Turkish students was around 79 thousand; 27,000 international students from 100 countries and 52,000 Turkish students (Ministry of education, 2017). Table 1 shows the number of international students based on their geographic area. International academic staffs are from 20 countries including the USA, UK, Hungary and some countries in the Middle East and Africa. Universities in North Cyprus follow international standards when they offer their programs (e.g. international curriculum) and English language is the teaching language for more than 200 programs for undergraduate and postgraduate studies.

This chapter aims to measure institutionalization of higher education in North Cyprus. The authors shed light on internationalization in the four oldest and largest universities in North Cyprus from institutionalization perspective. To achieve the aim of this study, the authors adapted a survey from IAU, this survey measure internationalization from institutionalization perspective. This chapter contributes to the literature review on internationalization in North Cyprus and indeed, it is the first attempt – to the best of authors' knowledge- to measure internationalization of higher education in North Cyprus from institutionalization perspective.

Theoretical Background

There are some studies which have been published about high education in North Cyprus from different perspectives e.g. motivations of international students to join universities in North Cyprus, impact of educational tourism on local community, impact of educational tourism on host population, environmental effects of educational tourism on domestic cities, effects of international students on the perception of Turkish students, energy consumption in higher education (Abubakar, Shneikat & Odai, 2014; Arici, Erturk & Orcan, 2014; Katircioglu, 2014; Shahgerdi, 2014; Ozsen, 2014). These studies in general focused on one side of internationalization that is international students (educational tourism).

Table 1. Number of international students according to their regions

Geographic Area	Total
Africa	11,085
Middle East	9,793
Central & South East Asia	2,446
Others	3674

Source: Researchers

However, one of the studies clarified the motivations of international students who come to study in North Cyprus. These motivations involved Accreditation, reputation, future job prospects, English as teaching medium, quality of education, travel and welcoming attitudes of the locals, tuition fees and scholarships, safety and low rate of discrimination in North Cyprus, easy to get visa, easy to get admission, recognition in the home country, qualified and friendly academic staff, natural and environmental factors, lack of availability of program in the home country, closeness to the home country (Abubakar, Shneikat & Odai, 2014). Arici, Erturk, and Orcan (2014) found that international students from Islamic countries have changed the perception of Turkish students on the following issues: development of positive sciences in other Islamic countries, social relations in Islamic countries, clothing styles in Islamic countries, foreign languages of Islamic countries, the role of women in social life, perception about Islamic culture, human rights and individual freedom in Islamic countries, the impact of religion in social life. Shahgerdi (2014) found that expansion of international students had negative impacts on the local environment. Ozsen (2012) found that educational tourism affects the local community positively and negatively in terms of socio-cultural, environmental and economic aspects. Aliyeva (2015) found that local students are strongly influenced by the cultural exchange that happens during interaction with international students, in addition to that, environmental, cultural, social and economic aspects of the local community were strongly affected by educational tourism.

Institutionalism as a distinctive approach used to study political, economic, and social phenomena (DiMaggio & Powell, 1991). Perrow (1979) stated that institutional theory is one of the best sociological perspectives in organization theory. Di Maggio and Powel (1991) clarified the differences between old and new institutionalism. In the old institutionalism, some issue such as power and informal structures, competing values, and influence were central (Clark, 1960; Selznick 1957). New institutionalism contrasts old institutionalism because it emphasizes on centrality of schema, routines and classification, embeddedness of organizational fields, and legitimacy (DiMaggio & Powell, 1991; Meyer & Rowan, 1977).

Institutional theory is not just a theory for organizational change (Greenwood & Hinings, 1996), it explains the isomorphism (similarity) and how organizational arrangements are stable in the field of organizations (Greenwood & Hinings, 1996). Ledford et al., (1989) stated that institutional theory doesn't offer much support for change. However, Dougherty (1994) posited that institutional theory a great basis for change because of it is definition for radical change which happens when the organization move from template to another.

Institutional pressures (e.g. internationalizing the HEIs) force organizations the use the same organizational template (Di Maggio & Powell, 1991). The idea of template is related to the "configurational research" for Meyer, Tsui and Hinings, (1993). Configurational researches seek to display similarities between organizations in terms of systems and structures (Drazin & Van de Ven, 1985; Mintzberg, 1983; Miller & Friesen, 1984). From new institutionalism perspective, configuration of organization's structure is provided by interpretive schemes that represent the underpinning values and ideas (Barley, 1986; Bartunek, 1983; Ranson, Hinings, & Greenwood, 1980).

The focus of new institutionalism theory is not on the individual organizations but on the organizations as a population in the field of organizations (Greenwood & Hinings, 1996). The theorists who support this theory usually see the organizations as horizontally and vertically interlinked organizations and therefore, prescriptions and pressures between these contexts can be applied to all pertinent organizations' classes (Greenwood & Hinings, 1996).

Rational choice (RI), sociological institutionalism (SI), and historical institutionalism (HI) represent the new versions of new institutionalism theory (Bell, 2011). RI concentrated on logic of calculations within institutions (Schmidt, 2010). Logic of calculations which means structures of incentives allows rational actors to track their preference. SI focuses on social agents (e.g. government, people) who take action based on logic of appropriateness. Logic of appropriateness is norms and rules that are culturally framed and socially constituted (Schmidt, 2010). HI provides details about the development of institutions (Schmidt, 2010). The authors believe that new institutionalism theory serves the aim of this chapter and thus, the theory is utilized in the literature review and discussion parts.

METHODOLOGY

In order to evaluate the rate of internationalization of HEIs in North Cyprus, the authors depended on a survey adapted from International Association of Universities (IAU). Eleven criteria were utilized (The survey includes 24 criteria- see appendix) from the survey and applied on the four oldest and largest universities in North Cyprus. The authors examined the websites of these universities to check their current situation of internationalization based on their institutional efforts to achieve internationalization. The websites were chosen because the website usually reflects all the university's activities, policies, and strategies, and as we know "the mirror of any organization". These criteria are:

1.   Is institutionalization a high priority in your institution?
2.   Has a policy or strategic plan for internationalization been elaborated at your institution?
3.   If there is a policy/strategy for internationalization, is it institution wide?
4.   Is there an office with overall institution responsibility for overseeing the implementation of the policy/strategy?
5.   Is there a specific budgetary provision made for implementing the internationalization policy/strategy?
6.   Does the internationalization policy/strategy include geographic priorities?
7.   Does a monitoring framework exist to review progress towards achieving the institutional objectives for the policy/strategy?
8.   Is the demand for courses/programs with significant international content on the rise?
9.   Is the demand for foreign language learning on the rise?
10. Is the impetus/demand for internationalization coming from students?
11. Are there funding programs at the national level to provide support to institutional internationalization efforts?.

   In regard to the first criterion, it will help us to check if really the top management of these universities are eager to internationalize their universities or not. Usually, internationalization should be among the most important priorities at these universities. The second criterion focuses on the strategic plan including their vision and mission. Vision and mission should reflect the importance of internationalization. Even if there is a policy or strategy for internationalization, Do these universities institutionalize this strategy and assign an independent office and budget to implement and monitor it?. This is reflected in criteria 3, 4, and 5. The sixth criterion sheds light on the geographical focus of the strategy (e.g. recruiting international students from a certain area- e.g. Africa). Strategic plan can't be achieved without institutionalization, so it is important to check the progress in achieving institutionalization and this is reflected in the seventh criterion. Criterion 8, 9, and 10 reflect the future trends for internationalization by focusing on the international students. Public support especially from the government is important to enable universities achieve full internationalization through institutionalization; Criterion 11 tries to investigate this support.

FINDINGS

After checking the websites of the four oldest and largest universities in North Cyprus, the authors found that all universities meet the overwhelming majority of these criteria. However, the first two criteria were met fully by one university and partially by other universities; the third criterion was met completely by one university and to some extent by other universities. The fourth criterion which is about the availability of an office with overall institution responsibility for overseeing the implementation of the policy/strategy was met partially by all universities. Criterion number five was met to some extent by all universities. The sixth criterion was achieved partially by all universities. Criterion number seven was met partially by all universities. The last four criteria were fully satisfied by all universities.

DISCUSSION

Many scholars have stressed the importance of internationalization of universities (e.g. de Witt & Knight, 1995). Internationalization of higher education seems to be a part of a broad view for universities in order to gain more success. In this chapter, the reviewers stress the importance of internationalization in general and the role of institutionalism in that through using institutionalism theory which interprets many faces of institutionalizations inside the universities such as isomorphism and organizational template, organizational arrangements, change, values and ideas, RI, HI, and SI.

Our findings prove that most of the universities being researched in this chapter focus on one side of internationalization which is recruiting international students. Jane knight stated that internationalization doesn't only mean recruiting international students. In addition to that, Most of the universities don't pay much attention to the important role of strategic plans or policies to implement internationalization by focusing on the institutionalization part. All universities need to establish independent office to have full responsibility for overseeing the implementation of the policy/strategy of internationalization and not just having an international office which is responsible for recruiting international students. Organizations tend to imitate each other (Liberman & Asaba, 2006) and universities are no exception. Greenwood and Hinings, (1996) explained the similarities (isomorphism) between organizations. The authors propose that universities tend to imitate each other; that is, if one university has full independence office that is responsible for implementing internationalization through institutionalization, other universities will try to imitate and therefore, establish the same office. So, at the end we will have what De Maggio and Powell (1991) called it "organizational template" as a response to the internationalization since internationalization represents an organizational pressure (De Maggio &

Powell, 1991). Creating these organizational templates will allow universities to move from template to another when they face radical change (e.g. establishing international office to achieve full internationalization as a response to the changes that competitors made) as suggested by Dougherty (1994). This response to the changes that competitors make in their environment proves that these organizations (e.g. universities) are vertically and horizontally interlinked (Greenwood & Hinings, 1996) and focus is on the population of universities and not on a certain university.

The budget that is allocated for internationalization policy and strategy is used mainly to recruit international students. Because of this, a lot of international promotion programs and activities such as booklets, leaflets, and advertisements in different languages especially English, Arabic, and Russian are implemented. This might be interpreted in three ways: First, internationalization is recruiting international students as some people think. Second, these universities are excluded from getting any kind of help from regional or international organizations. Third, institutions tend to imitate other in order to avoid falling behind other (Liberman & Asaba, 2006). Universities try to use their budget to recruit international universities to recruit similar number of international students as other universities. The competition between universities is based on the number of international students they recruit. Therefore, it seems that using the budget for any activity other than recruiting international students is wasting for financial resources.

For geographic priorities, again the universities more on recruiting students from some locations especially Africa, the Middle East, and Russian speaking countries. The monitoring framework to review the progress in achieving institutional objectives for the strategy should be given more attention by all universities. It is worth mentioning here that implementing internationalization will be resultant in a fully international university which will increase the opportunity for these universities to recruit more international students.

The four oldest and largest universities in North Cyprus still receive many applications from international students who want to join these universities because of international programs offered in English and the government of North Cyprus still supports these universities because it seems that the only connection between local people and foreigners is done through universities in the country, and these students when they go back home in their vacations or after graduation they tell their family members and friends about their happy times in North Cyprus. As a result, these people will have better understanding of the conflict in Cyprus. In addition to that, students in North Cyprus form a strong drive for the local economy which depends mainly on the students and service industries.

As mentioned above, all universities focus more on recruiting international students, these universities can't be blamed because they are excluded from international research projects and it is not easy for these universities to have mutual agreements or twinning programs with other universities in Europe or North America mainly. There is usually an "invisible hand" tries to block universities in North Cyprus from having international collaborations with other universities or organizations in other countries. Hence, the only source of revenue for these universities comes from students and therefore, it is not a surprise that these universities focus extensively on recruiting students from Turkey and other countries.

Implications

This chapter has some implications for policy makers and top management of the universities in North Cyprus. Politicians and policy makers in North Cyprus should be aware of increased competition from other countries which try to have internationalized and institutionalized universities; therefore, policy makers should recommend universities to have institutionalized and internationalized environment that help them to recruit more students from abroad. Top management of these universities should be aware of this; full independent office should be established to implement the all faces of internationalization because it will be easier to market these universities in the international market. Policy makers can direct universities to have strategic plan/policies for internationalization. Policy makers and politicians should stipulate higher standards for new granted licenses to establish universities in the country because the focus should be on the quality to allow the universities to compete in the international market. For example, new licenses can't be approved without indicating that there will be a strategic plan that reflects internationalization and an independent office to monitor the implementation of this strategy.

For top management of these universities, they should do more for internationalization. Training sessions for administrative and academic staff should be organized to have better understanding for internationalization and that is will help them to modify their behaviors according to internationalization. Achieving institutionalization seems to be vital to achieve internationalization; therefore, the principle of "the right man for the right place" should be fully implemented. If somebody has the art and science in management field, he/ she should be appointed in a managerial position because that will help the universities achieve institutionalization.

CONCLUSION

Internationalization of HEIs has become one of the most important factors in evaluating the performance of universities around the world. Universities and countries around the world compete each other to recruit international students, hire international academic staff, have international programs and curricula. When a university has a high level of internationalization, its ability to recruit international students and academic staff become better. In addition to that, the ability to start international and joint programs with universities abroad will be higher. This chapter tries to shed light on the concepts and parts of internationalization of higher education institutions with focus on North Cyprus. The chapter adapted a questionnaire to measure internationalization at the four oldest and largest universities in North Cyprus based on their website. The implementation of internationalization slightly differs from university to university. The policy makers and top management at these universities have a lot to do to maintain and enhance the level of internationalization at these universities.

REFERENCES

Abubakar, A. M., Shneikat, B. H. T., & Oday, A. (2014). Motivational factors for educational tourism: A case study in Northern Cyprus. *Tourism Management Perspectives*, *11*, 58–62. doi:10.1016/j.tmp.2014.04.002

Aktas, F. (2013). *The boom of international branch campuses: Western universities and the export of knowledge*. Retrieved from https://educationpolicytalk. com/2013/03/04/the-boom-of-international-branch-campuses-western-universities-and-the-export-of-knowledge/. Accessed online in May 11, 2017.

Aliyeva, G. (2015). *Impacts of Educational Tourism on Local Community: The Case of Gazimagusa, North Cyprus* (Master's thesis). Retrieved from http://i-rep.emu.edu.tr:8080/jspui/bitstream/11129/2258/1/aligun.pdf

Alpenidze, O. (2015). Conceptualizing internationalization strategies for higher education institutions. *Central and Eastern European Journal of Management and Economics*, *3*(3), 229–242.

Arici, H.E., Erturk, M., & Orcan, O. (2014) A Study on Educational Tourism: Impacts of Foreign Students on The Perception of Local Turkish Students: Evidence From Northern Cyprus. *Journal of Gastronomy and Studies, 2*(1), 3-12.

Barley, S. R. (1986). Technology as an occasion for structuring: Evidence from observations of CT scanners and the social order of radiology departments. *Administrative Science Quarterly*, *31*(1), 78–108. doi:10.2307/2392767 PMID:10281188

Bartunek, J. M. (1984). Changing interpretive schemes and organizational restructuring: The example of a religious order. *Administrative Science Quarterly*, *29*(3), 355–372. doi:10.2307/2393029

Beelen, J., & Jones, E. (2015). Redefining internationalisation at home. In A. Curai, L. Matei, & R. Castells (Eds.), *The Rise of the Network Society* (2nd ed.). Oxford, UK: Backwell.

Bell, S. (2011). Do We Really Need a New 'Constructivist Institutionalism' to Explain Institutional Change? *British Journal of Political Science*, *41*(4), 883–906. doi:10.1017/S0007123411000147

Chokheli, E. N., & Alpenidze, O. N. (2015). Strategy Of Internationalization For The Higher Education System (On The Example Of Georgia). *International Scientific Journal Theoretical & Applied Science*, *27*(7), 1–7.

Clark, B. R. (1960). *The open-door colleges: A case study*. New York: McGraw-Hill.

De Wit, H. (1995). Strategies for the Internationalization of Higher Education. A Comparative Study of Australia, Canada, Europe, and the United States of America. Amsterdam: European Association of International Education (EAIE).

De Wit, H. (1999). *Changing Rationales for the Internationalization of Higher Education*. Retrieved online from https://ejournals.bc.edu/ojs/index.php/ihe/article/viewFile/6477/5700

De Wit, H. (2000). *Changing rationales for the internationalization of higher education. Internationalization of higher education: An institutional perspective*. Bucharest, Romania: UNESCO/CEPES.

De Wit, H. (2002). *Internationalization of higher education in the united states of America and Europe: A historical, comparative and conceptual analysis*. Westport, CT: Greenwood Press.

De Wit, H. (2011). *Trends, issues, and challenges in internationalization of higher education*. Amsterdam: Center for applied research on economics and management, school of economics and management of the Hoge school van Amsterdam.

De Wit, H. (2011). Globaization and internationalization of higher education (Introduction to online monograph). *Revista de Universidad y Sociedad del Conocimiento, 8*(2), 241-248. Accessed online 13.01.2017 via http://rusc.uoc.edu/ojs/index.php/rusc/article/view/v8n2-dewit/v8n2-dewit-eng

De Wit, H. (2012). *Concepts, rationales, and interpretive frameworks in the internationalization of higher education. In The SAGE Handbook of International Higher Education* (pp. 27–42). London: SAGE.

DiMaggio, P. J., & Powell, W. W. (Eds.). (1991). *The new institutionalism in organizational analysis* (Vol. 17). Chicago, IL: University of Chicago Press.

Dougherty, D. (1994). Commentary. In P. Shrivastava, A. Huff, & J. Dutton (Eds.), Advances in strategic management. Greenwich, CT: JAI Press.

Drazin, R., & Van de Ven, A. H. (1985). Alternative forms of fit in contingency theory. *Administrative Science Quarterly, 30*(4), 514–539. doi:10.2307/2392695

Green, M. F. (2012). *Measuring and assessing internationalization*. Retrieved from http://www.nafsa.org/_/File/_/downloads/measuring_assessing.pdf

Greenwood, R., & Hinings, C. R. (1996). Understanding Radical Organizational Change: Bringing together the Old and the New Institutionalism. *Academy of Management Review*, *21*(4), 1022–1054. doi:10.5465/amr.1996.9704071862

HEIDA. (2017). *HEIDA -Data driven decision making for internationalization of higher education: Bridging the gap between faculty and admin using effective communication platforms*. Retrieved from https://heida.ku.edu.tr/sites/heida. ku.edu.tr/files/files/HEIDA_Project%20Output%201%20Literarture%20 Review%2025.5.2015.pdf

Jeptoo, M. L., & Razia, M. (2012). Internationalization of Higher Education: Rationale, Collaborations and its implications. *International Journal of Academic Research in Progressive Education and Development*, *1*, 4.

Katircioglu, S. T. (2014). Estimating higher education induced energy consumption: The case of Northern Cyprus. *Journal of Energy*, *66*, 831–838. doi:10.1016/j.energy.2013.12.040

Knight, J. (1997). Internationalization of Higher Education: A Conceptual Framework. In Internationalization of Higher Education in the Asia Pacific Countries. Amsterdam: European Association of International Education (EAIE).

Knight, J. (2004). Internationalization Remodeled: Definition, Approaches, and Rationales. *Journal of Studies in International Education*, *8*(1), 1, 5–31. doi:10.1177/1028315303260832

Knight, J. (2005). An Internationalization Model: Responding to New Realities and Challenges. V Higher education in Latin America: The international dimension. Washington, DC: The World Bank.

Knight, J. (2012). *Internationalization: Three Generations of Cross border Higher Education*. India International Center. Retrieved from http://www.iicdelhi. nic.in/ContentAttachments/Publications/DiaryFiles/53511July92012_IIC%20 Occasional%20Publication%2038.pdf

Knight, J. (2013). The changing landscape of higher education internationalization – for better or worse. *Perspectives: Policy and Practice in Higher Education*, *17*(3), 84-90.

Knight, J., & de Wit, H. (1995). *Strategies for internationalisation of higher education: Historical and conceptual perspectives*. Retrieved from: http://www. uni kassel.de/wz1/mahe/course/module6_3/10_knight95.pd

Ledford, G. E., Mohrman, A. M., & Lawler, E. E. (1989). The phenomenon of large-scale organizational change. In Large-scale organization change (pp. 1-31). San Francisco: Jossey-Bass.

Liberman, M. B., & Asaba, S. (2006). Why do firms imitate each other? *Academy of Management Review*, *31*(2), 366–385. doi:10.5465/amr.2006.20208686

Márquez, B. L. D., Torres, N. E. H., & Bondar, Y. (2011). Internationalization of Higher Education: Theoretical and Empirical Investigation of Its Influence on University Institution Rankings. *Globalisation and Internationalisation of Higher Education*, *8*(2), 265–284.

Marsh, J. A., Pane, J. F., & Hamilton, L. S. (2006). *Making Sense of Data -Driven Decision Making in Education*. Retrieved from: http://www.rand.org/content/dam/rand/pubs/occasional_papers/2006/RAND_OP170.pdf

Meyer, A. O., Tsui, A. S., & Hinings, C. R. (1993). Guest co-editors' introduction: Configurational approaches to organizational analysis. *Academy of Management Journal*, *36*, 1175–1195.

Meyer, J. W., & Rowan, B. (1977). Institutionalized organizations: Formal structure as myth and ceremony. *American Journal of Sociology*, *83*(2), 340–363. doi:10.1086/226550

Miller, D., & Friesen, P. H. (1984). *Organizations: A quantum view*. Englewood Cliffs, NJ: Pren-tice Hall.

Mintzberg, H. (1983). *Structure in fives: Designing effective organizations*. Englewood Cliffs, NJ: Prentice Hall.

OECD. (2009). Globalisation. *Higher Education*, 2030.

Ozsen, Z. S. (2012). *Impacts of Educational Tourism on Host Population: A Case of Famagusta, North Cyprus* (Master's thesis). Retrieved from http://i-rep.emu.edu.tr:8080/xmlui/bitstream/handle/11129/1590/ZeynepOzsen.pdf?sequence=1

Perrow, C. (1979). *Complex organizations: A critical essay* (2nd ed.). New York: Random House.

Pohl, H. (2015). *How to measure internationalization of higher education*. New perspectives on internationalization and competitiveness. DOI 10.1007/978-3-319-11979-3_4

Ranson, S., Hinings, C. R., & Greenwood, R. (1980). The structuring of organizational structures. *Administrative Science Quarterly*, *25*(1), 1–7. doi:10.2307/2392223

Schmidt, V. (2010). *Taking Ideas And Discourse Seriously: Explaining Change Through Discursive Institutionalism As The Fourth New Institutionalism.* Academic Press.

Selznick, P. (1957). *Leadership in administration.* Evanston, IL: Pow, Peterson.

Shahgerdi, A. (2014). *Environmental Impacts of Educational Tourism on the City of Famagusta, Northern Cyprus* (Master's thesis). Retrieved from http://i-rep. emu.edu.tr:8080/jspui/bitstream/11129/1702/1/ShahgerdiAmin.pdf

Slater, J. (2017). *Trump's immigration ban hinders recruitment by US hospitals and universities.* Retrieved from https://www.theglobeandmail.com/news/ world/us-politics/trumps-immigration-ban-hinders-recruitment-by-us-hospitals-universities/article34181949/

Van Der Wende, M. (2007). Internationalization of Higher Education in the OECD Countries: Challenges and Opportunities for the Coming Decade. *Journal of Studies in International Education, 11*(3-4), 274–289. doi:10.1177/1028315307303543

van Vught, F. A., van der Wende, M. C., & Westerheijden, D. F. (2002). Globalisation and internationalisation. Policy agendas compared. In J. Enders & O. Fulton (Eds.), *Higher education in a globalizing world. International trends and mutual observations* (pp. 103–121). Dordrecht, The Netherlands: Kluwer.

Yanosky, R. (2009). *Institutional Data Management in Higher Education.* Retrieved from: https://net.educause.edu/ir/library/pdf/ers0908/rs/ers0908w.pdf

Yemini, M., & Sagie, N. (2016). Research on internationalization in higher education – exploratory analysis. *Perspectives: Policy and Practice in Higher Education, 20*(23), 90–98. doi:10.1080/13603108.2015.1062057

Zong, J., & Batalova, J. (2016). *International Students in The USA.* Retrieved from http://www.migrationpolicy.org/article/international-students-united-states

KEY TERMS AND DEFINITIONS

Competition: The rivalry between two or more universities.

Competitive Advantage: The methods that can be used to put the universities a head of their competitors.

Cooperation: The association of two or more universities to achieve common goals.

Higher Education Institutions: The institutions that provide post-secondary education.

International Association of Universities: An Association that involves most of the universities in the world.

Internationalization: The process of utilizing the international dimension in delivering education.

North Cyprus: A country that was founded in 1983 whose inhabitants are Turkish Cypriots.

APPENDIX

Questionnaire

Institutional Questionnaire on Internationalization
of Higher Education

Table 2. Section 1:Institutional information

Name of the institution:	
Address:	
City:	Country:
Name of person completing questionnaire	
Position:	E-mail:

Table 3. Section 2: Internationalization policy

Is institutionalization a high priority in your institution?
Very Much ☐   Somewhat ☐   Very little ☐   Not at all ☐
If internationalization is a priority in your institution, please indicate why. Cite the three most important reasons:
a.
b.
c.
3. Has a policy or strategic plan for internationalization been elaborated at your institution?
Yes ☐ please send it to IAU or indicate the website where it is available for consultation   No ☐ If no, continue to question 9
4. If there is a policy/strategy for internationalization, is it institution wide?
Yes ☐   No ☐
5. Is there an office with overall institution responsibility for overseeing the implementation of the policy/strategy?
Yes ☐   No ☐
6. Is there a specific budgetary provision made for implementing the internationalization policy/strategy?
Yes ☐   No ☐
7. Does the internationalization policy/strategy include geographic priorities? If yes, please indicate to top three
a.
b.
c.
8. Does a monitoring framework exist to review progress towards achieving the institutional objectives for the policy/strategy?
Yes ☐   No ☐

Table4. Section 3: Internationalization priorities

9. On a scale of 1 to 5 (1= highest importance) , indicate the level of importance assigned to the following aspects of internationalization at your institution:	
a. Mobility of students	
b. Mobility of faculty members	
c. Introducing an international dimension into curriculum	
d. Strengthening international research collaboration	
e. International development projects, linkages, capacity building	
f. Extracurricular activities for international students	
g. Commercial export or import of educational programs	
h. Establishment of branch campuses abroad	
i. Development of twinning programs	
j. Offering joint academic programs with international partners	
k. Other aspects of internationalization, please specify:	

10. On a scale of 1 to 5 (1= highest emphasis) , for programs to stimulate student mobility, do you place most emphasis on:	
a. Welcoming international students?	
b. Sending students abroad?	
c. Reciprocal exchange?	

11. Please name three disciplines that you deem most internationalized in your institution.
a.
b.
c.

12. Is the demand for courses/programs with significant international content:		
On the rise ☐	Declining ☐	Steady ☐

13. Is the demand for foreign language learning:		
On the rise ☐	Declining ☐	Steady ☐

14. What is the most quickly expanding aspect of internationalization in your institution?

Table 5. Section 4: Facilitating factors and obstacles to internationalization

15. Is the impetus/demand for internationalization coming from:		
Students ⌐	Faculty ⌐	Administration ⌐
16. Where is the greatest resistance to internationalization?		
Among students ⌐	Among faculty ⌐	Among administration ⌐
17. On the scale of 1 to 5 (1= most important) indicate the level of importance of each obstacle of internationalization among these listed below:		
a. Lack of policy/strategy to facilitate the process		
b. Lack of financial support		
c. Administrative intertia or difficulties		
d. Competing priorities		
e. Issues of non-recognition of work done abroad		
f. Lack of reliable and comprehensive information		
g. Lack of opportunities		
h. Lack of understanding of what is involved		
i. Insufficiently trained or qualified staff to guide the process		
j. Other, please specify		

Table 6. Section 5: National/regional policy framework and internationalization

18. Are there policies in place at the international level to enhance the institutional efforts to internationalize?	
Yes ☐	No ☐
If yes, describe briefly:	

19. Are there funding programs at the national level to provide support to institutional internationalization efforts?	
Yes ☐	No ☐
If yes, describe briefly:	

20. Are there policies in place at the regional level to enhance the institutional efforts to internationalize?	
Yes ☐	No ☐
If yes, describe briefly:	

21. Are there funding programs at the regional level to provide support to institutional internationalization efforts?	
Yes ☐	No ☐
If yes, describe briefly:	

Table 7. Section 6: New developments, challenges and opportunities

22. What are the benefits and/or the risks of increasing internationalization? Please specify
Benefits:
Risks:
23. In your view, What new developments have taken place in this area during the past five years?
24. What aspects of internationalization should be discussed at the UNISCO WCHE + 5 meeting in 2003?

Chapter 8
The Role of International Student Mobility and Language Policies in the Process of Internationalization of Higher Education:
The Case of Turkey

Aylin Göztaş
Ege University, Turkey

Emel Kuşku Özdemir
Ege University, Turkey

Fusun Topsümer
Ege University, Turkey

ABSTRACT

The current study, based on the quantitative research approach, is structured on the basic question of whether participation in exchange programs and foreign language variables affect attitudes towards intercultural communication sensitivity. The research, which was conducted with the participation of university students from seven different geographical regions and from different educational fields, provides findings that support the existence of a relation between the contact with a foreign culture and language. Learning about different cultures and learning a foreign language in interaction with the culture reinforce individuals' language skills and improve their awareness about different cultures. Furthermore, it is remarked that the participants who acquired a foreign language through participating in an international exchange program are more confident and responsible in their interactions compared to the other group.

DOI: 10.4018/978-1-5225-5231-4.ch008

INTRODUCTION

As the process of globalisation has accelerated all over the earth, understanding of different cultures and interacting with them have gained importance in the context of improving international relations. Intercultural communication studies, developed as a common agenda and process across the world with new concepts such as pluralism, multiculturalism, diversity and alienation have substantially enhanced the importance of interculturality (Bekiroglu & Balci, 2014: 431). As a concept, intercultural communication refers to the communication and interaction between different cultures and subcultures. Furthermore, the term addresses a message in the context of intercultural dialogue. Improved mutual dialogue between different cultures may serve a number of primary purposes including democracy, human rights and rule of law and it also reinforces the global village concept which has become an unavoidable fact in our day.

While any nation, country or culture, which isolates itself from other cultures, cannot continue its existence at the present time, isolated individuals living solely in their own culture have begun giving way to multicultural societies. When individuals' tendencies towards intercultural communication sensitivity are observed, it is seen that people may adopt two different reactions in their relationship with target cultures: ethnocentric reaction and ethnorelative reaction. People with ethnocentric approach may deny cultural differences, defend their cultures against others, and deprecate different cultures. However, individuals with ethnorelative approach tend to accept and respect cultural differences (Bennett, 2004). At this point, one can mention significant indicatives such as learning new languages, speaking foreign languages and being in a different culture, with regard to understanding other cultures. Learning another language to comprehend the target culture is described as an important indicative, especially with a view to eliminate prejudices against a different culture and improve intercultural understanding; and it is argued that people may detach from ethnocentric behaviours through language learning (Er, 2006). In this context, the language becomes prominent within the scope of what to talk with whom, and when, where and under which circumstances to talk along with explaining the behaviours of other people belonging to the counterculture to maintain a positive communication process between individuals from different cultures (Edmonson & House, 1993: 82 as cited in Aktaş, 2004:93).

Intercultural communication, in regard to the relations between Turkey and the EU, is among the agenda topics of high importance, the demand for intercultural communication sensitivity continuously increase in terms of improving international relations and the integration process. Furthermore, academic, politic and social researches on this very topic gain more and more importance. When it is considered that each and every individual evaluates himself and the values of the society in which he lives according to his own culture. Thus, recognising and reading cultural differences stand out as a significant indicative in terms of correctly understanding different societies. At that point, language, which is one of the primary qualities people require to improve their ability to understand other individuals and societies with different cultures, has begun to be referred to as a precondition for success, especially in academic or professional life (Er, 2005), and it is described as a perquisite to keep pace with the globalising world (Şahin, 2000:42). In order to attain desired levels of success in the communication process, learning a language with the culture where it belongs is very important inasmuch as the learning processes of a language and a culture are identical and interconnected, and it is pointed out that it is not possible to teach a language isolated from the culture.

Former studies carried out in the field of intercultural communication describe language as a mirror and carrier of culture which cannot be addressed separately, and attribute great importance to language and language studies. Language and intercultural communication sensitivity studies are among the prominent topics especially in recognising different cultures and people with different lifestyles, and emphatically developing positive attitudes towards these people (Er, 2005:11).

This study was directed at determining attitudes of university students towards language knowledge and exchange programs in the context of intercultural communication sensitivity. In the study, which was conducted with the participation of university students from seven different geographical regions and from different educational field, the aim was to determine the participants' views on knowing a language, foreign languages they speak and their sensitivity tendencies towards interaction with other cultures.

CONCEPTUAL FRAMEWORK

The Concept of Internationalization and Its Reflections in the Field of Education

Globalization is defined as an integration process related to these fields in the world, as well as being a concept that is used to explain the recent changes and developments, politically, economically, socially, technologically and culturally experienced (Kürkçü, 2013: 2-3). In other words, it cannot simply be explained as politics, neither economical nor production alone. On the contrary, it is a concept that contains all of the aforementioned phenomenon within and signifies the integrated change of these fields (Dulupçu & Demirel, 2008:4). This era also called as the globalization process, gives birth to new circumstances for a lot of fields and make change an imperative (Akay, 2013: 320). The term internationalization, has came into prominence as a concept that appeared with globalization, and came to be used widely. Internationalization as a concept, has been acknowledged as a factor that contributes to the enlargement of the progressive and widening circle of globalization process, and defined within the terminology of the international organizations that back up this process. In this scope, this internationalization process brings onto the forefront international organizations that possess enough power to influence international political developments (United Nations, North Atlantic Treaty Organization (NATO), European Union which is the international economical union, etc.) (Dulupçu & Demirel, 2008:33).

Within this context, the globalization and internationalization movements which became an agenda and process that took the whole world under its influence, have paved the way open for the discussion of new concepts such as pluralism, multiculturalism, identity, diversity and variety. In addition to this, interculturality gained momentum with the network society infrastructure that raised its influence in the international field depending on the information technologies, also with the widespread use of environments and tools based on interactivity (Bekiroğlu & Balcı, 2014: 430). One of the fields that interculturality influences is education. It can be mentioned that educational approaches have evolved and changed with globalization. In this context, internationalization tendencies, which we may define as the driving force of globalization, have taken education under their influence. Yılmaz (2016:1191), mentions that there have been new economical and international tendencies in educational, research and social service missions of the universities, and points out that universities have become strategic fields as part of the economical and political agenda. For this reason, he refers to the widespread use of the term "strategy" instead of "activity" in the works conducted, to stress that the recent studies made in the scope of internationalization of education, involve process management, and he draws the attention to the planned, integrated and strategic nature of the processes in the name of internationalization in education.

Within the context of providing cultural integration in the international area, education is attributed an important role. Especially universities are institutions that come into prominence with regard to the internationalization of education. Şahin and Alkan (2016:298) mention that universities have sought harmony and balance in order to perform the duty of training qualified human resources that can operate in a global scale in parallel with the changes in education. Moreover, particularly in the USA and in the EU countries, in the reconstruction process of the higher education worldwide; universities have been attributed images such as entrepreneurial, innovative, open-minded, inquisitive and third generation universities. Kaya (2014:196), points out to the reforms in the field of education, discussed in universities of many countries as an obvious implication of this attribution, and to the appearance of educational strategies that enable the functioning of education language, students and academics in a multicultural environment, also enabling multiple and diverse cultural education opportunities through adjustments such as distance learning.

Internationalization Strategies of the EU Higher Education

In this era that we go through the information age, the adaptation of the strategies to be pursued in line with this scope, is among the top priorities of the European Union and many international institutions. Furthermore, particularly the educational policies of the EU, are conducted in cooperation with the inclusive action strategies that are developed accordingly. Especially in the matter of the internationalization of education, EU has serious implementations being conducted.

In a general sense, Gülcan (2013:13), claims that the core ambition of the internationalization strategies of EU in education, is to infuse the European identity to the individuals in EU countries. Additionally, 'equality of opportunity' and 'education for all' approaches in education, are the focus of EU educational policies. These ambitions were formalized in the "Maastricht Treaty" signed in 1992, and the other related clauses agreed upon were as follows;

- The development of Europe dimension in education, by the teaching and commonization of the member countries' languages,
- mutual recognition of degree and education periods,
- development of the changes occurring in student-teacher-academic member,
- improvement of cooperation between national and international educational institutions,
- improvement of distance learning,
- sharing of knowledge and experience in mutual problems regarding the educational systems of the countries,

- facilitation of introduction to vocational education, of occupational integration and of adaptation to labour market,
- incentives for cooperation among educational institutions and firms,
- initial and continuing vocational training for this integration.

Another study conducted by the EU in the context of internationalization of education, is the "Lisbon Treaty" signed by 29 countries in the year 1999. The main purpose of this treaty has been stated as creating the "Europe of Information". After the declaration that contained six main goals, three more new goals were added to these with the signing of the Prague Declaration in the year 2001. As of 2005, 45 countries have been in support of these common educational goals that include the EU higher education strategy. When the goals adopted by the EU countries are analysed (Akman, Akçay & Argün, 2011:19);

- Establishing a system in which the degrees can be easily understood and compared,
- Establishing a system that is cascaded as Undergraduate and Postgraduate,
- Establishing a credit system as in ECTS,
- Improving mobility by removing the factors that limit the freedom of movement of students and academic staff.
- Improving the cooperation of Europe in the field of quality assurance,
- Raising the consciousness of Europeanness required for higher education,
- Lifelong learning,
- Establishing a Europe Higher Education Area are observed to be among the goals.

When the studies regarding the internationalization of the EU higher education are analyzed, it is inferred that the youth is intensively targeted and topics; are discussed upon concepts such as language policies, student exchange, scholarships, lifelong learning etc. In this context, it can be said that exchange programs and efforts to create a lingua franca has been given prominence within the efforts of internationalization in education.

International Student Mobility

The internationalization of higher education refers to the international alumni mobility (exchange) (OECD, 2011). The leading EU initiative, giving the youth a chance of mobility, is ERASMUS programme. This programme, referring to a system that gives students and academic staff an opportunity of studying abroad, system (Kasalak, 2013:134); is composed of several areas of activity such as exchange organization, European Credit Transfer System and Diploma supplement, intensive programs, program development, academic expertise networks and intensive language preparation courses. According to Hasdemir and Çalıkoğlu (2011:68), another distinctive characteristic of the system is its attractive nature that enables people and ideas to change places.

According to UNESCO Report (2016), until today (in 15 years) four million students have participated in the exchange with this mobility program (Olcay & Nasır, 2016:288). These programs, as well as bringing important educational opportunities for the youth, is said to have contributed greatly to the countries by means of economic development and international competition (Tekelioğlu, Başar & Örtlek, 2012:191-192). Especially since the underdeveloped and developing countries' students arriving at the developed countries for the purpose of technological and informational data transfer, it is stated that developed nations started to make more investments on higher education sector.

When statistical data belonging to the international student exchange is analyzed within this context, in parallel with the data above, the student masses are mostly concentrated on the developed nations. In accordance with the 2013 international student exchange data, the order of the countries that accept the most students is stated as follows; USA (19), England (%10), France, Germany and Austria (ranging between 5-6%). The five developed world countries nearly corresponds to the half of the student mobility rate (46%). Turkey only makes up the 1% of the world total according to the same report. Similarly, according to UNESCO Statistical Institute's (UIS) current report (2016) on student mobility, the most international students go to the North American and Eastern European countries with 57%, and the order of the countries that make up this rate, are composed of USA, England, France and Germany (Olcay & Nasır, 2016:290-291). In this context, it would be appropriate to state that the five countries, accepting the most international students are in order, USA, England, Australia, France and Germany.

Lingua Franca

European Union is a project that combines various languages and cultures in its nature and one of the prominent goals of this project is the actualization of multilingualism. In this regard, EU education policies support the teaching of several foreign languages in the educational institutions. The framework of the progress made by EU in this matter, was determined with the Common European Framework of Reference (CEFR) for Languages program and the Common Language Portfolio.

Moreover, the year 2001 has been set as the "European Languages Year", this year has been supported with activities that encourage the individuals of EU to learn more than one language (Güler, 2005: 89-90). Other projects where language projects of EU Council are supported, are LINGUA, LEONARDO and SOCRATES Programs. These programs provide the teacher candidates the chance to go to and study in the country of the language they are learning (Genç 2003:181-182).

Today, including EU works, on a global scale, the choice of common language in a lot fields such as media, technology, tourism, trade and science is English (Oral, 2010:61). In the framework of higher education programs, the international students' choice of countries are mostly the countries which have universities that teach in English (IUC Report, 2016).

Works Conducted for the Internationalization of Turkish Higher Education

In Turkey too, the international organizations and studies on education are supported within the context of the internationalization of education. In this scope, one of the main goals is internationalization regarding the higher education strategy that is adopted within the internationalization of the higher education in Turkey (Şeremet, 2015:28). The main driving force in this matter is EU harmonization process that Turkey is in (Yalçınkaya, Güngör, Yanar & Arslan, 2013:13). Many institutions and organizations are conducting works within the scope of internationalization of higher education, in the framework of harmonization to EU educational policies (IUC Report, 2016). Especially with the works conducted by the Turkish National Agency, total involvement in the Erasmus program in 2004 has contributed greatly to this process, making the limited potentiality of studying abroad become accessible for a lot of students and academics, and became a driving force in increasing the quality of higher education (Hasdemir & Çalıkoğlu, 2011:68). Moreover, the works involving the modernization efforts in higher education have turned their focus on being an actor that attracts students from abroad, instead of being the country that sends students abroad (Yılmaz, 2016:1191). According to IUC Report, the number of foreign students studying in Turkish universities is showing increase day by day. In the year 2000, the foreign student number was stated as 15,803, for the

2014-2015 education year, this number was stated as 72,178 (2016). The number of students rising according to years indicates that works conducted with regard Turkey's claim fore becoming a country that is on demand, have given results.

Intercultural Communication and Dialogue in the Internationalization Process of Education

Kartarı (2014) defines the relationship between individual, society and communication as "Human is a social being; defines the social reality, forms his/her own identity within the framework of social relations and construct the meaning of life through various forms of communication". While communicating and interacting, humans are under the influence of specific variants. The most important of which is culture.

If we are to define culture as the pool of collective qualities of the society in which the individual lives in, the unstable, variant nature of culture is set forth. Kartarı (2014) mentions that the culture related problems are caused by the varying unknown cultural qualities rather than the common cultural qualities. He also adds that this situation leads to problems of people not making any sense of the other group of individuals' behaviour. As a reason for this, he points out to the unshared, dissimilar and inexperienced qualities not being included in the communication processes. The individuals being able to act properly outside their own context, is related to the requirement of knowing the contra culture's characteristics (2014:17). Knowing a foreign culture happens through being familiar with the norms and values of the culture.

Separate from our own culture, in the event that we are able to evaluate everything within the norms and values of the related culture, then it will be possible to realize intercultural communication successfully (Er, 2005:18). This intercultural adaptation condition is named as intercultural adequacy, and signifies a change in the individual's knowledge, skills and behaviour acquisition with regard to the related culture. For this acquisition and change to happen both in cognitive and affective levels, the individual interacting with a different culture or people from different cultures is highlighted (Eğinli & Yalçın, 2016:24).

Particularly depending on the change and development in communication and its technologies, today, as a result of people from different countries, languages, religion and ethnicity interacting more, highlights the importance of intercultural differences and intercultural communication (Bozkaya & Aydın, 2010:30). The increase in the number of businesses operating in the international scale and the multicultural structure of these businesses, are other changes that make acquiring intercultural adequacy a requirement for individuals that work or aim to work in these environments (Eğinli, 2011:215).

With the interaction in human relations showing increase, intercultural communication is within the operating field of many non-governmental organizations, especially in EU and the USA, specifically for providing peace in the world, a lot of prominence is attributed to exchange programs at this point (Gülnar, 2011:51). Especially, due to cultural diversity that is present in the EU, there are operations conducted in the name of sustaining the intercultural dialogue between the European societies. One of the initiatives is that the year 2008 brought forward by the European Union as "The Year of European Intercultural Dialogue". The Council, highlighted this year as the respectful and honest exchange of views, in a platform of mutual understanding and respect among individuals and groups that have different ethnic, cultural, religious, linguistic backgrounds and heritages (Council of Europe, 2008). The Intercultural dialogue, is defined as an understanding that recognizes both sides for the purpose of introducing different cultures to others, getting them close, and abolish the intercultural prejudices, and it is also defined as a prerequisite for healthy relations and communication to be established (Varol, 2013:10).

Exchange Programs and Multilingualism in the Development of Intercultural Communication Sensitivity

Intercultural sensitiveness is defined as "the individual possessing positive feelings before, during and after interacting with people from other cultures and respect the differences" (Eğinli, 2011:219). In other words, intercultural sensitivity signifies being open to change in the intercultural communication process. In some cases, the person having prejudice against different cultures causes the intercultural communication process to not function properly. Bennet (1993) explains this situation with the concept of ethnocentrism. Ethnocentric individuals are in the tendency of viewing their ethnicity as superior than others (Çakır, 2010: 81). These tendencies, as well as shaping the attitudes and behaviours of individuals towards people from other cultures, are the products of a process that involves time and experience. Furthermore, the collective experiences went through by the individuals that compose the society, besides the possibility of those transforming to values of judgement, there is also a possibility of an individual's experience can be arrogated to a culture. These value judgements have the power to influence the point of view towards the foreign people and intercultural relationship in time. Our points of view towards the foreign world consequentially contains ethnical and cultural boundaries, and these boundaries are generally conveyed and forced by the society (Akay, 2013: 312-313).

Rather than experience, the stereotypic perspectives towards foreign people can affect intercultural communication negatively. The increase in the number of intercultural contact points, is important in the name of knowing foreign cultures. With this regard, in the internationalization of higher education process, ERASMUS programs are in the forefront for the establishment of intercultural dialogue and intercultural communicative sensitiveness among people. The studies indicate that with the ERASMUS program, the individuals, finding a chance to live in a foreign culture, develop positive perception towards their own culture and the other cultures, and develop strategies with regard to resolving issues related to intercultural prejudice and intercultural communication. Furthermore, the findings of the study indicate that individuals participating in the ERASMUS program, gain skills regarding their knowledge of their own culture and being able to look at their own culture critically (Ersoy, 2013:163). However, in the process of intercultural communication, in order for the intercultural sensitiveness to be acquired, getting involved in ERASMUS programs alone is not enough. For this process to function properly, there is a need for language knowledge and skills. In this context, in order to know a culture, one needs to know the language of the culture.

Language learning is considered as an important key in understanding the values and attitudes related to culture and gaining intercultural competency (Eğinli, 2011:217). So, the widely accepted communicative approaches today, stress the relationship between language, culture and communication, and explain the communicative skills with an approach that encompasses cultural phenomenon (Çakır, 2010:76). Communicative skill is defined as "having the required skills to use the necessary information to communicate with a language society". In other words, it involves the meaningful usage of the language signs in various environments, in the right place and time. In this regard, communicative skill also includes the cultural rules and norms that form the basis for the context and content of the transactions in the communication and interaction process. Cultural elements qualify as transitive and an inseparable part of the culture (Aktaş, 2005:90).

Language teachers that adopt this approach, bring forward the social and cultural contexts where language is used in the scope of improving the foreign language teaching. Within this context, in the language learning process, they also attribute great importance to knowing about the culture that the language belongs, and defend that in the event of not learning about the culture, the language learning would not function properly. For this reason, as well as linguistic skills, cultural skills are also encouraged with communicational methods in language teaching. Language is described as an important tool for knowing other cultures and accepting them, in our day where subjects such as interculturality, multiculturality and cultural diversity are of great importance. In this context, as well as learning a language, knowing where and how to talk in various social environments requires communicational skills and those skills are considered as highly important with regard to learning a language. (Logie, 2004:177-178).

METHODS AND PROCEDURES

In the study which was designed to determine the attitudes towards knowledge of a language and exchange programs, in the context of intercultural communication sensitivity of university students, quantitative research approach was adopted. In the study, questionnaire method was used in order to provide quantitative data, and both open-ended and close-ended questions were asked. The questions, directed at describing the present situation and gathering general information, were prepared as dichotomous (Yes/No), and averages and percentages of negative and positive answers were based on while evaluating. In the questions that were prepared to determine the participants' attitudes and tendencies, 5 point Likert scale, specifying the participation rate, was used. In the questionnaire form, questions used were oriented at determining the participants'; views on knowing a language, known foreign languages, their sensitivity tendencies towards interaction with this culture and different cultures. In measuring the intercultural communication sensitivity, Chen and Starosta's (2000) Intercultural Sensitivity Scale was used, and Bekiroğu and Balcı's (2014) adaptation of the scale on Turkey, was also used. The sample group of the study is composed of university students, residing in seven different geographical regions of Turkey, and studying in different universities and departments. The process of gathering data was based upon online questionnaire method. Analysis were conducted through 101 questionnaires that were fully answered and returned according to the voluntary basis. In the analysis of the data gathered within the scope of the study, SPSS 20.0 statistical analysis program was used, and numerical data and tabulations were taken into consideration in the evaluation of the findings.

FINDINGS

Participants' Demographic Characteristics

53% of the participants were female, 47% were male students. The students, which made up the sample group, were 24% from science faculties, 25% from social sciences faculties, 19% from engineering and architecture faculties, 17% from medical schools and 15% were from art faculties. When the participants' residence ratio distribution in terms of the regions were 21% Inner Anatolia, 19% South-eastern Anatolia, 17% Marmara Region, 12% Mediterranean Region, 12% Aegean Region, 9% Eastern Anatolia and 7% Black Sea Region (Table 1). The sample group's representation by means of gender, field of study and region, was acquired.

Language Interest Level Results

Within the context of intercultural communication sensitivity, in the first part of the present study where the participant's interest towards and knowledge of the foreign language is evaluated; there are questions directed at determining the participant's interest towards language and language studies, spoken foreign languages, source of foreign language and attitudes towards knowing a foreign language. When the findings were analyzed, it was revealed that vast majority of the participants (96%) were interested in language and language studies (Figure 1).

Furthermore, the majority of participants interested in language and language studies (90%) have stated to know at least one foreign language (Figure 2). The second language of the majority of participant who knows at least one foreign language (89%) is English. The findings indicate that English is more commonly known among college students compared to other languages.

While more than half of participants only know English as a foreign language, 24 per cent of the participants know a second foreign language. Additionally, a relatively small percentage of participants (12%) speak three, four or five foreign languages (Figure 3).

When participants' ways of learning foreign languages are examined, language learning at school stands out as the primary method with 66 per cent. Apart from learning languages at school, participants are revealed to have learned foreign languages studying abroad, attending language courses and language schools in foreign countries. In this context, only a small percentage of participants (1%) have the opportunity go abroad for language training. Moreover, only quite a few participants (5%) have learned foreign languages with their personal efforts (Figure 4).

Table 1. Demographic characteristics of the participants

Region	N	%	Field	N	%
Aegean Region	12	12	Science	24	24
Black Sea region	7	7	Social science	26	25
Central Anatolia Region	21	21	Engineering and architecture	19	19
Eastern Anatolia Region,	9	9	Medical science	17	17
Marmara Region	17	17	Art	15	15
Mediterranean Region	16	16			
Southeastern Anatolia Region	19	19			
			Gender	N	%
			Women	54	53,4
			Men	47	46,6
Total	101	100%			
			Total	101	100%

Figure 1. Interest of foreign language

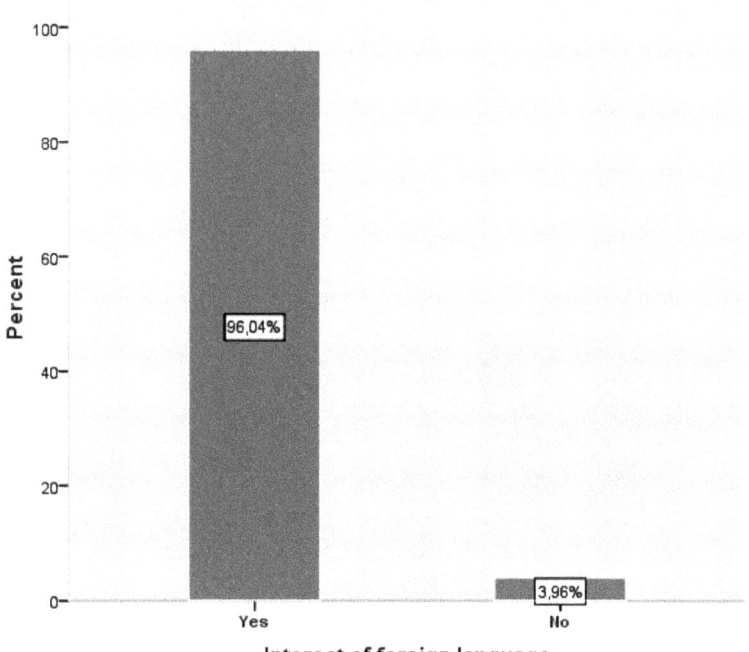

Figure 2. Knowledge of foreign language

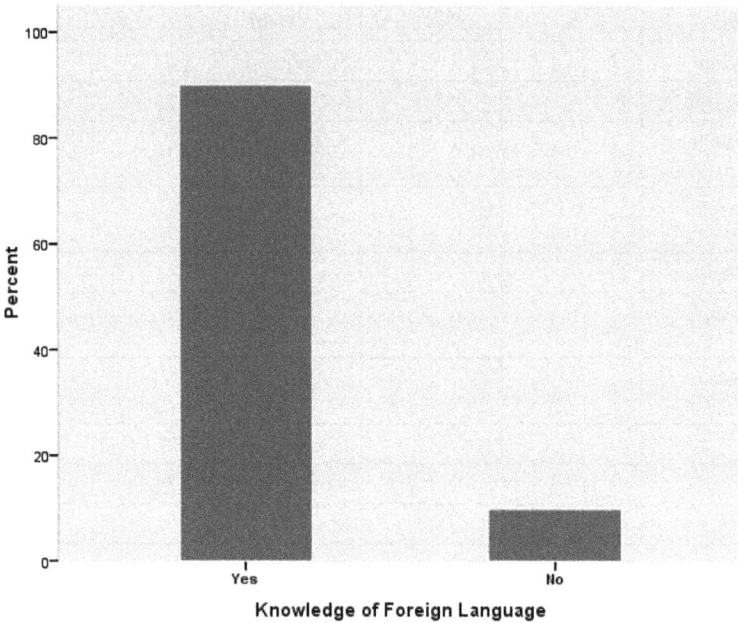

Figure 3. Known languages

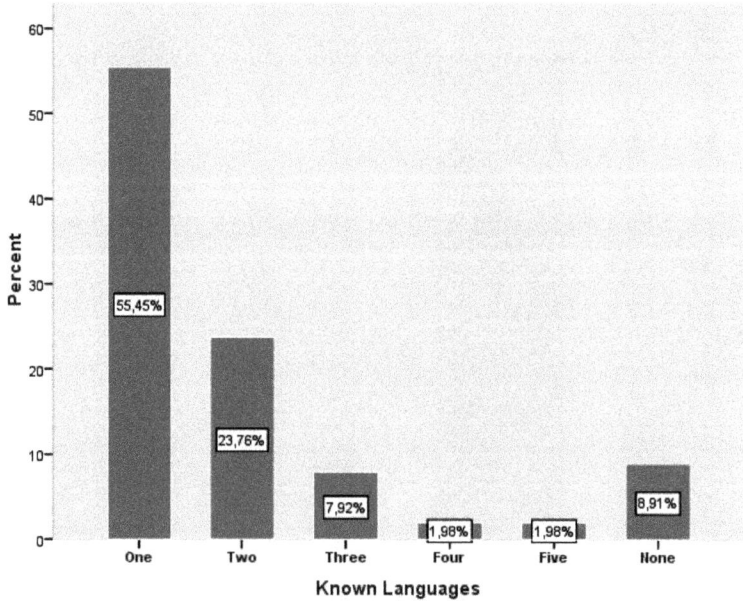

Figure 4. Way to learn English

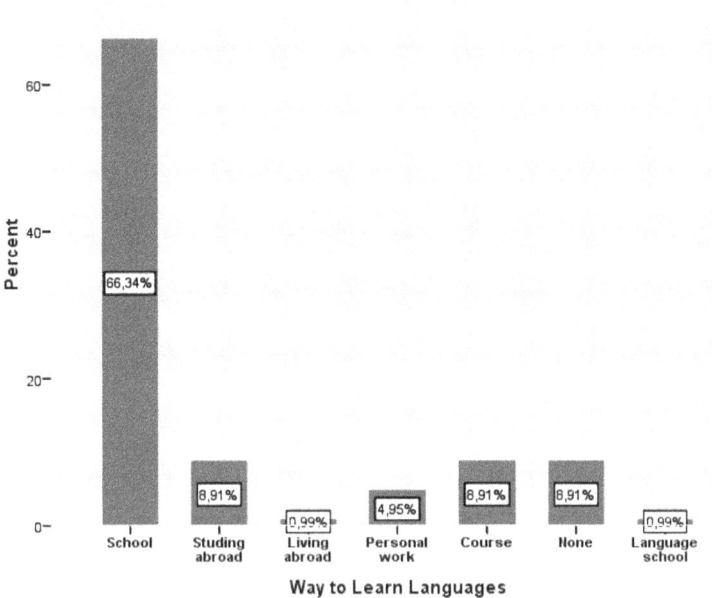

Figure 5. Participating in international exchange program

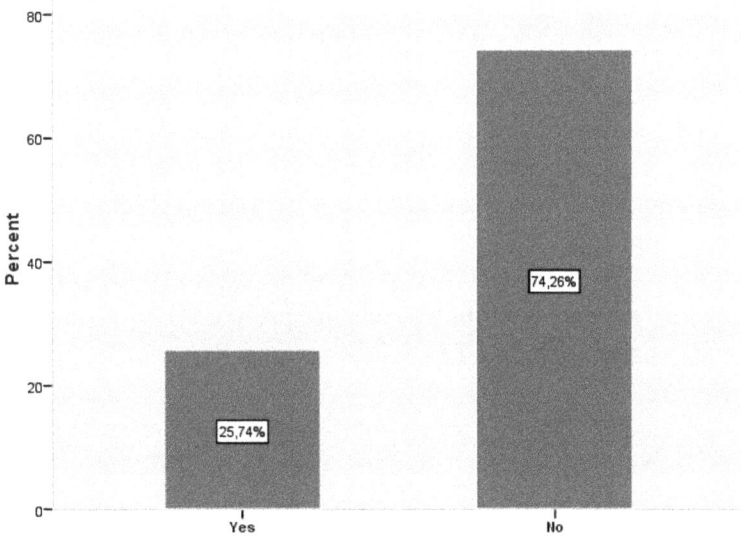

Findings Related to Perception of Exchange Programs

According to the findings, only 30 participants (26%) have been to foreign countries benefitting from international exchange programs such as Erasmus (Figure 5).

Additionally, students have considerably positive attitudes towards participating in international exchange programs (Mean=4.401) such as Erasmus. A large proportion of participants approve the statements about their objectives of participation. Participants leading objection of participating in student exchange programs is "to get to know the wealth and structures of different cultures" (Mean=4.643).

H1: Participants' perceptions towards knowing a language vary according to their status of participation in exchange programs.

When participants' interest in languages and language studies is considered, no difference has been observed (p=,810; p>0,05) between the students who participated in exchange programs (Mean=3,566) such as Erasmus and those who did not (Mean=3,5939). In other words, both students who participated in exchange programs (96%) and those who did not (91%) are highly interested languages and language studies.

H2: Participants' attitudes towards exchange programs vary due to their status of participation in an exchange program.

Furthermore, students who participated in international exchange programs exhibit more positive attitudes (Mean=4,604) towards their objective of participation compared to those who did not participate (Mean=4.330) in any exchange program.

H3: Participants' purposes of joining exchange programs vary according to their status of participation in an exchange program.

Moreover, students' participatory objectives vary depending on former experience of participation in such exchange programs. While the main objective of participation for those who have already taken a part in exchange programs (Mean=4,961) is "to get to know the wealth and structures of different cultures," the primary objective of the students who have not participated in any program (Mean=4,533) is to "improve their foreign languages and to develop self-confidence while speaking" (Figure 6). The findings support the existence of

Figure 6. Perception of participating in exchange programs

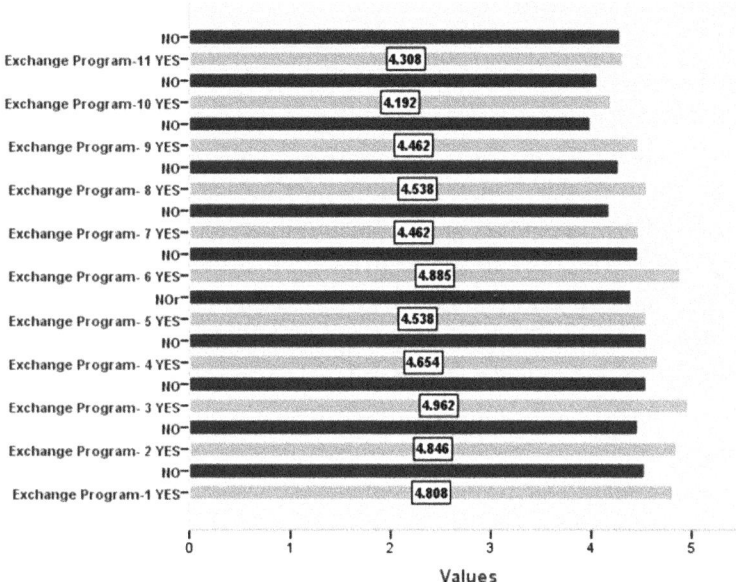

a relation between the contact with a foreign culture and language. Learning about different cultures and learning a foreign language in interaction with the culture reinforce individuals' language skills and improve their awareness about different cultures.

Intercultural Communication Sensitivity Results

The evaluation of the relation between intercultural communication sensitivity and knowledge of foreign languages is among the primary questions of the research. Thus, we employed a 20 item Intercultural Sensitivity Scale put forth by Chen and Starosta (2000) in order to determine participants' intercultural sensitivity levels. Cronbach's alpha coefficient is calculated as $\alpha=80$ for the responses to the forms used to asses participants' awareness about intercultural communication sensitivity, the value is proven to be reliable for this measure. The scale highlights four key factors for the evaluation of intercultural communication sensitivity: *responsibility and care in communication, confidence in interaction, respect for cultural differences* and *liking the interaction.*

In this context, the openness of the students who live in Turkey and participate in the survey to intercultural communication is described comparing their knowledge of foreign languages and experience of interaction with another culture in an effort to learn languages or to live abroad.

H4: There is difference among the participants' perceptions towards intercultural communication sensitivity.

When participants' intercultural communication sensitivity levels are observed, it is remarked that they adopt positive attitudes in terms of responsibility and care in their communication with different cultures, which is followed by confidence in communication. In this context, the participants are observed to have high confidence in their encounters with other individuals with different cultural backgrounds. However, they are stated to have a relatively negative attitude with regard to other intercultural communication sensitivity parameters (respect for cultural differences and liking the interaction) (Figure 7). Consequently, the students might be cited to have moderate levels of intercultural communication sensitivity (M=3.463). When the relation between intercultural communication sensitivity and language knowledge is inspected, participants who know foreign languages are observed to be more sensitive compared to those who cannot speak foreign languages.

Furthermore, it is remarked that the participants who acquired a foreign language through participating in an international exchange program are more confident and responsible in their interactions compared to the other group. When all findings are assessed, it is revealed that the individuals who have learned a

Figure 7. Intercultural communication sensitivity

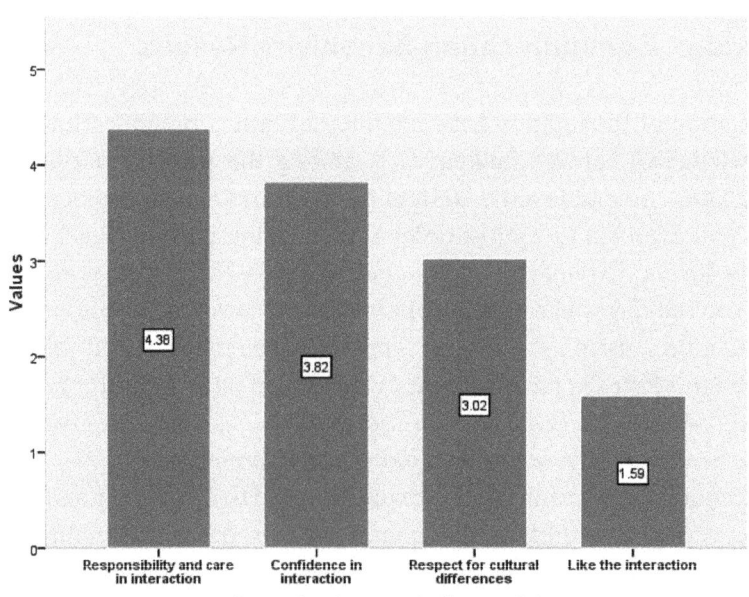

language participating in an exchange program and interacting with the target culture itself tend to have more advanced intercultural communication skills and cultural openness. Nevertheless, these variables do not affect the respect for cultural differences and liking the interaction parameters.

In addition to this, participants attribute great importance to learning a foreign language in the context of establishing intercultural communication in the internationalization process of higher education.

In the inter-cultural communication process, the participants were observed to have positive attitudes in the matters of:

- Improving intercultural relations more through learning different languages (Mean=4,455),
- Creating a better interaction environment with the help of language and communication with different cultures (Mean=4,455),
- Understanding the importance of language and communicative skills in the process of intercultural communication process (Mean=4,376),
- Understanding the meaning of being multilingual and multicultural (Mean=4,306),
- Understanding different lifestyles with the help of language (Mean=4,297),
- Removing the intercultural communication boundaries with the help of language (Mean=4,227).

DISCUSSION AND CONCLUSION

Today, when there are many changes and transformations on the axis of globalization, it is necessary to talk about education as a changing field. Particularly, the impact of globalization on the field of education constitutes a field of research which is worth investigating in the focus of providing intercultural communication and interaction in education. The focus of the studies on internationalization of education in the international field is consists of the development of information communication technologies, and the disappearance of borders in education, enabling education in a multilingual and multicultural environment. The main objective of these studies is to provide integration between cultures in all fields, especially education. In line with this basic aim, which is covered by the book, it is mentioned about a reconstructed understanding of education around the world, especially in the higher education system. Intercultural communication and dialogue studies that enable intercultural integration take place within the framework of the strategies that are followed in the new understanding adopted for higher education.

In order to maintain cross-cultural communication, first it is necessary to give the individuals the opportunities that will enable the recognition of counterculture. In order to achieve this integration in the context of students and education, a major role is given to international student mobility and common language studies which will enable foreign cultures and their educational approaches to be recognized. In this context, intercultural and intercultural interaction constitute an important dimension for today's students, not only in the field of education but also in the working life, where they will face all of the fields such as colleagues, working country, capital structure and ownership. In this context, the main problematic of the current research is built upon the interests and competencies of the Turkish students in the meaning of internationalization of education process and is studied the scope of to know a language, to participate in an international exchange program and to be open to foreign cultures in intercultural communication. With the findings obtained, it is aimed to contribute to the studies of internationalization of education in Turkey.

In the context of internationalization of higher education in Turkey, the findings of the study, where the impact of foreign language and student exchange programs in the process of improving the students' intercultural communication sensitivity, were analyzed under three headlines; knowledge of a foreign language, exchange programs and in the focus of these two variants, the evaluation of the students' level of intercultural communication sensitivity.

When the findings of the study regarding the knowledge of a foreign language are evaluated it can be claimed that:

- Interest towards foreign language is high in the sample group on which the study is made,
- Majority of the students with an interest toward foreign language (half of the participants), speak at least one foreign language.
- A great majority of the students speak english as a foreign language,
- Nearly 1/4 of the students know a second foreign language,
- Grammatical knowledge of the students mostly depend on the education given at schools,
- A small part of the participants (11%) have the chance for language education abroad.

When the findings regarding the exchange programs are analyzed, it can be said that:

- Participants have a fairly high degree of positive attitude in joining the exchange programs.

- Students who previously joined the programs have a more positive attitude compared to those who did not.
- The students who participated in exchange programs and the ones who did not, vary in terms of ambitions of participation,
- Whether previously included in an exchange program or not, the participants' interests towards knowing a foreign language did not differ significantly,
- Among the top of the reasons why the participants want to join these programs, "knowing the structure and existence of a different culture" came the first,
- The purposes of students who have never been involved in an exchange program before, "is to gain self-confidence in the development and usage of a foreign language.

When the findings regarding the intercultural communication sensitivity levels of students that compose the main research problem of the study were analyzed, it was revealed that:

- In a general sense, the students have a medium level tendency towards being sensitive in intercultural communication
- Sensitivities such as being responsible and careful about differences, and self-confidence in interaction lie in the basis of the communication of the participants with different cultures.
- Participants have high self confidence in face to face interaction from individuals from different cultures,
- Participants have a relatively more negative attitude in respect towards cultural differences in the communication they establish with the contra culture and their interest in the interaction established with people from different cultures,
- Participants who know a foreign language have a higher intercultural communicative sensitivity compared to the ones who don't.
- Participants who learnt a language through an exchange program act more responsibly while interacting with a foreign culture and have higher self-confidence in communication, compared to those who learnt a foreign language without attending to any exchange program.

From all these findings, it can be said that Turkish students have a high level of interest in learning foreign languages, which have a great role in the context of internationalization of education. Survey findings show that the vast majority of students involved in the study have at least one foreign language. It is determined that the commonly spoken language among the students is the English language that mentioned as the widely accepted language in the literature. In addition to this, as a sign of the progress of language studies in

Turkey in terms of internationalization of education, it is possible to show the increase of the second foreign language learners among the students and the formation of the language education in the school as the source of the language information of the students.

Another important finding from the survey is that the students have a high level of interest in participating in exchange programs. Findings have shown that the students who were involved in an exchange program had a higher desire to participate in an exchange program again than those who did not. In this respect, it can be said that the students who have participated in the exchange programs and lived this experience have increased their openness to foreign cultures. As an indication, it can be said that with the remarks of the students, the ultimate aim of the students to participate in exchange programs is their willing of "recognition of structures and assets of different cultures". In support of this finding, the learners stated that they have gained confidence in learning and using the language of the country they went through exchange programs. In this context, as mentioned in the literature, it can be said that language learning in the belonging culture gains importance for the students.

When the findings related to the level of intercultural communication sensitivity of the students constituting the basic research problem of the study are examined: It can be said that Turkish students have a moderate tendency in terms of their sensitive levels in intercultural communication. Moreover, in general terms, it can be mentioned that Turkish students have a high sense of self-confidence when there is a communication with an individual from foreign culture. However, in Turkey, which constitutes the main focus of the research, it has been determined that language and exchange programs are an important driving force in terms of internationalization of education and intercultural integration and increase in dialog. In support of this, it is possible to indicate that some different attitudes in the context of intercultural communication sensitivities of students who understand-cannot understand the language, who have previously participated-not participated in the exchange program can be shown as findings in the research. Thus, students who speak a foreign language, engage in vocabulary-based interaction in a cross-cultural communication, and have been involved in a foreign culture through an exchange program, are more open and sensitive to differences in intercultural interaction and more confident in communication. On the other hand, it can be said that the students who do not speak any foreign language, who cannot communicate with cross culture because of the lack of the language, and those who have not been able to range in a culture through an exchange program before, have more negative attitudes towards respecting and interacting with different cultures. When all the acquired findings are evaluated, students are observed to improve their intercultural communication sensitivity towards learning by interacting with the culture through language courses and exchange programs. The literature studies that to maintain the understanding of values and attitudes in intercultural communication and openness to foreign cultures (Eginli, 2011; Aktas, 2005, Logie, 2004). Again, it can be said that the findings such as participants who participated in the exchange programs are more willing to participate, different cultures are defined and interaction is clear, the self-confidence and xenophobia decrease mentioned in similar researches in the literature (Onder & Balci, 2010), prejudices and importance of dialogue (Ersoy, 2013, Demir & Demir, 2009) has been supported.

Finally, when the studies carried out in the scope of internationalization of education in Turkey and in the World are examined; as being mentioned before there are many dimensions such as recognition of diplomas and degrees of cooperation among national and international educational institutions, distance learning, life-long learning, common credit systems, and quality systems in education and so on. In the current research, it has been focused on the topics that constitutes the other important dimensions in the context of internationalization of education which are; sharing of knowledge and experiences with common language policies, student mobility that lifted the curtailment of education circulation, and creation of communication and dialogue for intercultural integration. The findings of the research have been limited within the scope of these issues and in the future studies related to the topic with the consideration of other aspects of the internationalization efforts in education, it may be suggested to provide a contribution to the literature upon the topic.

REFERENCES

Akay, R. (2013). Intercultural communication and communication competence. *Journal of Academic Inquiries*, *8*(3), 307–323.

Akman, E., Akçay, E. Y., & Argün, Ç. (2011). Youhts in the modifying structure of EU and youth policies of EU. *The Journal of Social Economic Research*, *15*(11), 1–31.

Aktaş, T. (2005). Communicative competence in foreign language teaching. *Journal of Language and Linguistic Studies*, *1*(1), 89–100.

Bekiroğlu, O., & Balcı, Ş. (2014). Looking for the clues of sensitivity of intercultural communication: A survey on the sample of communication faculty students. *Journal of Türkiyat Research*, 429-459.

Bennett, M. J. (1993). Towards ethnorelativism: A developmental model of intercultural sensitivity. In R. M. Paige (Ed.), *Education for the intercultural experience* (2nd ed.; pp. 21–71). Yarmouth, ME: Intercultural Press.

Bennett, M. J. (2004). From ethnocentrism to ethnorelativism. In J. S. Wurzel (Ed.), *Toward multiculturalism: A reader in multicultural education*. Newton, MA: Intercultural Resource Corporation.

Bozkaya, M., & Aydın, İ. E. (2010). Intercultural communiation apprehension: The case of Anadolu University for the Erasmus student exchange program. *Journal of Istanbul University Communication Faculty*, *1*(39), 29–42.

Çakır, M. (2010). Intercultural communication in a new perspective: The alienation of culture through the individual attitudes in intercultural communication. *Anatolia*, *21*(1), 75–84.

Chen, G. M., & Starosta, W. J. (2000). The development and validation of the intercultural communication sensitivity scale. *Human Communication*, *3*, 1–15.

Dulupçu, M., & Demirel, O. (2008). *Globalization and internationalization, ECOLAB: Economy and Labour World*. Comenuis.

Eğinli, A.T. (2011). The importance of the training of cultural diversity in-obtaining intercultural competency. *Öneri, 9* (35), 215-227.

Eğinli, A. T., & Yalçın, M. (2016). Developing intercultural competence and intercultural adjustment. *Global Media Journal*, *7*(13), 6–27.

Er, K. O. (2006). The effects of culture in foreign language curriculum. *Ankara University. Journal of Faculty of Educational Sciences*, *39*(1), 1–14.

Er, S. (2005). Intercultural communication, ethnocentrism and others. *Journal of Istanbul Kültür University*, *1*, 9–18.

Ersoy, A. (2013). Turkish teacher candidates' challenges regarding cross-cultural experiences: The case of Erasmus exchange program. *Education in Science*, *38*(168), 154–166.

Genç, A. (2003). *Türkiye'de geçmişten günümüze Almanca öğretimi*. Ankara, Turkey: Seçkin.

Gülcan, M. G. (2005). *AB ve eğitim süreci*. Ankara, Turkey: Anı.

Güler, G. (2005). The common european framework of reference: Learning, teaching, assessment and the foreign language education process in Turkey. *Journal of Social Science*, *6*(1), 89–106.

Gülnar, B. (2011). Acculturation and media using among foreign students. *Global Media Journal*, *2*(3), 51–68.

Hasdemir, F., & Çalıkoğlu, M. R. (2011). The European Union education programmes and the Change. *Journal of Higher Education and Science*, *1*(2), 66–68. doi:10.5961/jhes.2011.010

Kartarı, A. (2014). *Kültür, farklılık ve iletişim.* İstanbul, Turkey: İletişim.

Kasalak, G. (2013). Views of academic staff on Erasmus Teaching Staff Mobility: The case of Akdeniz University. *Journal of Higher Education and Science*, *3*(2), 133–141. doi:10.5961/jhes.2013.068

Kaya, G. T. (2014). Internationalisation of higher education and global mobility. *Journal of Educational Sciences*, *39*, 195–199.

Kürkçü, D.D. (2013). Küreselleşme kavramı ve küreselleşmeye yönelik yaklaşımlar. *The Turkish Online Journal of Design, Art and Communication*, *3*(2), 1-11.

Logie, N. N. (2004). Yabanci dil öğretiminde kültürel becerinin oluşturulmasinin önemi ve budunbilimsel boyut. *Hasan Ali Yücel Eğitim Fakültesi Dergisi*, *1*, 173–180.

OECD. (2011). *Education at a Glance 2011: OECD Indicators.* OECD Publishing.

Olcay, G. A., & Nasır, V. A. (2016). Internationalization in higher education: A look at the years 1999-2013 from the perspectives of the countries with the most international students and Turkey. *Journal of Higher Education and Science*, *6*(3), 288–297.

Onder, R.K., & Balcı, A. (2007). Erasmus öğrenci öğrenim hareketliliği programinin 2007 yilinda programdan yararlanan türk öğrenciler üzerindeki etkileri. *Ankara Avrupa Araştırmaları Dergisi*, *9*(2), 93-116.

Oral, Y. (2010). Türkiye'de yabancı dil eğitimi politikaları bağlamında İngilizce: Eleştirel bir çalışma. *Alternatif Eğitim e-Dergisi*, *1*, 59-68.

Şahin, K. (2009). *Küreselleşme tartışmaları ışığında ulus devlet.* İstanbul, Turkey: Yeniyüzyıl.

Şahin, M., & Alkan, R. M. (2016). Change and transformation course in higher education and expanding role of universities. *Journal of Research in Education and Teaching*, *5*(2), 297–307.

Şeremet, M. (2015). A comparative approach to Turkey and England higher education: The internationalism policy. *Journal of Higher Education and Science*, *5*(1), 27–31. doi:10.5961/jhes.2015.106

Tekelioğlu, F., Başer, H., Örtlek, M., & Aydınlı, C. (2012). Factors effecting the international students to select country and university: A case study of foundation university. *Organizasyon ve Yönetim Bilimleri Dergisi*, *4*(2), 191–200.

Varol, A. (2013). Kültürlerarası diyalogda halkla ilişkilerin rolü. *Sosyal Bilimler Dergisi*, *1*, 1–23.

Yalçınkaya, M., Güngör, A. A., Yanar, A. İ., & Arslan, M. (2013). Türkiye'deki üniversitelerin uluslararasılaşma stratejileri. *Proceedings of the Eighth National Conference on Education Congress,* 481-482.

Yılmaz, D. V. (2016). Internatıonalızatıon of turkısh state unıversıtıes: An evaluatıon over strategıc plans. Suleyman Demirel University. *The Journal of Faculty of Economics and Administrative Science*, *21*(4), 1191–1212.

Chapter 9
Internationalization of Higher Education in Kazakhstan:
National Capacity-Building Initiatives

Ainur Seitbattalovna Kenebayeva
University of International Business, Kazakhstan

ABSTRACT

This chapter highlights the internationalization of the higher education system in the Republic of Kazakhstan. It briefly discusses Kazakh national initiatives to enhance the country's global economic competitiveness through modernization and capacity-building in the field of higher education and science. National experience on integration to the international educational space by the consecutive implementation of Bologna principles is reflected. The importance of the Bolashak presidential scholarship program is addressed as a strategy for human capital development. This chapter also underlines trends, tendencies, and issues of internationalization of higher education in globalization. Key aspects of internationalization considered through the prism of the Kazakhstani experience include academic mobility, accreditation, university rankings, and research and development (R&D).

DOI: 10.4018/978-1-5225-5231-4.ch009

INTRODUCTION

This chapter discusses how globalization and internationalization have reshaped the traditional Soviet model higher education system and the state policy in developing modern Kazakhstan. It addresses Kazakhstan's main structural changes and policy reforms due to the integration of the international educational space. This chapter reflects on the strategic transition of modern Kazakhstan to international standards in education and science through visionary leadership and new economic goals. The country's national initiative to implement the Bologna Process and its main principles is discussed and analyzed. The prism of reliable statistics and data provides insight on the Kazakhstani experience in modernization of the national system of higher education. Kazakhstan's unique experience in integration and internationalization is an example through the Bolashak presidential scholarship programme. The objectives are:

1. Analyze and reflect on the influence of globalization processes on the internationalization of higher education in developing countries, particularly Kazakhstan
2. Discuss strategic reforms in the modernization of Kazakhstan's national higher education system within the context of the Bologna Process
3. Discuss the importance of the Bolashak scholarship program related to the integration of Kazakhstan as a competitive nation in the global community

Additionally, this chapter reflects on contemporary practices of Kazakhstan in a global educational space. To discuss key aspects of internationalization, it focuses on issues related to academic mobility, accreditation, university rankings, and R&D. This chapter contains many examples, comparisons, and statistical analyses to represent current situations in the local educational market. Finally, the chapter explores the image of the academic profession in the context of the Commonwealth of Independent States (CIS).

INTERNATIONALIZATION OF HIGHER EDUCATION TO FORM GLOBALLY COMPETITIVE NATIONAL ECONOMIES

The higher education system of developing countries is functioning and developing under the influence of inevitable factors, including globalization, internationalization, and liberalization. Globalization, which is one of the most significant tendencies of modern times, defines the development of countries worldwide, shapes intellectual capital of nations, and accelerates the process of sociocultural and economic integration. Global trends clearly define that any country in the world (especially underdeveloped states) are unable to progress separately. Strategic integration in the context of globalization is increasingly important. However, this is not true in developing countries. The universal effect of globalization has a considerable impact on both developing countries and the developed world. However, it is argued that developing states are more influenced by globalization because of country-specific issues related to political, sociocultural, and economic challenges (Al'abri, 2011). Globalization forces most developing countries to focus on integration. Therefore, priority is generally given to internationalization of the national educational system because the development of the educational sphere indicates a country's competitiveness. Internationalization is a key concept of state reform; it determines main principals of higher education in most countries.

Internationalization can be defined as a response to globalization through government policy executed in the form of state programs (Al'abri, 2011; UNESCO, 2009). In modern conditions, internationalization of education is a crucial stage of a deliberate policy of states aimed to solve national, political, social, and economic problems. The sphere of education is a vital institution of the state and society in facilitating human capital development. In this context, internationalization is quality improvement in higher education systems and modernization of a state economy. The internationalization of education contributes to a pool of qualified human resources, which improves the competitiveness of the nation (Qiang, 2003). In conditions of globalized economy, developing countries seek a competitive advantage by investing in people (Al'abri, 2011). On the other hand, developed countries also benefit from internationalization by accessing brain capital and ensuring revenue generation in the field of educational services (Jibeen & Khan, 2015). Currently, educational institutions compete for a market share and attract foreign students with an academic image promoted through advanced study programs emphasizing unique approaches in the formation of valuable competencies corresponding to the requirements of the labor market (Shafaei & Razak, 2016). It is reported that the global educational market is shared by leading players represented by the United States, the United Kingdom, Australia, and Canada (UEFISCDI, 2013).

Qiang (2003), in referring to Knight (1997), distinguished four rationales for internationalization: (1) political; (2) economic; (3) academic; and (4) sociocultural. The international educational space unites nations and continents.

Therefore, the political rationale can be interpreted as global stability due to the promotion of amity values between countries and the enhancement of cultural tolerance. The economic rationale illustrates how countries adapt to global change by exploiting market orientation opportunities through the internationalization of education. The academic rationale implies that governments are attaching an increased importance on internationalization to ensure global acceptance and multicultural competencies of a national academic staff in teaching and research. By doing so, developing countries integrate to the global knowledge economy. The sociocultural rationale reflects objectives associated with a preservation of national identity equally supporting cultural diversity. In this regard multilingual developing countries may benefit in terms of creating international networks and developing communications. Moreover, multilingualism is becoming one of most significant competitive advantages of countries and nations in the era of globalization. It is argued that multilingual nations progress quicker and positively adjust to changing conditions.

BOLOGNA PROCESS AND MODERNIZATION OF HIGHER EDUCATION IN KAZAKHSTAN

Implementation of Bologna Principles

Internationalization of higher education around the globe can be characterized by similar tendencies, including increased competition between educational institutions, redaction of state funding due to the underlining principle of university autonomy, lifelong learning, academic mobility, flexible approaches to teaching and learning, a cross-border corporative network, and the growing importance of quality assurance implemented by the accreditation system (Hénard, Diamond,& Roseveare, 2012; Rumbley, Altbach, & Reisberg, 2012; UEFISCDI, 2013). As an active member of the world community, Kazakhstan has also been involved in the internationalization process. Its orientation toward internationalization of education has been defined as a main direction of state policy. A series of reforms have been realized within the framework of laws and regulations issued by its government. Its normative documents are now main pillars of national strategic policy in the field of higher education in Kazakhstan. They include the "Law on Education - 2007", Conception of Education Development of the Republic of Kazakhstan till 2015, "State Program of Education Development for 2011-2020," National Plan – "The 100 concrete steps" set out by President

Nursultan Nazarbayev to implement the five institutional reforms and the state strategy "Kazakhstan-2050" designed as a new political course of successful country in an evolving world. State reforms, which focus on the modernization of the Kazakh system of education, aim to improve the quality of human capital based on standards of Organization for Economic Cooperation and Development (OECD) countries. In the Kazakh nation, education is viewed as the main economic asset and key driver of competitiveness in regard to the integration process. As defined by Omirbayev (2015), the main directions of Kazakh internationalization in higher education are:

- Dual diploma programs
- Joint establishment of international universities
- Teacher and student exchange programs
- International joint research projects
- Joint study programs (sandwich-programs)

The implementation of the Bologna principles is one of Kazakhstan's most significant strategic decisions regarding integration to the international educational space. Both policymakers and the local educational community perceive it as the next step in its integration to the world educational space. In addition, it meets the state's higher education system needs for quality improvement. Kazakhstan joined the Bologna process in March 2010. In the last seven years, fundamental parameters of the Bologna declaration have been realized. Due to modern transformations, Kazakhstan has joined the great charter of universities (currently signed by more than 650 universities). According to recent statistics provided by Independent Kazakh Agency for Quality Assurance in Education (IQAA), it was signed by more than 60 Kazakh universities. Furthermore, the three-tier system of education (bachelor's – master's - doctorate) was implemented in 2004. The national credit accumulation system was based on the European Credit Transfer and Accumulation System (ECTS) using the application of a conversion factor. If its application, combined with qualification frameworks, is based on educational outcomes to simplify the recognition procedures of qualifications and diplomas, the ECTS is considered an important condition to facilitate integration in higher education (Omirbayev, 2015). According to the report of the Ministry of Education and Science of the Republic of Kazakhstan, the Kazakh credit transfer model based on ECTS has been successfully applied by all universities to date (Ministry of Education & Science, 2015a).

According to new academic standards, the qualification framework is a distinctive feature of modern study programs in Kazakh universities. Qualification standards define and describe requirements for student competencies formed according to relevant levels of training. Prior to the implementation of the credit, study programs and curricula used by HEIs differed in content by 10% to 12%. Modern standards expand the autonomy of educational institutions in the formation of study programs. This is due to the elective components (Eligbayeva, 2015):

- 68% to 85% for basic and major disciplines at bachelor's level, respectively
- 50% to 60% for master's programs
- No less than 83% at the doctorate level.

The "State Programme of Education Development in the Republic of Kazakhstan for 2016-2019" discussed the expansion of the academic autonomy of HEIs by the year 2017. According to the report, the proportion of elective components in study programs will increase to 75% for a bachelor's degree, 85% for a master's; and 95% for a doctorate. This ensures university independence in the formation of educational programmes and general subjects, as well as independent development of integrated study modules (State Program for Education and Science Development in the Republic of Kazakhstan, 2016).

Academic Mobility

Internationalization of higher education requires academic mobility of teachers and students. It contributes to quality improvement of study programs, upgrades the research sector, and develops educational processes. Mobility in education and research is occurring in Kazakhstan according to the "Strategy of Academic Mobility for 2012-2020." According to statistics provided by the Ministry of Education and Science within the framework of mobility programs, more than 3,400 students have studied abroad between 2011-2015. The number of students studying for one semester in foreign university programs with academic mobility has been increasing since 2011 (see Figure 1). Additionally, more than 7,000 foreign professors and scientists from the U.S., Russia, Eastern Asian, and European countries have been invited by Kazakh universities to conduct lectures and research. Figure 1 demonstrates academic mobility and dynamics in Kazakhstan higher education.

Academic mobility is considered a leading trend of internationalization manifested in the Bologna Process. International academic mobility in Kazakhstan

Figure1. Student mobility and invited foreign professors
Based on data provided by The Ministry of Education and Science of the Republic of Kazakhstan
(Report about the realization of the State Program of Education Development for 2011-2020)

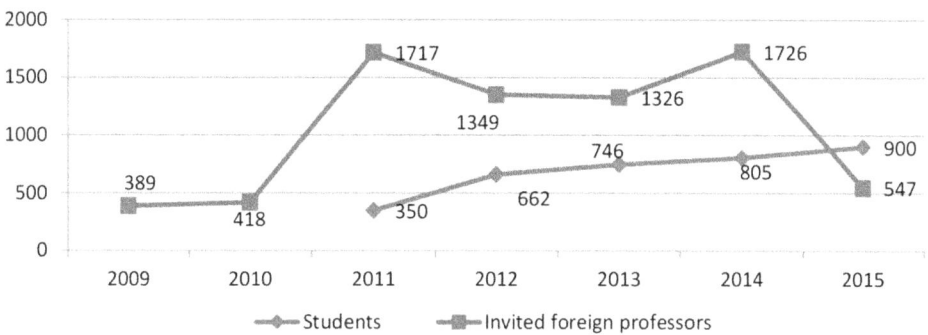

Figure 2. Academic mobility statistics under the Erasmus Mundus Programme (joint master's degrees)
Source: National Erasmus+ office in Kazakhstan

Erasmus Mundus Joint Master's Degrees

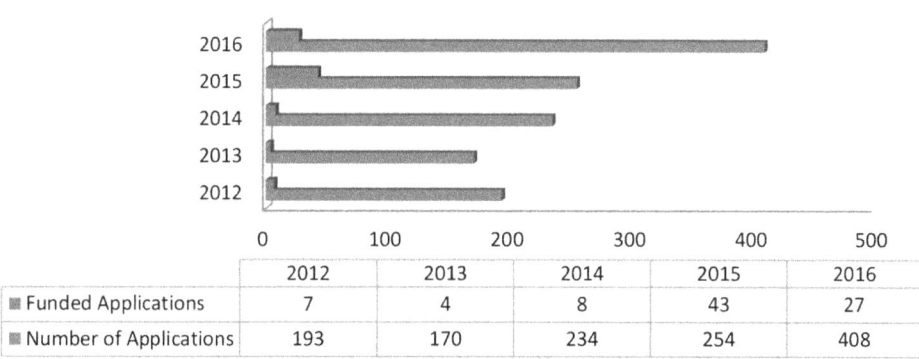

	2012	2013	2014	2015	2016
■ Funded Applications	7	4	8	43	27
■ Number of Applications	193	170	234	254	408

*For a more accurate representation see the electronic version.

is mainly implemented by Bolashak, Erasmus, and Erasmus+ programmes. In 2016, the Programme of Erasmus Mundus funded 27 applications for joint master's degrees and two applications for joint doctorates (see Figure 2 and Figure 3).

Active participation of local HEIs in the European Union (EU) programmes is one of the most important aspects of internationalization of higher education in Kazakhstan. Kazakhstan has been extensively involved in the Tempus Programme (implemented 1995-2013). The modernization of curricula has been realized through a number of these projects (EACEA, 2012). During this period, 76

Figure 3. Academic mobility statistics under the Erasmus Mundus Programme (joint doctorates)
Source: National Erasmus+ office in Kazakhstan

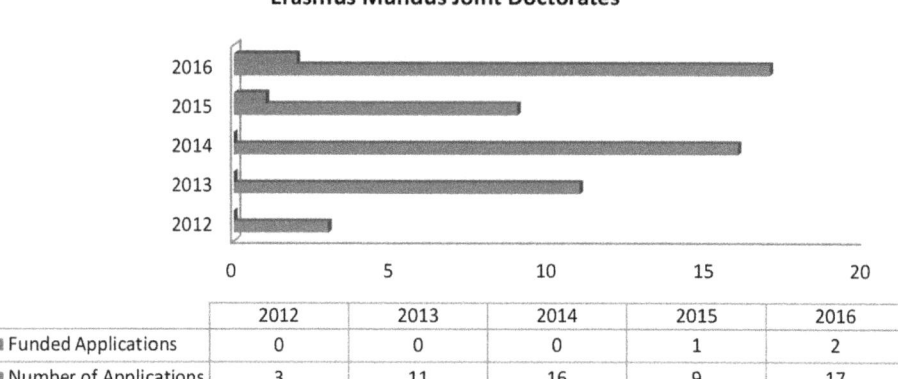

Erasmus Mundus Joint Doctorates

	2012	2013	2014	2015	2016
■ Funded Applications	0	0	0	1	2
■ Number of Applications	3	11	16	9	17

*For a more accurate representation see the electronic version.

Table 1. Kazakh universities with highest TEMPUS participation during TEMPUS IV (2008-2012)

Universities	Number of Projects	Universities	Number of Projects
Al-Farabi Kazakh National University	13	D. Serikbayev East Kazakhstan State Technical University	5
L.N.Gumilyov Eurasian National University	9	Korkyt Ata Kyzylorda State University	5
Auezov South Kazakhstan State University	6	A. Baitursynov Kostanay State University	5
Buketov Karaganda State University	6	Karaganda State Technical University	5
Sh. Ualikhanov Kokshetau State University	6	S.Seifullin Kazakh Agro Technical University	5

Source: National Erasmus+ office in Kazakhstan

projects with Kazakhstani partners were financed at a cost of 54 million Euros. Forty-six universities and 48 nonacademic partners participated in the projects. As a result, approximately 30% of Kazakh universities were engaged in the Tempus Programme (see Table 1).

Accreditation

Modern society expects more from the educational sphere. Due to growing demands and requirements, aspects of quality in education are becoming more crucial. Universities focused on quality improvement seek to gain a competitive advantage through accreditation. As international experience has shown, accreditation is essential for high-quality performance. It proves and measures general quality and reputation of higher educational institutions (HEIs).

The development and implementation of a quality assurance system in the field of higher education is a main goal of the national model of accreditation in Kazakhstan. Accreditation improves educational standards, ensures the mutual recognition of university degrees and professional qualifications, and facilitates integration into the global educational space within the Bologna process. A university's performance across different aspects (i.e., quality of teaching and study programs, research activity, resource base, and competitiveness) is evaluated through state certification, national accreditation, and international accreditation.

The Ministry of Education and Science of the Republic of Kazakhstan has established the national model of accreditation and ranking system to allow local HEIs to administer independent performance evaluations. The formation of the Kazakh National Register of Accreditation Institutions in May 2012 was a significant step forward. The register included six accreditation agencies with two national agencies (IQAA and the Independent Agency for Accreditation and Rating [IAAR]) and four foreign agencies (Accreditation, Certification, and Quality Assurance Institute [ACQUIN, German], ASIIN [German], AQA [Austrian], and the Accreditation Board for Engineering and Technology, Inc. [ABET, American] (Zhetpisbayeva, Arinova, & Asylbekuly, 2012). The list of foreign agencies has been extended and currently includes the Foundation for International Business Administration Accreditation (FIBAA), the Accreditation Council for Business Schools and Programs (ACBSP), the Middle States Association of Colleges and Schools (MSA-CESS), and The Institute of Marine Engineering, Science and Technology (IMaREST).

Attention is given to independent accreditation. These procedures are recognized by both national and international accreditation agencies. The number of licensed programs in 2016 was 4,687 (Ministry of Education & Science, 2016a). The percentage of accredited programs was 55.5%, which amounted to 2,603 (bachelor's – 1503, master's – 926, and PhD – 176) (IAAR, 2016). Detailed data addressed by each educational programme are presented in Table 2. (See Figure 4)

Figure 4. Number of accredited higher education programmes (2016)
Source: Independent Agency for Accreditation and Rating

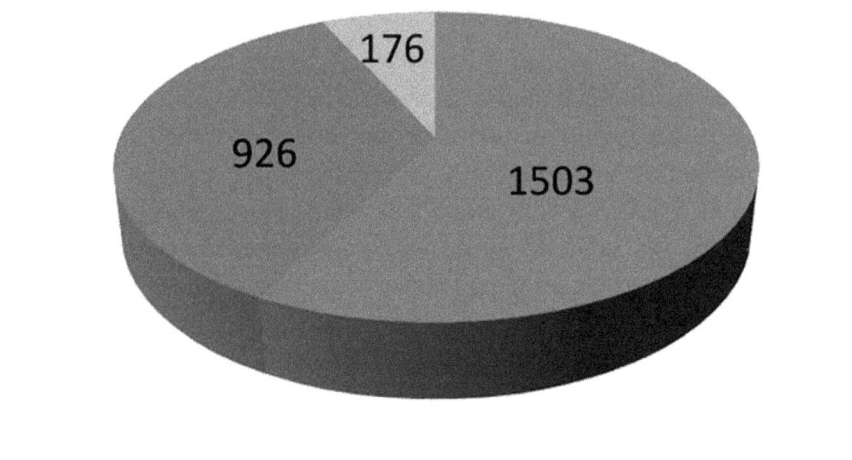

■ **Bachelor's**   ■ **Master's**   ▨ **PhD**

*For a more accurate representation see the electronic version.

Table 2. Educational programmes accredited by national and international agencies

Specialized Accreditation in National Agencies		Specialized International Accreditation	
Bachelor's	1,336	Bachelor's	167
Master's	800	Master's	126
PhD	162	PhD	14
Number of Educational Programmes	2,298	Number of Educational Programmes	307

Source: Independent Agency for Accreditation and Rating

In 2015, 343 specialties (higher education and postgraduate education) of 54 HEIs passed specialized national accreditation (Ministry of Education & Science, 2015a).This figure increased to 78 universities in 2016. In 2015, international accreditation was passed by 252 specialties (including higher and postgraduate education) of 30 Kazakh universities. The indicator for 2016 was 28 (Nurmagambetov, 2016).

International integration in the field of education and science is also developing in regard to the Bologna principles. Kazakh universities signed 453 agreements with foreign partner-universities. Currently, 443 joint educational programs have been implemented by local universities (bachelor's – 275; master's – 142;

PhD – 26). Moreover, 5,821 foreign students from CIS and abroad are studying at local universities (Ministry of Education & Science, 2015a). According to strategic goals set by the government and declared in the "State Programme of Education Development in the Republic of Kazakhstan for 2016-2019," the transition from a state certification of HEIs to accreditation is expected to be carried out by 2017. This implies that there will be a creation of an efficient quality assurance system of higher education, which will include internal and external quality control. Mechanisms for assessing internal quality assurance will also be developed; it will be the responsibility of HEIs to foster functional efficiency and quality assurance mechanisms.

A university ranking system will also be applied as an assessment mechanism to evaluate the competitiveness of local HEIs. Reliability and validity of ranking procedures are ensured by an independent assessment (Bishimbayev & Nurasheva, 2012). The procedures of institutional and programme accreditation are carried out by IQAA and realized in accordance with the European and international standards. The national system of accreditation is based on internationally

Table 3. Comparative data of Kazakh university rankings in the QS World University Rankings

University	Rank/2016	Rank/2015	Number of Students (2016)
Al-Farabi Kazakh National University	236	275	16,429
L.N. Gumilyov Eurasian National University	345	371	15,042
Satpaev Kazakh National Technical University	411-420	511-600	11,325
Abai Kazakh National Pedagogical University	501-550	601-650	8,035
M. Auezov South Kazakhstan State University	601-650	701+	13,804
Kazakh-British Technical University	651-700	701+	2,023
Buketov Karaganda State University	701+	701+	6,659
Kazakh Ablai Khan University of International Relations and World Languages	701+	701+	4,770

Source: QS World University Rankings, 2015-2016

accepted standards while considering national legitimacy.

In 2016, several Kazakh universities improved their positions in QS World University Rankings as compared with figures from 2015 (see Table 3). A main weakness of local universities was their focus on teaching vs. scientific and research development (OECD, 2016).

BOLASHAK PROGRAMME AS A STRATEGY OF INTELLECTUAL DEVELOPMENT OF KAZAKHSTAN

Another aspect of internationalization of higher education in Kazakhstan is the government-sponsored Bolashak programme. A presidential scholarship program, Bolashak (meaning "the future" in Kazakh language) was launched 1993 to train highly-qualified specialists in different sectors for the country's socioeconomic development. This unique international programme gives youth from Kazakhstan an opportunity to study at a leading foreign university, including Harvard, Columbia, Cambridge, Sorbonne, Oxford, and Manchester. Upon completion of their studies, Bolashak graduates must return to Kazakhstan and work in their specialty for three to five years.

During the decade since the implementation of the Bolashak programme (1994-2015), 11,352 scholarships have been awarded. As a result of the scholarships,

Figure 5. Number of Bolashak scholarship holders earning education abroad (broken down by study program)
Based on data provided by The Ministry of Education and Science of the Republic of Kazakhstan (Report about the realization of the State Program of Education Development for 2011-2020)

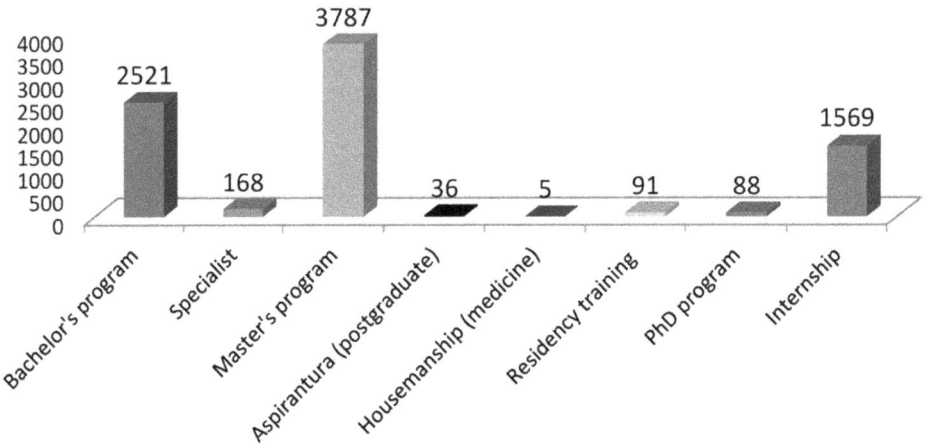

*For a more accurate representation see the electronic version.

8,265 specialists have been trained according to bachelor's, master's, and PhD programs. Other types of training include internship programs, bachelor's-level specialist training, aspirantura, postgraduate studies, housemanship, and residency training in the medical sphere. The number of students earning education abroad through the Bolashak program is illustrated in Figure 5. Currently, 1,395 students are studying abroad with the Bolashak scholarship. A considerable part of grant holders study in Great Britain and Ireland (46%), the U.S. and Canada (39.5%), Europe (7%), Asia and Oceania (4.5%), and Russia (3%).

R&D

Innovative development of the state economy requires quality improvements in the field of science and research. Kazakhstan continues to work toward accelerated development of research activities in universities. This includes the cooperation between science and business, as well as integration with the international academic community. In 2015, Kazakhstan passed the Law "On the commercialization of scientific and (or) scientific and technical activities". The objective of the law is to create conditions for the development of science from the perspective of the state economy and business (Ministry of Education & Science, 2016b). A new model of science management has been created in Kazakhstan. Financing mechanisms (i.e., basic, grants, programme-specific funds) for research projects have been identified. The independent expertise of research projects is carried out by the National Center of Science and Technology Evaluation. As a vital step toward the facilitation of research activities, technology and innovation are being fostered by the Technology Commercialization Project. This project, which is assisted by the World Bank, was completed by the government in 2015. Under this programme, 65 research projects and six licensing agreements have been implemented.

In Kazakhstan, R&D is realized by 392 scientific organizations, including 245 research institutions (Ministry of Education & Science, 2016b). The figures for 2015 show that 40% of the institutions belonged to the entrepreneurial sector represented by enterprises involved in the production of products or services. Compared to 2013, the number of organizations in this sector increased by 44 units. However, the higher education sector demonstrated negative trends. The number of R&D organizations in this sector decreased by nine units in comparison with indicators recorded in 2013. It decreased by two units compared to 2014. In general, higher education is represented by 103 R&D organizations, including universities (regardless of the source of funding and legal status), research

Table 4. Country rankings depending on publications (2011-2015)

Country	Rank	Number of Publications	% of Cited Documents
U.S.	1	3,081,687	53.88
China	2	1,484,026	53.83
Great Britain	3	883,708	54.02
UK	4	767,869	54.12
Germany	5	723,580	60.36
Japan	6	543,087	57.65
France	7	490,513	60.67
Canada	8	461,499	58.56
Italy	9	444,486	60.41
Russia	16	190,819	47.63
Belarus	74	7,112	50.15
Kazakhstan	**85**	**4,687**	**31.81**
Kyrgyzstan	143	595	46.89
Western Sahara	214	1	0

Source: InCites (Thomson Reuters)

institutes, experimental stations, and clinics. Ninety universities were engaged in R&D activities in 2015 (National Academy of Science of the Republic of Kazakhstan, 2016).

A prioritized quality indicator for Kazakhstan in the sector of science is the publication of Kazakhstani researchers in highly ranked academic journals. The number of publications in internationally accepted journals was 1,995 (in 2015): 976 in Scopus; 327 in Web of Science Core Collection (Thomson Reuters); and 692 simultaneously in both databases (Ministry of Education & Science, 2016b). The positive trend in 2015was three times higher compared to 2011. Although this rate was short of the target, it was the most positive dynamic of the Eurasian Economic Union (EAEU) countries (National Academy of Science of the Republic of Kazakhstan, 2016). According to the data presented by InCites (Thomson Reuters), which represents 214 countries, Kazakhstan placed 85[th]for the number of academic papers indexed in the Web of Science Core Collection between 2011 and 2015. Kazakhstan placed 108[th]for the total number of citations of these publications. Kazakhstan placed 207th for the average citation rate of a publication.

Despite progress, many pending problems exist in the field of education and science. Kazakhstan falls behind developed countries in terms of performance indicators in R&D. During the last five years, R&D expenditures have nearly tripled. However, these indicators are significantly lower than in OECD countries. In comparison, gross domestic expenditure on R&D is 14 times lower than in OECD countries. Sales of intellectual property rights in Kazakhstan are considerably lower than in Singapore and Russia (Ministry of Education & Science, 2016b). A large part of research projects remains unclaimed by business due to the underdeveloped cooperation between science and business. This prevents the implementation and application of research results in the production process. The majority of HEIs in Kazakhstan face problems related to the lack of pilot experimental base for research testing, lack of financial instruments for enterprises' interest in introducing innovations, and lack of mechanisms stimulating the work of researchers (Ministry of Education & Science, 2015b).

Creating a knowledge-intensive national economy in the next 10 to 15 years a priority defined in the "Development Strategy of Kazakhstan until 2050."A new model of scientist training programmes will be implemented. The split PhD will be implemented within the Bolashak presidential scholarship programme as an efficient instrument to accelerate integration into the world scientific and technological community. The aim of this project is to ensure science excellence and knowledge transfer, as well as develop research directions in Kazakhstan through training in modern methods of R&D. The split PhD project was launched and tested in 2014 at Nazarbayev University. The split PhD, which is a variety of doctoral programmes, carries out research activities based on two partner universities. This model of training implies different approaches to a comprehensive study of a research problem. It contributes to scientific capacity building among partner universities. This type of approach has been successfully practiced in Europe countries and the U.S. Several Great Britain universities (i.e., the University of Manchester, the University of Nottingham, and Durham University) have implemented this approach in two directions:

1. **Research Partnership:** Cooperation with commercial or industrial organizations
2. **Strengthening the Scientific Capacity:** Collaboration with other research institutes

U.S. universities have a highly developed research potential. Therefore, doctoral trainings are implemented based on a joint-PhD programme. The main features of the programme are:

1. Obtaining degrees from both partner universities
2. Formally enrolling in both partner universities

The implementation of the split PhD within the framework of the Bolashak programme offers Kazakhstan a unique opportunity to exploit the potential of leading global research centers with a focus on the development of the national economy (The Concept of Implementation of Split PhD, 2015).

The dynamics of social processes has recently increased. People in most countries demonstrate high mobility as an inevitable effect of globalization. This requires new knowledge and professional competencies. Knowledge acquired at a university does not guarantee a lifetime of social and professional adjustments. Therefore, lifelong learning is required. The implementation of the lifelong learning concept is a strategic state decision impacting the public. A steady progress toward technological and economic development in Kazakhstan requires highly qualified personnel to respond flexibly to changes in the labour market. To keep up with rapid changes, national specialists need advanced competencies (Narenova, Kenshibay & Usenbayeva, 2009).

SOLUTIONS AND RECOMMENDATIONS

Kazakhstan has successfully chosen a strategic path toward internationalization and modernization of the national higher education system aimed at qualitative improvements. Concrete examples discussed in this chapter represent timely transformations and adequate changes related to socioeconomic development in the Republic of Kazakhstan. The country has undertaken ambitious goals met through systematic actions.

Nevertheless, transformations and modern reforms place complicated conditions on national HEIs. Several problems hinder progressive results in the national higher education system. The most problematic drawback is a lack of balance between teaching and research activities. This is complicated by the imbalanced academic workload. For example, a recommended workload per year for teaching staff in a majority of Kazakhstan HEIs averages 550 hours. In fact, a considerable number of lecturers and assistant/associate professors teach between 725 and 825 hours per year. In Poland, teaching hours are 240 to 540 per year. Professors in Poland are less involved in teaching. In France, this indictor averages 126 hours for assistant/associate professors and 192 hours for teaching assistants (http://www.eui.eu).

All levels of academic staff members (i.e., teachers, head teachers, PhD, assistant/associate professors) in Kazakhstan conduct 20 to 25 hours of lectures and seminars per week. Highly qualified assistant/associate professors are required to teach in three languages—Kazakh, English, and Russian—for five to eight courses per semester. According to statistics provided by the European University Institute (2016), assistant professors in the U.S. teach two courses per semester (9 to 12 hours per week); associate professors teach six to nine hours per week.

On the other hand, PhDs and assistant/associate professors in Kazakhstan are actively involved in research, publish research in highly ranked international journals, and carry out social and administrative duties, including translations, students training, advisory support, and development of modular programmes. Instead of focusing on research, scientific staff spends a significant part of their time teaching, developing daily lecture materials, and performing tasks beyond their key responsibilities. Senior academic staff are not used efficiently. Efforts for quality improvements through R&D are not optimally implemented. The impact of working under such circumstances causes low motivation, low job enthusiasm, loss of working capacity, and low-quality work.

For a majority of HEIs, the creation of research-oriented faculties is a priority goal dictated by modern changes in a competitive educational environment. However, there is a discrepancy between ambitious goals and existing working conditions. Although expectations regarding research results and scientific productivity have significantly increased, both national and private HEIs have not succeeded in reforming human resource policies or motivating research-oriented staff. This kind of situation is common in CIS countries. Most universities are teaching-oriented; the research sector is considered less attractive for both universities and teachers. Moreover, research-related careers are perceived as low paying. For instance, the results of a recent survey in Russia revealed that "only 30.9% of the students that took research-oriented undergraduate courses wanted to go into science" (Kozmina, 2014, p.9).

Introducing a differentiated salary system redesigned for a capable research-focused staff is suggested as a solution for a transition period. This strategy enhances motivation, promotes involvement in research projects, and increases job satisfaction. These, in turn, directly impact work productivity. Additionally, daily tasks of junior staff must be eliminated from the duties of highly qualified senior research staff. This allows senior staff to concentrate on scientific work. Generally, within the context of global transformation, the reputation and image of the academic profession should be taken into consideration. Mechanisms surrounding university governance should ensure relevant working conditions along with the implementation of an efficient and transparent inducement system based on both monetary and nonmonetary rewards.

HEIs understand that research excellence is a vital indicator for measuring competitiveness at local and global scales. Therefore, producing high-quality publications, conducting research with evidential value, and discussing results in the world scientific arena are stirring concerns among Central Asian universities. This affects university governance and local HEIs as they move toward research and innovation while maintaining traditional teaching orientation.

CONCLUSION

Internationalization of higher education in a growing number of countries is becoming a strategic orientation of the state policy. Governments implement this as a solution for specific sociopolitical and economic issues. Sales in educational services at international levels have been intensifying. Some countries (i.e., U.S., UK, France, and Australia) exploit their opportunities in the international market by importing educational services. However, developing countries are increasing their export potential by educating domestic specialists abroad. In many cases, economic motives of strategic development have become important for those countries participating in internationalization because economic benefits are defined as the goal of developing international cooperation in the field of education. Economic stimuli force national systems of education to improve quality and attractiveness of study programmes. They also enhance graduate competitiveness in the labor market. In this regard, internationalization is important for developing economies. Firstly, the internationalization of higher education can stimulate the training of qualified specialists who operate in diverse cultural contexts and global professional environments. Secondly, internationalization shares national values and forms positive images of a country. Moreover, internationalization of higher education is an important factor in the modernization of developing economies. Foreign internships, double diploma programs, joint modules, and research projects allow countries to improve the quality of education. It also serves as an important source of attracting new technologies and knowledge.

Considering the perspectives of globalization, developing countries use the processes of internationalization as a positioning strategy to build a state's positive image and facilitate integration into the world community though global educational space. States implement the internationalization strategy based on individual political, social, economic, and technological capabilities. They consider the quality and potential of their system of education, as well as their experience in developing international collaborations and networks. National features of internationalization in the field of education are expressed though the language policy of Kazakhstan. This implies a gradual transition to study programs taught in English at high school and universities. It also enhances the export potential of Kazakh higher education.

The quality of higher education is a key factor of a country's global competitiveness and potential economic growth. Higher education is the foundation for human capacity development. A nation's competitiveness depends on human potential, which can be measured by a capability to innovate, take risks, and adapt to modern changes. National competitive advantage on a global scale is of interest to developing countries. It has become a visionary strategic goal in Kazakhstan. As the country passes through a period of intense ideological, political, and economic transformations, it successfully realizes modernization in the system of education at all levels. Kazakhstan is realizing continuous quality improvements in school education using Science, Technology, Engineering, Art, Mathematics (STEAM) strategies. As an integrated approach to learning, STEAM provides an arena for the study of academic, scientific, and technical concepts in the context of real life. This approach creates a sustainable link between school, society, work, and the world. It facilitates development in STEAM-literacy and competitiveness in the global economy.

In the era of globalization, knowledge has become a strategic asset in forming intellectual capital in the Kazakh nation. Kazakhstan is experiencing a third wave of modernization. President Nursultan Nazarbayev has set five key directions for reform. One of the directions focuses on strengthening human capital for competitive national economy needs. Over the last 25 years of accelerated transformation toward internationalization, Kazakhstan has gained a unique experience. Its integration into a global community goes forward with ambitious future expectations.

REFERENCES

Al'abri, K. (2011). The impact of globalization and education policy of developing countries: Oman as an example. *Literacy Information and Computer Education Journal*, 2(4), 491–502. doi:10.20533/licej.2040.2589.2011.0068

Bishimbayev, V., & Nurasheva, K. (2012). *Accreditation process in Kazakhstan: State regulation, procedures and prospects*. Retrieved from https://www.eurashe.eu/library/bishimbayev_nurasheva-pdf/

EACEA. (2012). *Higher Education in Kazakhstan*. Brussels, Belgium: European Commission.

Eligbayeva, G. Zh. (2015). Компетентностный подход в разработке образовательных программ [The competency approach in developing educational programs]. In Реализация Болонского процесса в Казахстане: модернизация подходов в контексте современных трендов. Научно - методический сборник [Realization of Bologna process in Kazakhstan: modernization of approaches in context of modern trends. Scientific and methodological collection]. National Office of Erasmus Mundus in Kazakhstan, Almaty. (in Russian)

Hénard, F., Diamond, L., & Roseveare, D. (2012). *Approaches to internationalisation and their implications for strategic management and institutional practice*. Paris, France: OECD Higher Education Program.

IAAR. (2016). *Accreditation*. Retrieved from https://issuu.com/iaarastana/docs/_2016

Jibeen, T., & Khan, M. S. (2015). Internationalization of higher education: Potential benefits and costs. *International Journal of Evaluation and Research in Education*, 4(4), 196–199. doi:10.11591/ijere.v4i4.4511

Knight, J. (1997). A shared vision? Stakeholders' perspectives on the internationalization of higher education in Canada. *Journal of Studies in International Education*, 1(1), 27–44. doi:10.1177/102831539700100105

Kozmina, Y. (2014). Attitudes towards research and teaching in the Russian public higher education institutions. *Higher Education in Russia and Beyond*, 2, 8–9.

Ministry of Education & Science of the Republic of Kazakhstan. (2015a). *Report about the realization of the State Program of Education Development for 2011-2020*. Author.

Ministry of Education & Science of the Republic of Kazakhstan. (2015b). *The Concept of Implementation of Split PhD by the Programme "Bolashak."* Author.

Ministry of Education & Science of the Republic of Kazakhstan. (2016a). *Repot about the realization of strategic plans for 2014-2018.* Author.

Ministry of Education & Science of the Republic of Kazakhstan. (2016b). The state Program for Development of Education and Science of the Republic of Kazakhstan for 2016 – 2019. Author.

Narenova, M. N., Kenshibay, T. I., & Usenbayeva, G. D. (2009). *Реформирование высшего образования в Казахстане и Болонский процесс: Информационные материалы для практических действий* [Higher education reforms in Kazakhstan and Bologna Process: Information materials for practical actions]. Almaty: National Office of Tempus Program in Kazakhstan (in Russian)

National Academy of Science of the Republic of Kazakhstan. (2016). *National science report.* Author.

Nurmagambetov, A. (2016). National system of quality assurance sustainability. *Education. IAAR Magazine, 1,* 14–18.

OECD. (2016). *Boosting Kazakhstan' national intellectual property system for innovation.* Paris, France: OECD.

Omirbayev, S. K. (2015). Интернационализация высшего образования в Республике Казахстан [Internationalization of higher education in the Republic of Kazakhstan]. In Реализация Болонского процесса в Казахстане: модернизация подходов в контексте современных трендов. Научно - методический сборник [Realization of Bologna process in Kazakhstan: modernization of approaches in context of modern trends. Scientific and methodological collection]. National Office of Erasmus Mundus in Kazakhstan. (in Russian)

Qiang, Z. (2003). Internationalization of higher education: Towards a conceptual framework. *Policy Futures in Education, 1*(2), 248–270. doi:10.2304/pfie.2003.1.2.5

Rumbley, L. E., Altbach, P. G., & Reisberg, L. (2012). Internationalisation within the higher education context. In D. K. Deardorff, H. de Wit, J. D. Heyl, & T. Adams (Eds.), *The SAGE handbook of international higher education* (pp. 3–26). Thousand Oak, CA: SAGE. doi:10.4135/9781452218397.n1

Shafaei, A., & Razak, N. A. (2016). Internationalization of higher education: Conceptualizing the antecedents and outcomes of cross-cultural adaptation. *Policy Futures in Education, 14*(6), 701–720. doi:10.1177/1478210316645017

UEFISCDI. (2013). *Internationalization of higher education in Romania* [Project report]. Higher Education Evidence Based Policy Making: A Necessary Premise for Progress in Romania, code34912.

UNESCO. (2009). *Trends in Global Higher Education: Tracking an Academic Revolution.* Paris: UNESCO.

Zhetpisbayeva, B. A., Arinova, O. T., & Asylbekuly, D. A. (2012). Об опыте международной аккредитации образовательных программ КарГУ им. Е.А. Букетова [On the experience of international accreditation of educational programs in Buketov Karaganda State University]. *Вестник КарГУ, 4*(68), 23–26.

KEY TERMS AND DEFINITIONS

Academic Mobility: Training students in an international partner-university for an academic period.

Accreditation: Recognition maintained by an institution regarding standards and quality levels.

Bolashak: International scholarship established by Republic of Kazakhstan president Nazarbayev in November 1993 to grant its citizens study privileges in 200 upstanding universities in 33 countries.

EACEA: Education, audiovisual, and culture executive agency.

ECTS: The European credit transfer and accumulation system.

EU: European Union.

IAAR: Independent Agency for Accreditation and Rating.

Split PhD: Doctoral programs to carry out research using two partner universities.

STEAM (Science, Technology, Engineering, Art, and Mathematics): An integrated approach to learning in which academic, scientific, and technical concepts are studied in the context of real life.

Compilation of References

Abou-dagga, S., & El-Holy, A. (2014). Enhancement of Quality in Palestinian Higher Education Institutions: The Case of Islamic University of Gaza (IUG). *The Online Journal of Quality Higher Education*, *1*(2), 53–59.

Abraham, J. M. (1999). Identifying and Managing Risk. *New Directions for Higher Education, 1999*(107), 83–89.

Abubakar, A. M., Shneikat, B. H. T., & Oday, A. (2014). Motivational factors for educational tourism: A case study in Northern Cyprus. *Tourism Management Perspectives*, *11*, 58–62. doi:10.1016/j.tmp.2014.04.002

Abu-Lughod, I. (2000). Palestinian Higher Education: National identity, liberation and globalization. *Boundary 2*, *27*(1), 75–95. doi:10.1215/01903659-27-1-75

Abushawish, H. F., Ali, A. J. B., & Jamil, H. B. (2013). Key predictors of organizational effectiveness in Palestinian higher education: What matters for outcome. *Journal of Education Policy, Planning and Administration*, *2*(2), 55–80.

Adams, C. (2017a). Universities blame Brexit for fall in foreign students. *The Telegraph*. Retrieved February 17th, 2018 at https://www.telegraph.co.uk/news/2017/11/27/universities-blame-brexit-fall-foreign-students/

Adams, R. (2017b). UK universities 'face disaster within weeks' without clear Brexit plan. *The Guardian*. Retrieved April 3rd, 2018 at https://www.theguardian.com/education/2017/nov/22/uk-universities-disaster-weeks-brexit-plan-eu-citizens

ADB. (2009). *Good practice in information and communication technology for education. Mandaluyong City*. Asian Development Bank.

Akay, R. (2013). Intercultural communication and communication competence. *Journal of Academic Inquiries*, *8*(3), 307–323.

Akman, E., Akçay, E. Y., & Argün, Ç. (2011). Youhts in the modifying structure of EU and youth policies of EU. *The Journal of Social Economic Research*, *15*(11), 1–31.

Aktas, F. (2013). *The boom of international branch campuses: Western universities and the export of knowledge*. Retrieved from https://educationpolicytalk.com/2013/03/04/the-boom-of-international-branch-campuses-western-universities-and-the-export-of-knowledge/. Accessed online in May 11, 2017.

Aktaş, T. (2005). Communicative competence in foreign language teaching. *Journal of Language and Linguistic Studies*, *1*(1), 89–100.

Al Abri, K. (2011). The impact of globalization on education policy of developing countries: Oman as an example. *Literacy Information and Computer Education Journal*, *2*(4), 491–502. doi:10.20533/licej.2040.2589.2011.0068

Al Harthy, M. (2011). *Private higher education in the Sultanate of Oman: Rationales, development and challenges* (Doctoral dissertation). The University of Kassel, Hessen, Germany. Retrieved from http://d-nb.info/1013197429/34

Al Shmeli, S. (2009). *Higher education in the Sultanate of Oman: planning in the context of the globalization*. Paper presented at the IIEP Policy Forum: Tertiary Education in Small States: Planning in the context of globalization. Retrieved from http://www.iiep.unesco.org/fileadmin/user_upload/Policy_Forums/2009/Alshmeli_Oman.pdf

Albrecht, K. (1983). New systems view of the organization. In *Organization Development* (pp. 44–59). Englewood Cliffs, NJ: Prentice-Hall.

Alfoqahaa, S. (2015). Economics of Higher Education under Occupation: The Case of Palestine. *Journal of Arts and Humanities*, *4*(10), 25–43.

Ali, A. (2012). *Surviving the 21st century in Southeast Asia: open and distance learning for human capital development*. SEAMEO SEAMOLEC and HOU international seminar on open and distance learning: Southeast Asian open and distance learning in the 21st century, Danang City, Vietnam.

Aliyeva, G. (2015). *Impacts of Educational Tourism on Local Community: The Case of Gazimagusa, North Cyprus* (Master's thesis). Retrieved from http://i-rep. emu.edu.tr:8080/jspui/bitstream/11129/2258/1/aligun.pdf

Alkın, E., Tuğrul, S., & Akman, V. (2001). *Entering Risk Management in Banks*. İstanbul: Çetin Typography.

Al-Masri, N. (2014). Imagine you are a Palestinian academic or student. *Mondoweiss*. Available online at: http://mondoweiss.net/2014/08/palestinian-academic-student/

Al-Mughrabi, N., & Sawafta, A. (2017). Fatah, Hamas to discuss security in Gaza under unity deal. *Reuters*. Available online at: https://www.reuters.com/article/us-palestinians-reconciliation/fatah-hamas-to-discuss-security-in-gaza-under-unity-deal-idUSKBN1CE17Q

Alpenidze, O. (2015). Conceptualizing internationalization strategies for higher education institutions. *Central and Eastern European Journal of Management and Economics*, *3*(3), 229–242.

Altbach, P. G. (2005). Globalization and the University: Myths and Realities in an Unequal World. *The NEA 2005 Almanac of Higher Education*. Retrieved from http://www.nea.org/assets/ img/PubAlmanac/ALM_05_06.pdf

Altbach, P., Reisberg, L., & Rumbley, L. (2009). *Trends in Global Higher Education, Tracking an Academic Revolution*. Paris: UNESCO.

Anderson, R. (2016). Report of the Council on the financial position and budget of the University, recommending allocations from the Chest for 2016–17. *Reporter*. Retrieved March 14th, 2018, at http://www.admin.cam.ac.uk/reporter/2015-16/weekly/6426/section6.shtml

Annan, K. (2000). Secretary-general salutes international workshop on human security in Mongolia. *Two-Day Session in Ulaanbaatar*, 8-10.

Aras, G. (2007). Relations between Institutional Management and Internal Inspection. *Internal Inspection Magazine, 19*, 90-95.

Arici, H.E., Erturk, M., & Orcan, O. (2014) A Study on Educational Tourism: Impacts of Foreign Students on The Perception of Local Turkish Students: Evidence From Northern Cyprus. *Journal of Gastronomy and Studies, 2*(1), 3-12.

Ashwill, M. (2016). Vietnamese student numbers growing in the US. *WebNews*. Accessed at http://www.universityworldnews.com/article.php?story=2016011313585113

Atshan, S. (2015). Introduction. In *Impediments to education in the occupied Palestinian territories*. AURDIP. Available online at http://aurdip.fr/les-entraves-a-l-education-dans.html?lang=en

Aydın, A. (2010). *The Usage of Derivative Financial Tools in Risk Management Within the Banking Sector and Entering it in Accounts at International Accounting Standards* (Unpublished Post-graduate Thesis). Gazi Uni. Institution of Social Sciences, Business Majors, Accounting Sciences, Ankara, Turkey.

Ayeni, M. A. (2010). Higher Education Research and Environmental Development. *European Journal of Educational Studies*, 2(3), 211–216.

Baporikar, N., & Shah, I. (2012). Quality of higher education in 21st century – A case of Oman. *Journal of Educattional and Instructional Studies in the World*, 2(2), 9–18.

Barley, S. R. (1986). Technology as an occasion for structuring: Evidence from observations of CT scanners and the social order of radiology departments. *Administrative Science Quarterly*, 31(1), 78–108. doi:10.2307/2392767 PMID:10281188

Bartunek, J. M. (1984). Changing interpretive schemes and organizational restructuring: The example of a religious order. *Administrative Science Quarterly*, 29(3), 355–372. doi:10.2307/2393029

Beecher, B. & Streitwieser, T. B. (2017). A Risk Management Approach for the Internationalization of Higher Education. *Journal of the Knowledge Economy*.

Beelen, J., & Jones, E. (2015). Redefining internationalisation at home. In A. Curai, L. Matei, & R. Castells (Eds.), *The Rise of the Network Society* (2nd ed.). Oxford, UK: Backwell.

Bekhradnia, B. (2009). Battered but unbowed. *Times Higher Education*. Available online at: https://www.timeshighereducation.com/features/battered-but-unbowed/409752.article

Bekiroğlu, O., & Balcı, Ş. (2014). Looking for the clues of sensitivity of intercultural communication: A survey on the sample of communication faculty students. *Journal of Türkiyat Research*, 429-459.

Bell, S. (2011). Do We Really Need a New 'Constructivist Institutionalism' to Explain Institutional Change? *British Journal of Political Science, 41*(4), 883–906. doi:10.1017/S0007123411000147

Bennett, M. J. (1993). Towards ethnorelativism: A developmental model of intercultural sensitivity. In R. M. Paige (Ed.), *Education for the intercultural experience* (2nd ed.; pp. 21–71). Yarmouth, ME: Intercultural Press.

Bennett, M. J. (2004). From ethnocentrism to ethnorelativism. In J. S. Wurzel (Ed.), *Toward multiculturalism: A reader in multicultural education*. Newton, MA: Intercultural Resource Corporation.

Ben-Tsur, D. (2009). The impact of conflict on international student mobility: A case study of international students studying in Israel. *International Studies in Sociology of Education, 19*(2), 135–149. doi:10.1080/09620210903257257

Beringer, A. (2006). Campus sustainability audit research in Atlantic Canada: Pioneering the campus sustainability assessment framework. *International Journal of Sustainability in Higher Education, 7*(4), 437–455. doi:10.1108/14676370610702235

Birzeit University. (2017). *About the PAS Programme*. Available online at: http://sites.birzeit.edu/pas/about

Bishimbayev, V., & Nurasheva, K. (2012). *Accreditation process in Kazakhstan: State regulation, procedures and prospects.* Retrieved from https://www.eurashe.eu/library/bishimbayev_nurasheva-pdf/

Bloom, D. E. (2006). Education in a globalized world. *Globalization and Education, Political Academy of Sciences, Extra Series 28.* Available online at http://www.pas.va/content/dam/accademia/pdf/es28/es28-bloom.pdf

Bolton, P. (2012). Education: historical statistics. *House of Commons Library, 27.*

Bozkaya, M., & Aydın, İ. E. (2010). Intercultural communiation apprehension: The case of Anadolu University for the Erasmus student exchange program. *Journal of Istanbul University Communication Faculty*, *1*(39), 29–42.

Brandenburg, T. (2012). *Bridging the knowledge gap: Internationalization and privatization of higher education in the State of Qatar and the Sultanate of Oman. (Doctoral dissertation), The Johannes Gutenberg University of Mainz.* Mainz: Rhineland Palatinate, Germany. Retrieved from http://scholar.google.com.au/scholar?q=Dissertation%2C+Bridging+the+Knowledge+Gap%3A+Internationalization+and+Privatization+of+Higher+Education+in+the+State+of+Qatar+and+the+Sultanate+of+Oman&btnG=&hl=en&as_sdt=0%2C5

Bridgestock, L. (2017). What Does Brexit Mean for Students? *QS Top Universities*. Retrieved February 16th, 2018 at https://www.topuniversities.com/student-info/university-news/what-does-brexit-mean-students

Britannica online Encyclopedia. (2017). *Southeast Asia*. Retrieved from https://www.britannica.com/print/article/556489

Bruhn, C. (2006). Higher Education as Empowerment: The Case of Palestinian Universities. *The American Behavioral Scientist*, *48*(8), 1125–1142. doi:10.1177/0002764205284722

Buchan, L. (2018). Brexit: more than 2,300 EU academics resign amid warning over UK university 'Brexodus'. *The Independent*. Retrieved on April 12th at https://www.independent.co.uk/news/uk/politics/brexit-latest-news-uk-university-eu-academics-resign-immigration-brexodus-citizens-europe-a8143796.html

Çakır, M. (2010). Intercultural communication in a new perspective: The alienation of culture through the individual attitudes in intercultural communication. *Anatolia*, *21*(1), 75–84.

Calderon, A. (2012, September 2). *Massification continues to transform higher education*. Retrieved from University World News: http://www.universityworldnews.com/article.php?story=20120831155341147

Calder, W., & Clugston, R. M. (2003). Progress toward sustainability in higher education. *Environmental Law Reporter News and Analysis*, *33*(1), 10003–10022.

Carroll, M., & Palermo, J. (2006). *Increasing national capability for quality higher education the case of the Sultanate of Oman.* Paper presented at the AAIR 2006: Community, Customers, Clients, Colleagues and Competitors: Defining relationships through institutional research, Coffs Harbour, Australia.

Cassar, A. Z., & Bruch, C. E. (2003). Transboundary environmental impact assessment in international watercourse management. *NYU Envtl. LJ, 12,* 169.

Çelik, T., & Kaplan, M. (2005). *Competition in the Turkish Insurance Sector:2002-2004.* İstanbul: Aves Publications.

CESR Office. (2014). *Comprehensive Education Sector Review Phase (2) Report (Draft): Consultation Meeting for Development Partners (presentation).* Yangon: Comprehensive Education Sector Review Office.

Chen, G. M., & Starosta, W. J. (2000). The development and validation of the intercultural communication sensitivity scale. *Human Communication, 3,* 1–15.

Childress, L. K. (2009). Internationalization Plans for Higher Education Institutions. *Journal of Studies in International Education, 13*(3), 289–309. doi:10.1177/1028315308329804

Chitoran, D. (2010). *The Peace Programme: A Unique Interuniversity cooperation network.* Global University Network for Innovation. Retrieved from http://www.guninetwork.org/articles/peace-programme-unique-interuniversity-cooperation-network

Chokheli, E. N., & Alpenidze, O. N. (2015). Strategy Of Internationalization For The Higher Education System (On The Example Of Georgia). *International Scientific Journal Theoretical & Applied Science, 27*(7), 1–7.

Chou, M., & Ravinet, P. (2017). Higher education regionalism in Europe and Southeast Asia: Comparing policy ideas. *Policy and Society, 36*(1), 143–159. doi: 10.1080/14494035.2017.1278874

Clark, B. R. (1960). *The open-door colleges: A case study.* New York: McGraw-Hill.

Çolak, Ö. F., & Yiğidim, A. (2001). *Crisis in Turkish Banking.* Ankara: Nobel Publication Distribution.

Corbett, A., & Gordon, C. (2015). *The university challenge: what type of Brexit would work for Higher Education?* British Politics and Policy at LSE.

Cressey, D. (2016a). Academics across Europe join 'Brexit' debate. *Nature*, *530*(7588), 15. doi:10.1038/530015a PMID:26842034

Cressey, D. (2016b). Scientists say 'no' to UK exit from Europe in Nature poll. *Nature*, *531*(7596), 559–559. doi:10.1038/531559a PMID:27029257

Davidovitch, N. (2012). Academic Capitalism in Higher Education – A Cross Cultural Perspective: CIS – Israel. *International Journal of Academic Research in Progressive Education and Development*, *1*(4), 326–339.

Dayan, V. (2006). *Developments in the Field of Risk Management in the Exchange Market for Forward Transaction and Option, Basel II Standards and Application Examples* (Unpublished post-graduate thesis). Celal Bayar University Institution of Social Sciences Business Majors, Manisa.

De Wit, H. (1995). Strategies for the Internationalization of Higher Education. A Comparative Study of Australia, Canada, Europe, and the United States of America. Amsterdam: European Association of International Education (EAIE).

De Wit, H. (1999). Changing Rationales for the Internationalization of Higher Education. *International Higher Education*, *15*.

De Wit, H. (1999). *Changing Rationales for the Internationalization of Higher Education.* Retrieved online from https://ejournals.bc.edu/ojs/index.php/ihe/article/viewFile/6477/5700

De Wit, H. (2011). Globaization and internationalization of higher education (Introduction to online monograph). *Revista de Universidad y Sociedad del Conocimiento, 8*(2), 241-248. Accessed online 13.01.2017 via http://rusc.uoc.edu/ojs/index.php/rusc/article/view/v8n2-dewit/v8n2-dewit-eng

De Wit, H. (2011). *Trends, issues, and challenges in internationalization of higher education.* Amsterdam: Center for applied research on economics and management, school of economics and management of the Hoge school van Amsterdam.

De Wit, H. (2000). *Changing rationales for the internationalization of higher education. Internationalization of higher education: An institutional perspective.* Bucharest, Romania: UNESCO/CEPES.

De Wit, H. (2002). *Internationalization of higher education in the united states of America and Europe: A historical, comparative and conceptual analysis.* Westport, CT: Greenwood Press.

De Wit, H. (2012). *Concepts, rationales, and interpretive frameworks in the internationalization of higher education. In The SAGE Handbook of International Higher Education* (pp. 27–42). London: SAGE.

Derici, O., Tüysüz, Z., & Sarı, A. (2008). Institutional Risk Management and Audit Office Application. *Audit Office Magazine, 65,* 70.

Digital Marketing, Q. S. (2018). Emerging Student Markets in South and South East Asia. *Web News.* accessed from http://www.qs.com/emerging-student-markets-in-south-and-south-east-asia/

DiMaggio, P. J., & Powell, W. W. (Eds.). (1991). *The new institutionalism in organizational analysis* (Vol. 17). Chicago, IL: University of Chicago Press.

Donn, G., & Al Manthri, Y. (2010). *Globalisation and higher education in the Arab Gulf States.* Oxford, UK: *Symposium Books.* 10.15730/books.73

Dougherty, D. (1994). Commentary. In P. Shrivastava, A. Huff, & J. Dutton (Eds.), Advances in strategic management. Greenwich, CT: JAI Press.

Drazin, R., & Van de Ven, A. H. (1985). Alternative forms of fit in contingency theory. *Administrative Science Quarterly, 30*(4), 514–539. doi:10.2307/2392695

Dulupçu, M., & Demirel, O. (2008). *Globalization and internationalization, ECOLAB: Economy and Labour World.* Comenuis.

Dutt, A. (2016). *University of Manchester: Post-Brexit Reality.* Panel Discussion Brodcast Live. Retrieved on February 19th, 2018 at https://www.youtube.com/watch?v=xFBsbQEYd-g&t=3390s

EACEA. (2012). *Higher Education in Kazakhstan*. Brussels, Belgium: European Commission.

Eğinli, A.T. (2011). The importance of the training of cultural diversity in-obtaining intercultural competency. *Öneri, 9* (35), 215-227.

Eğinli, A. T., & Yalçın, M. (2016). Developing intercultural competence and intercultural adjustment. *Global Media Journal, 7*(13), 6–27.

El Fadel, M., Rachid, G., El-Samra, R., Boutros, G. B., & Hashisho, J. (2013). Knowledge management mapping and gap analysis in renewable energy: Towards a sustainable framework in developing countries. *Renewable & Sustainable Energy Reviews, 20*, 576–584. doi:10.1016/j.rser.2012.11.071

Elghawi, U., & Shames, H. (2016). Management of Radioactive Waste in Libya: Case Study. *Journal of Hazardous, Toxic and Radioactive Waste, 20*(3), 04016003. doi:10.1061/(ASCE)HZ.2153-5515.0000314

Eligbayeva, G. Zh. (2015). Компетентностный подход в разработке образовательных программ [The competency approach in developing educational programs]. In Реализация Болонского процесса в Казахстане: модернизация подходов в контексте современных трендов. Научно - методический сборник [Realization of Bologna process in Kazakhstan: modernization of approaches in context of modern trends. Scientific and methodological collection]. National Office of Erasmus Mundus in Kazakhstan, Almaty. (in Russian)

El-Namey, S. (2016, October 14). Hamas-Fatah feud stalls Gaza higher education. *The Electronic Intifada*.

Emhan, A. (2009). Risk Management Process and Techniques used in Managing. *Atatürk University Economics and Administrative Sciences Magazine, Volume, 23*(3), 209–220.

Erdoğan, M. (2000). *Business*. Eskişehir: Anadolu University Publications.

Erdogan, M., & Usak, M. (2009). Curricular and extra-curricular activities to develop the environmental awareness of young students: A case from Turkey. *Educational Sciences. Odgojne Znanosti, 11*(1).

Er, K. O. (2006). The effects of culture in foreign language curriculum. *Ankara University. Journal of Faculty of Educational Sciences, 39*(1), 1–14.

Er, S. (2005). Intercultural communication, ethnocentrism and others. *Journal of Istanbul Kültür University, 1*, 9–18.

Ersoy, A. (2013). Turkish teacher candidates' challenges regarding cross-cultural experiences: The case of Erasmus exchange program. *Education in Science, 38*(168), 154–166.

European Commission. (2014). *ECTS and diploma supplement label holders 2011 & 2012: Internationalisation in Europe's universities*. EU Publications. Retrieved from https://publications.europa.eu/en/publication-detail/-/publication/a3713d20-71dd-4b06-b19f-796972dd86e9

European Union. (2014). *The Erasmus Impact Study: Effects of mobility on the skills and employability of students and the internationalisation of higher education institutions*. Accessed from http://ec.europa.eu/dgs/education_culture/repository/education/library/study/2014/erasmus-impact_en.pdf

Ferguson, R., Barzilai, S., Ben-Zvi, D., Chinn, C. A., Herodotou, C., Hod, Y., ... Whitelock, D. (2017). *Innovating Pedagogy 2017: Open University Innovation Report 6*. Milton Keynes, UK: The Open University.

Francis, A. (1993). *Facing the future: the internationalization of post-secondary institutions in British Colombi*. Vancouver: Centre for International Education.

Gannon, F. (2016). Brexit and research: Goodbye EU money and colleagues? *EMBO Reports*. PMID:27466322

Genç, A. (2003). *Türkiye'de geçmişten günümüze Almanca öğretimi*. Ankara, Turkey: Seçkin.

Gerner, D. J., & Schrodt, P. A. (1999). Into the New Millennium: Challenges facing Palestinian higher education in the Twenty First Century. *Arab Studies Quarterly, 21*(4), 17–33.

Green, M. F. (2012). *Measuring and assessing internationalization*. Retrieved from http://www.nafsa.org/_/File/_/downloads/measuring_assessing.pdf

Greenwood, R., & Hinings, C. R. (1996). Understanding Radical Organizational Change: Bringing together the Old and the New Institutionalism. *Academy of Management Review*, *21*(4), 1022–1054. doi:10.5465/amr.1996.9704071862

Gülcan, M. G. (2005). *AB ve eğitim süreci*. Ankara, Turkey: Anı.

Güler, G. (2005). The common european framework of reference: Learning, teaching, assessment and the foreign language education process in Turkey. *Journal of Social Science*, *6*(1), 89–106.

Gülnar, B. (2011). Acculturation and media using among foreign students. *Global Media Journal*, *2*(3), 51–68.

Güzel, V. (2007). *Numerical Methods Used When Determining Financial Risk Values: ISE applications with ARCH/GARCH Models* (Unpublished post-graduate thesis). Marmara University Institution of Social Sciences Business Majors Branch Financial Markets and Investment Management Science Branch, İstanbul, Turkey.

Hammond, K. (2012). Lifelong learning in Palestine. *Journal of Holy Land and Palestine Studies*, *11*(1), 79–85. doi:10.3366/hls.2012.0031

Hasdemir, F., & Çalıkoğlu, M. R. (2011). The European Union education programmes and the Change. *Journal of Higher Education and Science*, *1*(2), 66–68. doi:10.5961/jhes.2011.010

Hassi, A., & Storti, G. (2012). *Globalization and Culture: The Three H Scenarios*. Retrieved from https://www.intechopen.com/books/globalization-approaches-to-diversity/globalization-and-culture-the-three-h-scenarios

HEIDA. (2017). *HEIDA -Data driven decision making for internationalization of higher education: Bridging the gap between faculty and admin using effective communication platforms*. Retrieved from https://heida.ku.edu.tr/sites/heida.ku.edu.tr/files/files/HEIDA_Project%20Output%201%20Literarture%20Review%2025.5.2015.pdf

Held, D. (2000). Global Transformations: Politics, Economics and Culture. In C. Pierson & S. Tormey (Eds.), *Politics at the Edge, Political Studies Association Yearbook Series*. London: Palgrave Macmillan. doi:10.1057/9780333981689_2

Henard, F., Diamond, L., & Roseveare, D. (2012). *Approachers to Internationalisation and their Implications for Strategic Management and Institutional Practice: A Guide for Higher Education Institutions.* OECD Higher Education Programme IMHE. Retrieved from http://www.oecd.org/education/imhe/Approaches%20to%20 internationalisation%20-%20final%20-%20web.pdf

Hénard, F., Diamond, L., & Roseveare, D. (2012). *Approaches to internationalisation and their implications for strategic management and institutional practice.* Paris, France: OECD Higher Education Program.

Henley, J. (2015). Leaving EU would be a 'disaster', British universities warn. *The Guardian.* Retrieved on March 18th, 2018 at https://www.theguardian.com/ politics/2015/nov/11/leaving-eu-would-be-a-disaster-british-universities-warn

HESA. (2018a). *Higher Education Student Statistics: UK, 2016/17 - Where students come from and go to study.* Retrieved April 10th, 2018 at https://www.hesa.ac.uk/ news/11-01-2018/sfr247-higher-education-student-statistics/location

HESA. (2018b). *Staff numbers and characteristics.* Retrieved April 10th, 2018 at https://www.hesa.ac.uk/data-and-analysis/staff

Heylighen, F., & Joslyn, C. (1992). What is Systems Theory. In F. Heylighen, C. Joslyn, & V. Turchin (Eds.), *Principia Cybernetica Web.* Retrieved March 18th, 2018, at URL: http://cleamc11.vub.ac.be/SYSTHEOR.html

Hicks, G. H., & Gullet, C. R. (1975). *Organizations: Theory and Behaviour.* New York, NY: McGraw-Hill. See.

Hilal, M. A. (1998). *The compatibility of higher education with the local labor market: Analytical study. Palestinian Ministry of Finance, No.9.* Nablus.

Hogwood, B. W., & Gunn, L. A. (1984). *Policy analysis for the real world. Oxford.* New York: Oxford University Press.

Horta, H. (2009). Global and national prominent universities: Internationalization, competitiveness and the role of the state. *Higher Education*, *58*(3), 387–405. doi:10.100710734-009-9201-5

IAAR. (2016). *Accreditation.* Retrieved from https://issuu.com/iaarastana/docs/_2016

IAU. (2016). *Higher Education in ASEAN.* The International Association of Universities. Accessed from https://www.iau-aiu.net/IMG/pdf/iau_higher_education_in_asean-2.pdf

ICEF Monitor. (2015). Indonesia looks to education to help drive growth. *Webnews.* Accessed from http://monitor.icef.com/2015/05/indonesia-looks-to-education-to-help-drive-growth/

International Atomic Energy Agency. (2005). *INFCIRC/640: Multilateral Approaches to the Nuclear Fuel Cycle.* Vienna: International Atomic Energy Agency.

International Network for Cooperation with Palestinian Universities. (1999). *Peace Programme: Palestinian/European/American Cooperation in Education.* Retrieved from: http://unesdoc.unesco.org/images/0011/001176/117620Eo.pdf

Jadhav, A. S., Jadhav, V. V., & Raut, P. D. (2014). Role of Higher Education Institutions in Environmental Conservation and Sustainable Development: A case study of Shivaji University, Maharashtra, India. *Journal of Environment and Earth Science.*

Jeptoo, M. L., & Razia, M. (2012). Internationalization of Higher Education: Rationale, Collaborations and its implications. *International Journal of Academic Research in Progressive Education and Development, 1*, 4.

Jibeen, T., & Khan, M. S. (2015). Internationalization of higher education: Potential benefits and costs. *International Journal of Evaluation and Research in Education, 4*(4), 196–199. doi:10.11591/ijere.v4i4.4511

Jones, E., & de Wit, H. (2012). Globalization of Internationalization: Thematic and regional reflections on a traditional concept. *The International Journal of Higher Education and Democracy, 3*, 35–54.

Jung, I. S., & Latchem, C. (2007). Assuring quality in Asian open and distance learning. *Open Learning, 22*(3), 235–250. doi:10.1080/02680510701619885

Karekezi, S., Kithyoma, W., & Initiative, E. (2003, June). Renewable energy development. In Workshop on African Energy Experts on Operationalizing the NEPAD Energy Initiative (pp. 2-4). Academic Press.

Kartarı, A. (2014). *Kültür, farklılık ve iletişim*. İstanbul, Turkey: İletişim.

Kasalak, G. (2013). Views of academic staff on Erasmus Teaching Staff Mobility: The case of Akdeniz University. *Journal of Higher Education and Science, 3*(2), 133–141. doi:10.5961/jhes.2013.068

Katircioglu, S. T. (2014). Estimating higher education induced energy consumption: The case of Northern Cyprus. *Journal of Energy, 66*, 831–838. doi:10.1016/j.energy.2013.12.040

Kaya, G. T. (2014). Internationalisation of higher education and global mobility. *Journal of Educational Sciences, 39*, 195–199.

Kerr, C. (2001). *The uses of the university*. Harvard University Press.

Khalaf Al'Abri, K.M. (2015). *Higher education policy architecture and policy-making in the Sultanate of Oman: Towards a critical understanding MA in Educational Studies: Leadership*. The University of Queensland in 2015 The School of Education.

Killwick, C. A. P., & Cuddeford, V. (2016). *How Universities can continue to attract the best minds post Brexit*. Academic Press.

Knight, J. (1997). Internationalization of Higher Education: A Conceptual Framework. In Internationalization of Higher Education in the Asia Pacific Countries. Amsterdam: European Association of International Education (EAIE).

Knight, J. (2005). An Internationalization Model: Responding to New Realities and Challenges. V Higher education in Latin America: The international dimension. Washington, DC: The World Bank.

Knight, J. (2012). *Internationalization: Three Generations of Cross border Higher Education*. India International Center. Retrieved from http://www.iicdelhi.nic.in/ContentAttachments/Publications/DiaryFiles/53511July92012_IIC%20Occasional%20Publication%2038.pdf

Knight, J. (2013). The changing landscape of higher education internationalization – for better or worse. *Perspectives: Policy and Practice in Higher Education, 17*(3), 84-90.

Knight, J., & de Wit, H. (1995). *Strategies for internationalisation of higher education: Historical and conceptual perspectives*. Retrieved from: http://www.uni kassel.de/wz1/mahe/course/module6_3/10_knight95.pd

Knight, J. (1997). A shared vision? Stakeholders' perspectives on the internationalization of higher education in Canada. *Journal of Studies in International Education, 1*(1), 27–44. doi:10.1177/102831539700100105

Knight, J. (2004). Internationalization Remodeled: Definition, Approaches, and Rationales. *Journal of Studies in International Education, 8*(1), 1, 5–31. doi:10.1177/1028315303260832

Knight, J. (2006). Cross-border education: Conceptual confusion and data deficits. *Perspectives in Education, 24*(4), 15–27.

Knight, J. (2012). Student mobility and internationalization: Trends and tribulations. *Research in Comparative and International Education, 7*(1), 20–33. doi:10.2304/rcie.2012.7.1.20

Knight, J., & de Wit, H. (1997). *Internationalisation of Higher Education in Asia Pacific Countries*. Amsterdam: European Association for International Education.

Kozmina, Y. (2014). Attitudes towards research and teaching in the Russian public higher education institutions. *Higher Education in Russia and Beyond, 2*, 8–9.

Kürkçü, D.D. (2013). Küreselleşme kavramı ve küreselleşmeye yönelik yaklaşımlar. *The Turkish Online Journal of Design, Art and Communication, 3*(2), 1-11.

Landesman, L. Y. (2005). *Public health management of disasters: the practice guide*. American public health association.

Ledford, G. E., Mohrman, A. M., & Lawler, E. E. (1989). The phenomenon of large-scale organizational change. In Large-scale organization change (pp. 1-31). San Francisco: Jossey-Bass.

Liberman, M. B., & Asaba, S. (2006). Why do firms imitate each other? *Academy of Management Review, 31*(2), 366–385. doi:10.5465/amr.2006.20208686

Lieber, D. (2016, August). Ramallah invalidates new degrees from top Gaza university. *Times of Israel, 10*. Retrieved from http://www.timesofisrael.com/ramallah-invalidates-new-degrees-from-top-gaza-university/

Logie, N. N. (2004). Yabanci dil öğretiminde kültürel becerinin oluşturulmasinin önemi ve budunbilimsel boyut. *Hasan Ali Yücel Eğitim Fakültesi Dergisi*, *1*, 173–180.

Lokumcu, S. (2009). *Financial Risk Management* (Post-graduate Thesis). Yıldız Technical Universitesi Institution of Science and Technology, İstanbul, Turkey.

Macpherson, S. (2017). *Brexit: Higher Education in Scotland*. Scottish Parliament Information Centre (SPICe).

Marginson, S. (2017). Brexit: Challenges for Universities in Hard Times. *International Higher Education*, (88), 8-10.

Márquez, B. L. D., Torres, N. E. H., & Bondar, Y. (2011). Internationalization of Higher Education: Theoretical and Empirical Investigation of Its Influence on University Institution Rankings. *Globalisation and Internationalisation of Higher Education*, *8*(2), 265–284.

Marsh, J. A., Pane, J. F., & Hamilton, L. S. (2006). *Making Sense of Data -Driven Decision Making in Education*. Retrieved from: http://www.rand.org/content/dam/rand/pubs/occasional_papers/2006/RAND_OP170.pdf

Menendez Alvarez Hevia, D., & Zotzman, K. (2017). *Brexit and the Internationalisation of UK Universities: The Experiences of Academic Staff from EU Member States*. Academic Press.

Meyer, A. O., Tsui, A. S., & Hinings, C. R. (1993). Guest co-editors' introduction: Configurational approaches to organizational analysis. *Academy of Management Journal*, *36*, 1175–1195.

Meyer, J. W., & Rowan, B. (1977). Institutionalized organizations: Formal structure as myth and ceremony. *American Journal of Sociology*, *83*(2), 340–363. doi:10.1086/226550

Miller, D., & Friesen, P. H. (1984). *Organizations: A quantum view*. Englewood Cliffs, NJ: Pren-tice Hall.

Ministry of Education & Science of the Republic of Kazakhstan. (2015a). *Report about the realization of the State Program of Education Development for 2011-2020*. Author.

Ministry of Education & Science of the Republic of Kazakhstan. (2015b). *The Concept of Implementation of Split PhD by the Programme "Bolashak."* Author.

Ministry of Education & Science of the Republic of Kazakhstan. (2016a). *Repot about the realization of strategic plans for 2014-2018.* Author.

Ministry of Education & Science of the Republic of Kazakhstan. (2016b). The state Program for Development of Education and Science of the Republic of Kazakhstan for 2016 – 2019. Author.

Ministry of National Economy (MONE). (2005). *Oman: The development experience and investment climate* (5th ed.). Muscat, Oman: Ministry of National Economy.

Mintzberg, H. (1983). *Structure in fives: Designing effective organizations.* Englewood Cliffs, NJ: Prentice Hall.

Mitchell, D. E., & Nielsen, S. Y. (2012). *Internationalization and Globalization in Higher Education.* Retrieved from http://cdn.intechopen.com/pdfs-wm/38270.pdf

Mitchell, N. (2018). Some UK universities are shaking off the Brexit blues. *University World News.* Retrieved March 20th, 2018 at http://www.universityworldnews.com/article.php?story=20180119062806710

Morrison, K. (2016). *A rough guide to Southeast Asia for BC Institutions.* Available online http://bccie.bc.ca/wp-content/uploads/2016/06/ascendance-of-southeast-asia.pdf

Moughrabi, F. (2004). Palestinian Universities Under Siege. *International Higher Education, 36,* 9-10.

Narenova, M. N., Kenshibay, T. I., & Usenbayeva, G. D. (2009). *Реформирование высшего образования в Казахстане и Болонский процесс: Информационные материалы для практических действий* [Higher education reforms in Kazakhstan and Bologna Process: Information materials for practical actions]. Almaty: National Office of Tempus Program in Kazakhstan (in Russian)

National Academy of Science of the Republic of Kazakhstan. (2016). *National science report.* Author.

National Erasmus Office Palestine. (2017a). *2015-2016 Statistics on Key Action 1.* Retrieved from: http://www.erasmusplus.ps/page-703-en.html

National Erasmus Office. (2017b). *Project Summaries (2008-2012).* Retrieved from http://www.erasmusplus.ps/page-577-en.html

Nedera, M. (2016). *University of Manchester: Post-Brexit Reality.* Panel Discussion Brodacast Live. Retrieved on February 19th, 2018 at https://www.youtube.com/watch?v=xFBsbQEYd-g&t=3390s

NMC Horizon Report, . (2012). *2012 Higher Education Edition.* Austin, TX: The New Media Consortium.

Nurmagambetov, A. (2016). National system of quality assurance sustainability. *Education. IAAR Magazine, 1*, 14–18.

OECD. (2009). Globalisation. *Higher Education*, 2030.

OECD. (2011). *Education at a Glance 2011: OECD Indicators.* OECD Publishing.

OECD. (2016). *Boosting Kazakhstan' national intellectual property system for innovation.* Paris, France: OECD.

OECD. (2017). *Economic Outlook for Southeast Asia, China and India 2017: Addressing Energy Challenges.* Paris: OECD Publishing.

Olcay, G. A., & Nasır, V. A. (2016). Internationalization in higher education: A look at the years 1999-2013 from the perspectives of the countries with the most international students and Turkey. *Journal of Higher Education and Science, 6*(3), 288–297.

Omirbayev, S. K. (2015). Интернационализация высшего образования в Республике Казахстан [Internationalization of higher education in the Republic of Kazakhstan]. In Реализация Болонского процесса в Казахстане: модернизация подходов в контексте современных трендов. Научно - методический сборник [Realization of Bologna process in Kazakhstan: modernization of approaches in context of modern trends. Scientific and methodological collection]. National Office of Erasmus Mundus in Kazakhstan. (in Russian)

Onder, R.K., & Balcı, A. (2007). Erasmus öğrenci öğrenim hareketliliği programının 2007 yilinda programdan yararlanan türk öğrenciler üzerindeki etkileri. *Ankara Avrupa Araştırmaları Dergisi, 9*(2), 93-116.

Oral, Y. (2010). Türkiye'de yabancı dil eğitimi politikaları bağlamında İngilizce: Eleştirel bir çalışma. *Alternatif Eğitim e-Dergisi, 1*, 59-68.

Öznacar, B., & Dagli, G. (2016). Evaluation of Risks for School Directors in Education in Developed/Developing Countries. *The Anthropologist, 23*(1-2), 1-10.

Öznacar, B., & Dericioglu, S. (2017). The role of school administrators in the use of technology. Eurasia Journal of Mathematics. *Science & Technology Education, 13*, 1.

Ozsen, Z. S. (2012). *Impacts of Educational Tourism on Host Population: A Case of Famagusta, North Cyprus* (Master's thesis). Retrieved from http://i-rep.emu.edu.tr:8080/xmlui/bitstream/handle/11129/1590/ZeynepOzsen.pdf?sequence=1

Perrow, C. (1979). *Complex organizations: A critical essay* (2nd ed.). New York: Random House.

Phillps, J. (2009). *Project Management Professional Study Guide* (3rd ed.). McGraw-Hill.

Pohl, H. (2015). *How to measure internationalization of higher education.* New perspectives on internationalization and competitiveness. DOI 10.1007/978-3-319-11979-3_4

Qiang, Z. (2003). Internationalization of Higher Education: Towards a conceptual framework. *Policy Futures in Education, 1*(2), 248–270. doi:10.2304/pfie.2003.1.2.5

QS. (2018). *QS World University Rankings.* Retrieved January-April, 2018 at https://www.topuniversities.com/university-rankings/world-university-rankings/2018

Qumsiyeh, M., & Jad, I. (2012). Research and Development in the Occupied Palestinian Territories: Challenges and opportunities. *Arab Studies Quarterly, 34*(3), 158–172.

Ranson, S., Hinings, C. R., & Greenwood, R. (1980). The structuring of organizational structures. *Administrative Science Quarterly, 25*(1), 1–7. doi:10.2307/2392223

Rastogi, V., Tamboto, E., Tong, D., & Sinburimsit, T. (2013). Indonesia's Rising Middle-Class and Affluent Consumers: Asia's Next Big Opportunity. *Webnews.* Accessed from https://www.bcg.com/publications/2013/center-consumer-customer-insight-consumer-products-indonesias-rising-middle-class-affluent-consumers.aspx

Redman, E. (2013). Advancing Educational Pedagogy for Sustainability: Developing and Implementing Programs to Transform Behaviors. *International Journal of Environmental and Science Education*, 8(1), 1–34.

Rhema, A. (2013). *An analysis of experiences and perceptions of technology-based learning in higher education institutions in Libya: informing the advancement of e-learning* (Doctoral dissertation). Victoria University.

Rimmon-Kenan, S. (2014). *Discourse in Psychoanalysis and Literature (Routledge Revivals).* Routledge.

Robbins, L. R. B. (1963). *Higher Education: Report of the Committee appointed by the Prime Minister under the chairmanship of Lord Robbins, 1961-63* (No. 2). HM Stationery Office. Accessed at http://www.educationengland.org.uk/documents/robbins/robbins1963.html

Robinson, D. (2010). The Status of Higher Education Teaching Personnel in Israel, the West Bank and Gaza. *Education International.* Retrieved from www.ei-ie.org

Rumbley, L. E., Altbach, P. G., & Reisberg, L. (2012). Internationalisation within the higher education context. In D. K. Deardorff, H. de Wit, J. D. Heyl, & T. Adams (Eds.), *The SAGE handbook of international higher education* (pp. 3–26). Thousand Oak, CA: SAGE. doi:10.4135/9781452218397.n1

Sadiman, A. S. (2006). *Challenges in education in Southeast Asia.* Paper presented at the International Seminar on "Towards Cross Border Cooperation between South and Southeast Asia: The Importance of India's North East Playing Bridge and Buffer Role", Kaziranga, India. Available online at http://www.seameo.org/vl/library/dlwelcome/publications/paper/india0

Şahin, K. (2009). *Küreselleşme tartışmaları ışığında ulus devlet.* İstanbul, Turkey: Yeniyüzyıl.

Şahin, M., & Alkan, R. M. (2016). Change and transformation course in higher education and expanding role of universities. *Journal of Research in Education and Teaching*, *5*(2), 297–307.

Schmidt, V. (2010). *Taking Ideas And Discourse Seriously: Explaining Change Through Discursive Institutionalism As The Fourth New Institutionalism*. Academic Press.

Scott, R. A. (1992). *Campus developments in response to the challenges of internationalization: The case of Ramapo College of New Jersey*. Springfield: CBIS Federal.

Selznick, P. (1957). *Leadership in administration*. Evanston, IL: Pow, Peterson.

Şeremet, M. (2015). A comparative approach to Turkey and England higher education: The internationalism policy. *Journal of Higher Education and Science*, *5*(1), 27–31. doi:10.5961/jhes.2015.106

Seyidoğlu, S. (1999). Activities in the Financial Market of Financial Risk and Risk Management. Economic Approach org.

Shafaei, A., & Razak, N. A. (2016). Internationalization of higher education: Conceptualizing the antecedents and outcomes of cross-cultural adaptation. *Policy Futures in Education*, *14*(6), 701–720. doi:10.1177/1478210316645017

Shahgerdi, A. (2014). *Environmental Impacts of Educational Tourism on the City of Famagusta, Northern Cyprus* (Master's thesis). Retrieved from http://i-rep.emu.edu.tr:8080/jspui/bitstream/11129/1702/1/ShahgerdiAmin.pdf

Sharples, M., de Roock, R., Ferguson, R., Gaved, M., Herodotou, C., Koh, E., ... Wong, L. H. (2016). *Innovating Pedagogy 2016: Open University Innovation Report 5*. Milton Keynes, UK: The Open University.

Shraim, K., & Khlaif, Z. (2012). An e-learning approach to secondary education in Palestine: Opportunities and challenges. *Information Technology for Development*, *16*(3), 159–173. doi:10.1080/02681102.2010.501782

Silman, F., Gokcekus, H., & İsman, A. (2012). A study on quality assurance activities in higher education in North Cyprus. *International Online Journal of Educational Sciences*, *4*(1), 31–38.

Singh, J. P. (2010). *United Nations Educational, Scientific, and Cultural Organization (UNESCO): creating norms for a complex world*. Routledge.

Slater, J. (2017). *Trump's immigration ban hinders recruitment by US hospitals and universities*. Retrieved from https://www.theglobeandmail.com/news/world/us-politics/trumps-immigration-ban-hinders-recruitment-by-us-hospitals-universities/article34181949/

Sowula, T. (2015). Why Palestinian Universities are looking abroad. *The British Council*. Retrieved from: https://www.britishcouncil.org/voices-magazine/why-palestinian-universities-are-looking-abroad

Tan, V. (2018). Why more Southeast Asian students are choosing China for higher education. *Web News*. Accessed at https://www.channelnewsasia.com/news/asia/why-more-southeast-asian-students-are-choosing-china-for-higher-10042118

Tekelioğlu, F., Başer, H., Örtlek, M., & Aydınlı, C. (2012). Factors effecting the international students to select country and university: A case study of foundation university. *Organizasyon ve Yönetim Bilimleri Dergisi*, *4*(2), 191–200.

TEMPUS. (2012). *Higher Education in the Occupied Palestinian Territories*. Retrieved from: http://eacea.ec.europa.eu/tempus/participating_countries/overview/oPt.pdf

Teng, A. (2015, November 12). *NIE to offer courses on open online platform*. Retrieved from Straits Times: http://www.straitstimes.com/singapore/education/nie-to-offer-courses-on-open-online-platform

Times Higher Education (THE). (2018). *World University Rankings*. Retrieved from https://www.timeshighereducation.com/world-university-rankings

Toor, W. (2003). The Road Less Traveled: Sustainable Transportation for Campuses. *Planning for Higher Education*, *31*(3), 131–141.

Trevor-Roper, S., Razvi, S., & Goodliffe, T. (2013). *Academic affiliations between foreign and Omani higher education institutions: Learning from OAAA quality audits.* Paper presented at the INQAAHE Conference, Taipei, Taiwan. Retrieved from http://www.oaaa.gov.om/Conference/1paper_trevor-roper-razvi-goodliffe%20final2.pdf

UEFISCDI. (2013). *Internationalization of higher education in Romania* [Project report]. Higher Education Evidence Based Policy Making: A Necessary Premise for Progress in Romania, code34912.

Uhawenimana, T. C. (2012, August 26). Higher education needs to engage in outreach-based research. *University World News.*

UNESCO Bangkok and SEAMEO. (2006). *Higher education in Southeast Asia.* Bangkok: UNESCO Asia and Pacific Regional Bureau for Education.

UNESCO Institute for Statistics (UIS). (2016). *Global Flow of Tertiary-Level Students.* Retrieved from http://uis.unesco.org/ en/uis-student-flow

UNESCO. (2003). *Synthesis of Country Case Studies, South East Asian ICT Advocacy and Planning Workshop for Policy Makers.* Bangkok: UNESCO Asia and Pacific Regional Bureau of Education.

UNESCO. (2009). *Trends in Global Higher Education: Tracking an Academic Revolution.* Paris: UNESCO.

UNESCO. (2011). *ICT in higher education: Case studies from Asia and the Pacific.* Bangkok: UNESCO Bangkok.

UNESCO. (2017). *Outbound internationally mobile students by host region.* Retrieved from: http://data.uis.unesco.org/Index.aspx?queryid=172

UUK. (2015). *International Undergraduate Students: The UK's Competitive Advantage.* Retrieved April 12th, 2018 http://www.universitiesuk.ac.uk/policy-and-analysis/reports/Documents/International/international-undergraduate-students-uk-competitive-advantage.pdf

UUK. (2017). *Brexit FAQS.* Retrieved March 18th, 2018 at http://www.universitiesuk.ac.uk/policy-and-analysis/brexit/Pages/brexit-faqs.aspx

UUK. (2018). *How Can the Government Ensure Universities are Best Placed to Maximise Their Contribution to a Successful and Global UK Post-EU Exit?* Retrieved April 6th, 2018 at http://www.universitiesuk.ac.uk/policy-and-analysis/reports/Documents/2018/brexit-briefing-march-18.pdf

Van Der Wende, M. (2007). Internationalization of Higher Education in the OECD Countries: Challenges and Opportunities for the Coming Decade. *Journal of Studies in International Education*, *11*(3-4), 274–289. doi:10.1177/1028315307303543

van Vught, F. A., van der Wende, M. C., & Westerheijden, D. F. (2002). Globalisation and internationalisation. Policy agendas compared. In J. Enders & O. Fulton (Eds.), *Higher education in a globalizing world. International trends and mutual observations* (pp. 103–121). Dordrecht, The Netherlands: Kluwer.

Varghese, N. V. (2008). *Globalization of higher education and cross-border student mobility*. IIEP Research Papers. Retrieved from http://www.iiep.unesco.org/en

Varol, A. (2013). Kültürlerarası diyalogda halkla ilişkilerin rolü. *Sosyal Bilimler Dergisi*, *1*, 1–23.

Vasilevska, D., Rivza, B., Alekneviciene, B., & Parlinska, A. (2017). Analysis of the Demand for Distance Education at Eastern and Central European Higher Education Institutions. *Journal of Teacher Education for Sustainability*, *19*(1), 106–116. doi:10.1515/jtes-2017-0007

Visweswaran, K. (2015, September). Palestinian universities and everyday life under occupation. *American Association of University Professors Academe*.

Von Bertalanffy, L. (1951, December). General systems theory: a new approach to the unit of science. *Human Biology*.

Whitfield, R. N. (2003). *Managing İnstitutional Risks: A Framework*. *EdD*. University of Pennsylvania.

Wilcock, J., & Miller, A. (2016). The truth and consequences of Brexit: Could a catastrophe for academia be an opportunity for publishers? *Insights*, *29*(3), 216–223. doi:10.1629/uksg.328

Wilkinson, R., & Al Hajry, A. (2007). The global higher education market: The case of Oman. In M. Martin (Ed.), Cross-border higher education: Regulation quality assurance and impact. Chile, Oman, Philippines, South Africa. New Trends in Higher Education. Paris: International Institute for Educational Planning (IIEP) UNESCO.

Wilkins, S. (2011). Who benefits from foreign universities in the Arab Gulf States? *Australian Universities Review, 53*(1), 73–83.

World Bank. (2007). *West Bank and Gaza Public Expenditure Review. Vol. 1: From Crisis to Greater Fiscal Independence.* Report No. 38207-WBG. Retrieved from: http://unispal.un.org/pdfs/38207WBGVol1.pdf

World Bank. (2017). *Tertiary Education Project.* Retrieved from: http://projects. worldbank.org/P083767/wbg-tertiary-education-project?lang=en

Yalçınkaya, M., Güngör, A. A., Yanar, A. İ., & Arslan, M. (2013). Türkiye'deki üniversitelerin uluslararasılaşma stratejileri. *Proceedings of the Eighth National Conference on Education Congress,* 481-482.

Yanosky, R. (2009). *Institutional Data Management in Higher Education.* Retrieved from: https://net.educause.edu/ir/library/pdf/ers0908/rs/ers0908w.pdf

Yemini, M., & Sagie, N. (2016). Research on internationalization in higher education – exploratory analysis. *Perspectives: Policy and Practice in Higher Education, 20*(23), 90–98. doi:10.1080/13603108.2015.1062057

Yen, E. (2015). Internationals at Birzeit University. *Palestine-Israel Journal of Politics, Economics and Culture.* Retrieved from: http://www.pij.org/details. php?blog=1&id=329

Yerkes, R., & Haras, K. (1997). *Outdoor education and environmental responsibility. Clearinghouse on Rural Education and Small Schools.* Appalachia Educational Laboratory.

Yılmaz, D. V. (2016). Internationalization of turkish state universities: An evaluation over strategic plans. Suleyman Demirel University. *The Journal of Faculty of Economics and Administrative Science, 21*(4), 1191–1212.

Zelkowitz, I. (2014). Education, Revolution and evolution: The Palestinian universities as initiators of national struggle 1972-1995. *Journal of the History of Education Society*, *43*(3), 387–407. doi:10.1080/0046760X.2014.889226

Zhetpisbayeva, B. A., Arinova, O. T., & Asylbekuly, D. A. (2012). Об опыте международной аккредитации образовательных программ КарГУ им. Е.А. Букетова [On the experience of international accreditation of educational programs in Buketov Karaganda State University]. *Вестник КарГУ*, *4*(68), 23–26.

Zong, J., & Batalova, J. (2016). *International Students in The USA*. Retrieved from http://www.migrationpolicy.org/article/international-students-united-states

Related References

To continue our tradition of advancing academic research, we have compiled a list of recommended IGI Global readings. These references will provide additional information and guidance to further enrich your knowledge and assist you with your own research and future publications.

Aburezeq, I. M., & Dweikat, F. F. (2017). Cloud Applications in Language Teaching: Examining Pre-Service Teachers' Expertise, Perceptions and Integration. *International Journal of Distance Education Technologies*, *15*(4), 39–60. doi:10.4018/IJDET.2017100103

Adera, B. (2017). Supporting Language and Literacy Development for English Language Learners. In J. Keengwe (Ed.), *Handbook of Research on Promoting Cross-Cultural Competence and Social Justice in Teacher Education* (pp. 339–354). Hershey, PA: IGI Global. doi:10.4018/978-1-5225-0897-7.ch018

Ahamer, G. (2011). How Technologies Can Localize Learners in Multicultural Space: A Newly Developed "Global Studies" Curriculum. *International Journal of Technology and Educational Marketing*, *1*(2), 1–24. doi:10.4018/ijtem.2011070101

Ahamer, G. (2015). Conclusions from Social Dynamics in Collaborative Environmental Didactics. *International Journal of Technology and Educational Marketing*, *5*(2), 68–92. doi:10.4018/IJTEM.2015070105

Ahamer, G. (2015). Designing and Analyzing Social Dynamics for Collaborative: Environmental Didactics. *International Journal of Technology and Educational Marketing*, *5*(2), 46–67. doi:10.4018/IJTEM.2015070104

Ahamer, G. (2017). Quality Assurance for a Developmental "Global Studies" (GS) Curriculum. In I. Management Association (Ed.), *Educational Leadership and Administration: Concepts, Methodologies, Tools, and Applications* (pp. 438-477). Hershey, PA: IGI Global. doi:10.4018/978-1-5225-1624-8.ch023

Ahamer, G. (2017). Quality Assurance for a Developmental "Global Studies" (GS) Curriculum. In I. Management Association (Ed.), *Educational Leadership and Administration: Concepts, Methodologies, Tools, and Applications* (pp. 438-477). Hershey, PA: IGI Global. doi:10.4018/978-1-5225-1624-8.ch023

Alegre de la Rosa, O. M., & Angulo, L. M. (2017). Social Inclusion and Intercultural Values in a School of Education. In S. Mukerji & P. Tripathi (Eds.), *Handbook of Research on Administration, Policy, and Leadership in Higher Education* (pp. 518–531). Hershey, PA: IGI Global. doi:10.4018/978-1-5225-0672-0.ch020

Ambikairajah, E., Sethu, V., Eaton, R., & Sheng, M. (2014). Evolving Use of Educational Technologies: Enhancing Lectures. In F. Alam (Ed.), *Using Technology Tools to Innovate Assessment, Reporting, and Teaching Practices in Engineering Education* (pp. 241–258). Hershey, PA: IGI Global. doi:10.4018/978-1-4666-5011-4.ch018

Anderson, K. M. (2017). Preparing Teachers in the Age of Equity and Inclusion. In I. Management Association (Ed.), *Medical Education and Ethics: Concepts, Methodologies, Tools, and Applications* (pp. 1532-1554). Hershey, PA: IGI Global. doi:10.4018/978-1-5225-0978-3.ch069

Awdziej, M. (2017). Case Study as a Teaching Method in Marketing. In D. Latusek (Ed.), *Case Studies as a Teaching Tool in Management Education* (pp. 244–263). Hershey, PA: IGI Global. doi:10.4018/978-1-5225-0770-3.ch013

Bain, B. (2014). Exploring Assessment of Critical Thinking Learning Outcomes in Online Higher Education. In V. Wang (Ed.), *Handbook of Research on Education and Technology in a Changing Society* (pp. 1191–1202). Hershey, PA: IGI Global. doi:10.4018/978-1-4666-6046-5.ch089

Banas, J. R., & York, C. S. (2017). Pre-Service Teachers' Motivation to Use Technology and the Impact of Authentic Learning Exercises. In L. Tomei (Ed.), *Exploring the New Era of Technology-Infused Education* (pp. 121–140). Hershey, PA: IGI Global. doi:10.4018/978-1-5225-1709-2.ch008

Bariso, E. U. (2015). Educational Policy Analysis Debates and New Learning Technologies in England. In M. Khosrow-Pour (Ed.), *Encyclopedia of Information Science and Technology* (3rd ed.; pp. 2371–2378). Hershey, PA: IGI Global. doi:10.4018/978-1-4666-5888-2.ch230

Beycioglu, K., & Wildy, H. (2015). Principal Preparation: The Case of Novice Principals in Turkey. In K. Beycioglu & P. Pashiardis (Eds.), *Multidimensional Perspectives on Principal Leadership Effectiveness* (pp. 1–17). Hershey, PA: IGI Global. doi:10.4018/978-1-4666-6591-0.ch001

Beycioglu, K., & Wildy, H. (2017). Principal Preparation: The Case of Novice Principals in Turkey. In I. Management Association (Ed.), Educational Leadership and Administration: Concepts, Methodologies, Tools, and Applications (pp. 1152-1169). Hershey, PA: IGI Global. doi:10.4018/978-1-5225-1624-8.ch054

Bharwani, S., & Musunuri, D. (2018). Reflection as a Process From Theory to Practice. In M. Khosrow-Pour, D.B.A. (Ed.), Encyclopedia of Information Science and Technology, Fourth Edition (pp. 1529-1539). Hershey, PA: IGI Global. doi:10.4018/978-1-5225-2255-3.ch132

Bisschoff, T., & Rhodes, C. (2011). Transformation through Marketing: A Case of a Secondary School in South Africa. In P. Tripathi & S. Mukerji (Eds.), *Cases on Innovations in Educational Marketing: Transnational and Technological Strategies* (pp. 263–272). Hershey, PA: IGI Global. doi:10.4018/978-1-60960-599-5.ch016

Bodomo, A. B. (2010). Educational Technologies (WebCT): Creating Constructivist and Interactive Learning Communities. In A. Bodomo (Ed.), *Computer-Mediated Communication for Linguistics and Literacy: Technology and Natural Language Education* (pp. 252–290). Hershey, PA: IGI Global. doi:10.4018/978-1-60566-868-0.ch010

Bohjanen, S. L., Cameron-Standerford, A., & Meidl, T. D. (2018). Capacity Building Pedagogy for Diverse Learners. In J. Keengwe (Ed.), *Handbook of Research on Pedagogical Models for Next-Generation Teaching and Learning* (pp. 195–212). Hershey, PA: IGI Global. doi:10.4018/978-1-5225-3873-8.ch011

Brewer, J. C. (2018). Measuring Text Readability Using Reading Level. In M. Khosrow-Pour, D.B.A. (Ed.), Encyclopedia of Information Science and Technology, Fourth Edition (pp. 1499-1507). Hershey, PA: IGI Global. doi:10.4018/978-1-5225-2255-3.ch129

Brown, S. L. (2017). A Case Study of Strategic Leadership and Research in Practice: Principal Preparation Programs that Work – An Educational Administration Perspective of Best Practices for Master's Degree Programs for Principal Preparation. In V. Wang (Ed.), *Encyclopedia of Strategic Leadership and Management* (pp. 1226–1244). Hershey, PA: IGI Global. doi:10.4018/978-1-5225-1049-9.ch086

Brzozowski, M., & Ferster, I. (2017). Educational Management Leadership: High School Principal's Management Style and Parental Involvement in School Management in Israel. In V. Potocan, M. Üngan, & Z. Nedelko (Eds.), *Handbook of Research on Managerial Solutions in Non-Profit Organizations* (pp. 55–74). Hershey, PA: IGI Global. doi:10.4018/978-1-5225-0731-4.ch003

Cannaday, J. (2017). The Masking Effect: Hidden Gifts and Disabilities of 2e Students. In P. Dickenson, P. Keough, & J. Courduff (Eds.), *Preparing Pre-Service Teachers for the Inclusive Classroom* (pp. 220–231). Hershey, PA: IGI Global. doi:10.4018/978-1-5225-1753-5.ch011

Capobianco, B. M., & Lehman, J. D. (2010). Fostering Educational Technology Integration in Science Teacher Education: Issues of Teacher Identity Development. In J. Yamamoto, J. Kush, R. Lombard, & C. Hertzog (Eds.), *Technology Implementation and Teacher Education: Reflective Models* (pp. 245–257). Hershey, PA: IGI Global. doi:10.4018/978-1-61520-897-5.ch014

Chao, G. H., Hsu, M. K., & Scovotti, C. (2013). Predicting Donations from a Cohort Group of Donors to Charities: A Direct Marketing Case Study. In J. Wang (Ed.), *Optimizing, Innovating, and Capitalizing on Information Systems for Operations* (pp. 196–214). Hershey, PA: IGI Global. doi:10.4018/978-1-4666-2925-7.ch010

Chauhan, A. (2015). Beyond the Phenomenon: Assessment in Massive Open Online Courses (MOOCs). In E. McKay & J. Lenarcic (Eds.), *Macro-Level Learning through Massive Open Online Courses (MOOCs): Strategies and Predictions for the Future* (pp. 119–140). Hershey, PA: IGI Global. doi:10.4018/978-1-4666-8324-2.ch007

Coffman, T. L., & Klinger, M. B. (2013). Managing Quality in Online Education. In G. Kurubacak & T. Yuzer (Eds.), *Project Management Approaches for Online Learning Design* (pp. 220–233). Hershey, PA: IGI Global. doi:10.4018/978-1-4666-2830-4.ch011

Contreras, E. C., & Contreras, I. I. (2018). Development of Communication Skills through Auditory Training Software in Special Education. In M. Khosrow-Pour, D.B.A. (Ed.), Encyclopedia of Information Science and Technology, Fourth Edition (pp. 2431-2441). Hershey, PA: IGI Global. doi:10.4018/978-1-5225-2255-3.ch212

Cook, R. G. (2011). Educational Marketing: Coming Down from the Cloud Using Landing Gear. In U. Demiray & S. Sever (Eds.), *Marketing Online Education Programs: Frameworks for Promotion and Communication* (pp. 26–31). Hershey, PA: IGI Global. doi:10.4018/978-1-60960-074-7.ch003

Cook, R. G., & Ley, K. (2015). Past, Future and Presents: Meeting New Online Challenges with Primal Marketing Solutions. *International Journal of Technology and Educational Marketing*, 5(2), 19–33. doi:10.4018/IJTEM.2015070102

Cooley, D., & Whitten, E. (2017). Special Education Leadership and the Implementation of Response to Intervention. In F. Topor (Ed.), *Handbook of Research on Individualism and Identity in the Globalized Digital Age* (pp. 265–286). Hershey, PA: IGI Global. doi:10.4018/978-1-5225-0522-8.ch012

Cosner, S., Tozer, S., & Zavitkovsky, P. (2017). Enacting a Cycle of Inquiry Capstone Research Project in Doctoral-Level Leadership Preparation. In I. Management Association (Ed.), Educational Leadership and Administration: Concepts, Methodologies, Tools, and Applications (pp. 1460-1481). Hershey, PA: IGI Global. doi:10.4018/978-1-5225-1624-8.ch067

Crawford, C. M. (2018). Instructional Real World Community Engagement. In M. Khosrow-Pour, D.B.A. (Ed.), Encyclopedia of Information Science and Technology, Fourth Edition (pp. 1474-1486). Hershey, PA: IGI Global. doi:10.4018/978-1-5225-2255-3.ch127

Crosby-Cooper, T., & Pacis, D. (2017). Implementing Effective Student Support Teams. In P. Dickenson, P. Keough, & J. Courduff (Eds.), *Preparing Pre-Service Teachers for the Inclusive Classroom* (pp. 248–262). Hershey, PA: IGI Global. doi:10.4018/978-1-5225-1753-5.ch013

Curran, C. M., & Hawbaker, B. W. (2017). Cultivating Communities of Inclusive Practice: Professional Development for Educators – Research and Practice. In C. Curran & A. Petersen (Eds.), *Handbook of Research on Classroom Diversity and Inclusive Education Practice* (pp. 120–153). Hershey, PA: IGI Global. doi:10.4018/978-1-5225-2520-2.ch006

Dass, S., & Dabbagh, N. (2018). Faculty Adoption of 3D Avatar-Based Virtual World Learning Environments: An Exploratory Case Study. In I. Management Association (Ed.), Technology Adoption and Social Issues: Concepts, Methodologies, Tools, and Applications (pp. 1000-1033). Hershey, PA: IGI Global. doi:10.4018/978-1-5225-5201-7.ch045

Davison, A. M., & Scholl, K. G. (2017). Inclusive Recreation as Part of the IEP Process. In C. Curran & A. Petersen (Eds.), *Handbook of Research on Classroom Diversity and Inclusive Education Practice* (pp. 311–330). Hershey, PA: IGI Global. doi:10.4018/978-1-5225-2520-2.ch013

DeCoito, I. (2018). Addressing Digital Competencies, Curriculum Development, and Instructional Design in Science Teacher Education. In M. Khosrow-Pour, D.B.A. (Ed.), Encyclopedia of Information Science and Technology, Fourth Edition (pp. 1420-1431). Hershey, PA: IGI Global. doi:10.4018/978-1-5225-2255-3.ch122

DeCoito, I., & Richardson, T. (2017). Beyond Angry Birds™: Using Web-Based Tools to Engage Learners and Promote Inquiry in STEM Learning. In I. Levin & D. Tsybulsky (Eds.), *Digital Tools and Solutions for Inquiry-Based STEM Learning* (pp. 166–196). Hershey, PA: IGI Global. doi:10.4018/978-1-5225-2525-7.ch007

Delmas, P. M. (2017). Research-Based Leadership for Next-Generation Leaders. In R. Styron Jr & J. Styron (Eds.), *Comprehensive Problem-Solving and Skill Development for Next-Generation Leaders* (pp. 1–39). Hershey, PA: IGI Global. doi:10.4018/978-1-5225-1968-3.ch001

Demiray, U., & Ekren, G. (2018). Administrative-Related Evaluation for Distance Education Institutions in Turkey. In K. Buyuk, S. Kocdar, & A. Bozkurt (Eds.), *Administrative Leadership in Open and Distance Learning Programs* (pp. 263–288). Hershey, PA: IGI Global. doi:10.4018/978-1-5225-2645-2.ch011

Dickenson, P. (2017). What do we Know and Where Can We Grow?: Teachers Preparation for the Inclusive Classroom. In P. Dickenson, P. Keough, & J. Courduff (Eds.), *Preparing Pre-Service Teachers for the Inclusive Classroom* (pp. 1–22). Hershey, PA: IGI Global. doi:10.4018/978-1-5225-1753-5.ch001

Dickerson, J., & Coleman, H. V. (2012). Technology, E-Leadership and Educational Administration in Schools: Integrating Standards with Context and Guiding Questions. In V. Wang (Ed.), *Encyclopedia of E-Leadership, Counseling and Training* (pp. 408–422). Hershey, PA: IGI Global. doi:10.4018/978-1-61350-068-2.ch030

Dickerson, J., Coleman, H. V., & Geer, G. (2012). Thinking like a School Technology Leader. In V. Wang (Ed.), *Technology and Its Impact on Educational Leadership: Innovation and Change* (pp. 53–63). Hershey, PA: IGI Global. doi:10.4018/978-1-4666-0062-1.ch005

Donne, V., & Hansen, M. (2017). Teachers' Use of Assistive Technologies in Education. In L. Tomei (Ed.), *Exploring the New Era of Technology-Infused Education* (pp. 86–101). Hershey, PA: IGI Global. doi:10.4018/978-1-5225-1709-2.ch006

Donne, V., & Hansen, M. A. (2018). Business and Technology Educators: Practices for Inclusion. In I. Management Association (Ed.), Business Education and Ethics: Concepts, Methodologies, Tools, and Applications (pp. 471-484). Hershey, PA: IGI Global. doi:10.4018/978-1-5225-3153-1.ch026

Dreon, O., Shettel, J., & Bower, K. M. (2017). Preparing Next Generation Elementary Teachers for the Tools of Tomorrow. In M. Grassetti & S. Brookby (Eds.), *Advancing Next-Generation Teacher Education through Digital Tools and Applications* (pp. 143–159). Hershey, PA: IGI Global. doi:10.4018/978-1-5225-0965-3.ch008

Drinka, D., Voge, K., & Yen, M. Y. (2005). From Principles to Practice: Analyzing a Student Learning Outcomes Assessment System. *Journal of Cases on Information Technology*, 7(3), 37–56. doi:10.4018/jcit.2005070103

Durak, H. Y., & Güyer, T. (2018). Design and Development of an Instructional Program for Teaching Programming Processes to Gifted Students Using Scratch. In J. Cannaday (Ed.), *Curriculum Development for Gifted Education Programs* (pp. 61–99). Hershey, PA: IGI Global. doi:10.4018/978-1-5225-3041-1.ch004

Egorkina, E., Ivanov, M., & Valyavskiy, A. Y. (2018). Students' Research Competence Formation of the Quality of Open and Distance Learning. In V. Mkrttchian & L. Belyanina (Eds.), *Handbook of Research on Students' Research Competence in Modern Educational Contexts* (pp. 364–384). Hershey, PA: IGI Global. doi:10.4018/978-1-5225-3485-3.ch019

Ekren, G., Karataş, S., & Demiray, U. (2017). Understanding of Leadership in Distance Education Management. In I. Management Association (Ed.), Educational Leadership and Administration: Concepts, Methodologies, Tools, and Applications (pp. 34-50). Hershey, PA: IGI Global. doi:10.4018/978-1-5225-1624-8.ch003

Elmore, W. M., Young, J. K., Harris, S., & Mason, D. (2017). The Relationship between Individual Student Attributes and Online Course Completion. In K. Shelton & K. Pedersen (Eds.), *Handbook of Research on Building, Growing, and Sustaining Quality E-Learning Programs* (pp. 151–173). Hershey, PA: IGI Global. doi:10.4018/978-1-5225-0877-9.ch008

Ercegovac, I. R., Alfirević, N., & Koludrović, M. (2017). School Principals' Communication and Co-Operation Assessment: The Croatian Experience. In I. Management Association (Ed.), Educational Leadership and Administration: Concepts, Methodologies, Tools, and Applications (pp. 1568-1589). Hershey, PA: IGI Global. doi:10.4018/978-1-5225-1624-8.ch072

Everhart, D., & Seymour, D. M. (2017). Challenges and Opportunities in the Currency of Higher Education. In K. Rasmussen, P. Northrup, & R. Colson (Eds.), *Handbook of Research on Competency-Based Education in University Settings* (pp. 41–65). Hershey, PA: IGI Global. doi:10.4018/978-1-5225-0932-5.ch003

Farmer, L. S. (2017). Managing Portable Technologies for Special Education. In V. Wang (Ed.), *Encyclopedia of Strategic Leadership and Management* (pp. 977–987). Hershey, PA: IGI Global. doi:10.4018/978-1-5225-1049-9.ch068

Farmer, L. S. (2018). Optimizing OERs for Optimal ICT Literacy in Higher Education. In J. Keengwe (Ed.), *Handbook of Research on Mobile Technology, Constructivism, and Meaningful Learning* (pp. 366–390). Hershey, PA: IGI Global. doi:10.4018/978-1-5225-3949-0.ch020

Fındık, L. Y. (2017). Self-Assessment of Principals Based on Leadership in Complexity. In I. Management Association (Ed.), Educational Leadership and Administration: Concepts, Methodologies, Tools, and Applications (pp. 978-991). Hershey, PA: IGI Global. doi:10.4018/978-1-5225-1624-8.ch047

Flor, A. G., & Gonzalez-Flor, B. (2018). Dysfunctional Digital Demeanors: Tales From (and Policy Implications of) eLearning's Dark Side. In I. Management Association (Ed.), The Dark Web: Breakthroughs in Research and Practice (pp. 37-50). Hershey, PA: IGI Global. doi:10.4018/978-1-5225-3163-0.ch003

Floyd, K. K., & Shambaugh, N. (2017). Instructional Design for Simulations in Special Education Virtual Learning Spaces. In T. Kidd & L. Morris Jr., (Eds.), *Handbook of Research on Instructional Systems and Educational Technology* (pp. 202–215). Hershey, PA: IGI Global. doi:10.4018/978-1-5225-2399-4.ch018

Giovannini, J. M. (2017). Technology Integration in Preservice Teacher Education Programs: Research-based Recommendations. In M. Grassetti & S. Brookby (Eds.), *Advancing Next-Generation Teacher Education through Digital Tools and Applications* (pp. 82–102). Hershey, PA: IGI Global. doi:10.4018/978-1-5225-0965-3.ch005

Good, S., & Clarke, V. B. (2017). An Integral Analysis of One Urban School System's Efforts to Support Student-Centered Teaching. In J. Keengwe & G. Onchwari (Eds.), *Handbook of Research on Learner-Centered Pedagogy in Teacher Education and Professional Development* (pp. 45–68). Hershey, PA: IGI Global. doi:10.4018/978-1-5225-0892-2.ch003

Grobler, B. (2015). The Relationship between Emotional Competence and Instructional Leadership and Their Association with Learner Achievement. In K. Beycioglu & P. Pashiardis (Eds.), *Multidimensional Perspectives on Principal Leadership Effectiveness* (pp. 373–407). Hershey, PA: IGI Global. doi:10.4018/978-1-4666-6591-0.ch017

Hamidi, F., Owuor, P. M., Hynie, M., Baljko, M., & McGrath, S. (2017). Potentials of Digital Assistive Technology and Special Education in Kenya. In C. Ayo & V. Mbarika (Eds.), *Sustainable ICT Adoption and Integration for Socio-Economic Development* (pp. 125–151). Hershey, PA: IGI Global. doi:10.4018/978-1-5225-2565-3.ch006

Heavin, C., & Neville, K. (2015). Addressing the Learning Needs of Future IS Security Professionals through Social Media Technology. In M. Khosrow-Pour (Ed.), *Encyclopedia of Information Science and Technology* (3rd ed.; pp. 4766–4775). Hershey, PA: IGI Global. doi:10.4018/978-1-4666-5888-2.ch468

Henderson, L. K. (2017). Meltdown at Fukushima: Global Catastrophic Events, Visual Literacy, and Art Education. In R. Shin (Ed.), *Convergence of Contemporary Art, Visual Culture, and Global Civic Engagement* (pp. 80–99). Hershey, PA: IGI Global. doi:10.4018/978-1-5225-1665-1.ch005

Hismanoglu, M. (2012). Important Issues in Online Education: E-Pedagogy and Marketing. In I. Management Association (Ed.), E-Marketing: Concepts, Methodologies, Tools, and Applications (pp. 676-701). Hershey, PA: IGI Global. doi:10.4018/978-1-4666-1598-4.ch041

Howard, B. C. (2008). Common Features and Design Principles Found in Exemplary Educational Technologies. *International Journal of Information and Communication Technology Education, 4*(4), 31–52. doi:10.4018/jicte.2008100104

Howard, B. C., & Tomei, L. A. (2008). The Classroom of the Future and Emerging Educational Technologies: Introduction to the Special Issue. *International Journal of Information and Communication Technology Education, 4*(4), 1–8. doi:10.4018/jicte.2008100101

Hudgins, T., & Holland, J. L. (2018). Digital Badges: Tracking Knowledge Acquisition Within an Innovation Framework. In I. Management Association (Ed.), Wearable Technologies: Concepts, Methodologies, Tools, and Applications (pp. 1118-1132). Hershey, PA: IGI Global. doi:10.4018/978-1-5225-5484-4.ch051

Ion, G., Tomàs, M., Castro, D., & Salat, E. (2015). Analysis of the Tasks of School Principals in Secondary Education in Catalonia: Case Study. In K. Beycioglu & P. Pashiardis (Eds.), *Multidimensional Perspectives on Principal Leadership Effectiveness* (pp. 39–58). Hershey, PA: IGI Global. doi:10.4018/978-1-4666-6591-0.ch003

Janus, M., & Siddiqua, A. (2018). Challenges for Children With Special Health Needs at the Time of Transition to School. In I. Management Association (Ed.), *Autism Spectrum Disorders: Breakthroughs in Research and Practice* (pp. 339-371). Hershey, PA: IGI Global. doi:10.4018/978-1-5225-3827-1.ch018

Jesus, R. A. (2018). Screencasts and Learning Styles. In M. Khosrow-Pour, D.B.A. (Ed.), Encyclopedia of Information Science and Technology, Fourth Edition (pp. 1548-1558). Hershey, PA: IGI Global. doi:10.4018/978-1-5225-2255-3.ch134

Kaplan-Rakowski, R., & Rakowski, D. (2011). Educational Technologies for the Neomillennial Generation. In E. Dunkels, G. Franberg, & C. Hallgren (Eds.), *Interactive Media Use and Youth: Learning, Knowledge Exchange and Behavior* (pp. 12–31). Hershey, PA: IGI Global. doi:10.4018/978-1-60960-206-2.ch002

Karpinski, A. C., D'Agostino, J. V., Williams, A. K., Highland, S. A., & Mellott, J. A. (2018). The Relationship Between Online Formative Assessment and State Test Scores Using Multilevel Modeling. In M. Khosrow-Pour, D.B.A. (Ed.), Encyclopedia of Information Science and Technology, Fourth Edition (pp. 5183-5192). Hershey, PA: IGI Global. doi:10.4018/978-1-5225-2255-3.ch450

Kats, Y. (2017). Educational Leadership and Integrated Support for Students with Autism Spectrum Disorders. In I. Management Association (Ed.), *Educational Leadership and Administration: Concepts, Methodologies, Tools, and Applications* (pp. 101-114). Hershey, PA: IGI Global. doi:10.4018/978-1-5225-1624-8.ch007

Kaya, G., & Altun, A. (2018). Educational Ontology Development. In M. Khosrow-Pour, D.B.A. (Ed.), Encyclopedia of Information Science and Technology, Fourth Edition (pp. 1441-1450). Hershey, PA: IGI Global. doi:10.4018/978-1-5225-2255-3.ch124

Keough, P. D., & Pacis, D. (2017). Best Practices Implementing Special Education Curriculum and Common Core State Standards using UDL. In P. Dickenson, P. Keough, & J. Courduff (Eds.), *Preparing Pre-Service Teachers for the Inclusive Classroom* (pp. 107–123). Hershey, PA: IGI Global. doi:10.4018/978-1-5225-1753-5.ch006

Kilburn, M., Henckell, M., & Starrett, D. (2018). Factors Contributing to the Effectiveness of Online Students and Instructors. In M. Khosrow-Pour, D.B.A. (Ed.), Encyclopedia of Information Science and Technology, Fourth Edition (pp. 1451-1462). Hershey, PA: IGI Global. doi:10.4018/978-1-5225-2255-3.ch125

Konecny, L. T. (2017). Hybrid, Online, and Flipped Classrooms in Health Science: Enhanced Learning Environments. In I. Management Association (Ed.), Flipped Instruction: Breakthroughs in Research and Practice (pp. 355-370). Hershey, PA: IGI Global. doi:10.4018/978-1-5225-1803-7.ch020

Kowch, E. G. (2013). Towards Leading Diverse, Smarter and More Adaptable Organizations that Learn. In J. Lewis, A. Green, & D. Surry (Eds.), *Technology as a Tool for Diversity Leadership: Implementation and Future Implications* (pp. 11–34). Hershey, PA: IGI Global. doi:10.4018/978-1-4666-2668-3.ch002

Krezmien, M., Powell, W., Bosch, C., Hall, T., & Nieswandt, M. (2017). The Use of Tablet Technology to Support Inquiry Science for Students Incarcerated in Juvenile Justice Settings. In I. Levin & D. Tsybulsky (Eds.), *Optimizing STEM Education With Advanced ICTs and Simulations* (pp. 267–295). Hershey, PA: IGI Global. doi:10.4018/978-1-5225-2528-8.ch011

Leach, L. F., Winn, P., Erwin, S., & Benedict, L. P. (2015). What 21st Century Students Want: Factors that Influence Student Selection of Educational Leadership Graduate Programs. *International Journal of Technology and Educational Marketing*, *5*(1), 15–28. doi:10.4018/ijtem.2015010102

Leng, H. K. (2014). An Update on the Use of Facebook as a Marketing Tool by Private Educational Institutions in Singapore. In I. Lee (Ed.), *Trends in E-Business, E-Services, and E-Commerce: Impact of Technology on Goods, Services, and Business Transactions* (pp. 191–205). Hershey, PA: IGI Global. doi:10.4018/978-1-4666-4510-3.ch011

Leone, S. (2018). An Open Learning Format for Lifelong Learners' Empowerment. In M. Khosrow-Pour, D.B.A. (Ed.), Encyclopedia of Information Science and Technology, Fourth Edition (pp. 1517-1528). Hershey, PA: IGI Global. doi:10.4018/978-1-5225-2255-3.ch131

Ley, K., & Gannon-Cook, R. (2010). Marketing a Blended University Program: An Action Research Case Study. In S. Mukerji & P. Tripathi (Eds.), *Cases on Technology Enhanced Learning through Collaborative Opportunities* (pp. 73–90). Hershey, PA: IGI Global. doi:10.4018/978-1-61520-751-0.ch005

Loose, W., & Marcos, T. (2016). Instructional Design for Millennials: Instructor Efficiency in Streamlining Content, Assignments, and Assessments. In P. Dickenson & J. Jaurez (Eds.), *Increasing Productivity and Efficiency in Online Teaching* (pp. 1–25). Hershey, PA: IGI Global. doi:10.4018/978-1-5225-0347-7.ch001

Lovell, K. L. (2017). Development and Evaluation of Neuroscience Computer-Based Modules for Medical Students: Instructional Design Principles and Effectiveness. In J. Stefaniak (Ed.), *Advancing Medical Education Through Strategic Instructional Design* (pp. 262–276). Hershey, PA: IGI Global. doi:10.4018/978-1-5225-2098-6.ch013

Manuel, N. N. (2016). Angolan Higher Education, Policy, and Leadership: Towards Transformative Leadership for Social Justice. In N. Ololube (Ed.), *Handbook of Research on Organizational Justice and Culture in Higher Education Institutions* (pp. 164–188). Hershey, PA: IGI Global. doi:10.4018/978-1-4666-9850-5.ch007

Marouchou, D. V. (2015). The Impact of Academic Beliefs on Student Learning. In M. Khosrow-Pour (Ed.), *Encyclopedia of Information Science and Technology* (3rd ed.; pp. 4796–4804). Hershey, PA: IGI Global. doi:10.4018/978-1-4666-5888-2.ch471

McCormack, V. F., Stauffer, M., Fishley, K., Hohenbrink, J., Mascazine, J. R., & Zigler, T. (2018). Designing a Dual Licensure Path for Middle Childhood and Special Education Teacher Candidates. In D. Polly, M. Putman, T. Petty, & A. Good (Eds.), *Innovative Practices in Teacher Preparation and Graduate-Level Teacher Education Programs* (pp. 21–36). Hershey, PA: IGI Global. doi:10.4018/978-1-5225-3068-8.ch002

McDaniel, R. (2017). Strategic Leadership in Instructional Design: Applying the Principles of Instructional Design through the Lens of Strategic Leadership to Distance Education. In V. Wang (Ed.), *Encyclopedia of Strategic Leadership and Management* (pp. 1570–1584). Hershey, PA: IGI Global. doi:10.4018/978-1-5225-1049-9.ch109

Memon, R. N., Ahmad, R., & Salim, S. S. (2018). Critical Issues in Requirements Engineering Education. In I. Management Association (Ed.), Computer Systems and Software Engineering: Concepts, Methodologies, Tools, and Applications (pp. 1953-1976). Hershey, PA: IGI Global. doi:10.4018/978-1-5225-3923-0.ch081

Mendenhall, R. (2017). Western Governors University: CBE Innovator and National Model. In K. Rasmussen, P. Northrup, & R. Colson (Eds.), *Handbook of Research on Competency-Based Education in University Settings* (pp. 379–400). Hershey, PA: IGI Global. doi:10.4018/978-1-5225-0932-5.ch019

Mense, E. G., Griggs, D. M., & Shanks, J. N. (2018). School Leaders in a Time of Accountability and Data Use: Preparing Our Future School Leaders in Leadership Preparation Programs. In E. Mense & M. Crain-Dorough (Eds.), *Data Leadership for K-12 Schools in a Time of Accountability* (pp. 235–259). Hershey, PA: IGI Global. doi:10.4018/978-1-5225-3188-3.ch012

Mense, E. G., Griggs, D. M., & Shanks, J. N. (2018). School Leaders in a Time of Accountability and Data Use: Preparing Our Future School Leaders in Leadership Preparation Programs. In E. Mense & M. Crain-Dorough (Eds.), *Data Leadership for K-12 Schools in a Time of Accountability* (pp. 235–259). Hershey, PA: IGI Global. doi:10.4018/978-1-5225-3188-3.ch012

Mestry, R., & Naicker, S. R. (2017). Exploring Distributive Leadership in South African Public Primary Schools in the Soweto Region. In I. Management Association (Ed.), Educational Leadership and Administration: Concepts, Methodologies, Tools, and Applications (pp. 1041-1064). Hershey, PA: IGI Global. doi:10.4018/978-1-5225-1624-8.ch050

Monaghan, C. H., & Boboc, M. (2017). (Re) Defining Leadership in Higher Education in the U.S. In V. Wang (Ed.), *Encyclopedia of Strategic Leadership and Management* (pp. 567–579). Hershey, PA: IGI Global. doi:10.4018/978-1-5225-1049-9.ch040

Muthee, J. M., & Murungi, C. G. (2018). Relationship Among Intelligence, Achievement Motivation, Type of School, and Academic Performance of Kenyan Urban Primary School Pupils. In M. Khosrow-Pour, D.B.A. (Ed.), Encyclopedia of Information Science and Technology, Fourth Edition (pp. 1540-1547). Hershey, PA: IGI Global. doi:10.4018/978-1-5225-2255-3.ch133

Naranjo, J. (2018). Meeting the Need for Inclusive Educators Online: Teacher Education in Inclusive Special Education and Dual-Certification. In D. Polly, M. Putman, T. Petty, & A. Good (Eds.), *Innovative Practices in Teacher Preparation and Graduate-Level Teacher Education Programs* (pp. 106–122). Hershey, PA: IGI Global. doi:10.4018/978-1-5225-3068-8.ch007

Nkabinde, Z. P. (2017). Multiculturalism in Special Education: Perspectives of Minority Children in Urban Schools. In J. Keengwe (Ed.), *Handbook of Research on Promoting Cross-Cultural Competence and Social Justice in Teacher Education* (pp. 382–397). Hershey, PA: IGI Global. doi:10.4018/978-1-5225-0897-7.ch020

Nkabinde, Z. P. (2018). Online Instruction: Is the Quality the Same as Face-to-Face Instruction? In J. Keengwe (Ed.), *Handbook of Research on Digital Content, Mobile Learning, and Technology Integration Models in Teacher Education* (pp. 300–314). Hershey, PA: IGI Global. doi:10.4018/978-1-5225-2953-8.ch016

O'Connor, J. R. Jr, & Jackson, K. N. (2017). The Use of iPad® Devices and "Apps" for ASD Students in Special Education and Speech Therapy. In Y. Kats (Ed.), *Supporting the Education of Children with Autism Spectrum Disorders* (pp. 267–283). Hershey, PA: IGI Global. doi:10.4018/978-1-5225-0816-8.ch014

Okolie, U. C., & Yasin, A. M. (2017). TVET in Developing Nations and Human Development. In U. Okolie & A. Yasin (Eds.), *Technical Education and Vocational Training in Developing Nations* (pp. 1–25). Hershey, PA: IGI Global. doi:10.4018/978-1-5225-1811-2.ch001

Paciga, K. A., & Hoffman, J. L. (2015). Realizing the Potential of e-Books in Early Education. In M. Khosrow-Pour (Ed.), *Encyclopedia of Information Science and Technology* (3rd ed.; pp. 4787–4795). Hershey, PA: IGI Global. doi:10.4018/978-1-4666-5888-2.ch470

Paulson, E. N. (2017). Adapting and Advocating for an Online EdD Program in Changing Times and "Sacred" Cultures. In I. Management Association (Ed.), Educational Leadership and Administration: Concepts, Methodologies, Tools, and Applications (pp. 1849-1876). Hershey, PA: IGI Global. doi:10.4018/978-1-5225-1624-8.ch085

Petersen, A. J., Elser, C. F., Al Nassir, M. N., Stakey, J., & Everson, K. (2017). The Year of Teaching Inclusively: Building an Elementary Classroom for All Students. In C. Curran & A. Petersen (Eds.), *Handbook of Research on Classroom Diversity and Inclusive Education Practice* (pp. 332–348). Hershey, PA: IGI Global. doi:10.4018/978-1-5225-2520-2.ch014

Pfannenstiel, K. H., & Sanders, J. (2017). Characteristics and Instructional Strategies for Students With Mathematical Difficulties: In the Inclusive Classroom. In C. Curran & A. Petersen (Eds.), *Handbook of Research on Classroom Diversity and Inclusive Education Practice* (pp. 250–281). Hershey, PA: IGI Global. doi:10.4018/978-1-5225-2520-2.ch011

Preast, J. L., Bowman, N., & Rose, C. A. (2017). Creating Inclusive Classroom Communities Through Social and Emotional Learning to Reduce Social Marginalization Among Students. In C. Curran & A. Petersen (Eds.), *Handbook of Research on Classroom Diversity and Inclusive Education Practice* (pp. 183–200). Hershey, PA: IGI Global. doi:10.4018/978-1-5225-2520-2.ch008

Randolph, K. M., & Brady, M. P. (2018). Evolution of Covert Coaching as an Evidence-Based Practice in Professional Development and Preparation of Teachers. In V. Bryan, A. Musgrove, & J. Powers (Eds.), *Handbook of Research on Human Development in the Digital Age* (pp. 281–299). Hershey, PA: IGI Global. doi:10.4018/978-1-5225-2838-8.ch013

Rawlins, P., & Kehrwald, B. (2010). Education Technology in Teacher Education: Overcoming Challenges, Realizing Opportunities. In R. Luppicini & A. Haghi (Eds.), *Cases on Digital Technologies in Higher Education: Issues and Challenges* (pp. 50–63). Hershey, PA: IGI Global. doi:10.4018/978-1-61520-869-2.ch004

Rell, A. B., Puig, R. A., Roll, F., Valles, V., Espinoza, M., & Duque, A. L. (2017). Addressing Cultural Diversity and Global Competence: The Dual Language Framework. In L. Leavitt, S. Wisdom, & K. Leavitt (Eds.), *Cultural Awareness and Competency Development in Higher Education* (pp. 111–131). Hershey, PA: IGI Global. doi:10.4018/978-1-5225-2145-7.ch007

Riel, J., Lawless, K. A., & Brown, S. W. (2017). Defining and Designing Responsive Online Professional Development (ROPD): A Framework to Support Curriculum Implementation. In T. Kidd & L. Morris Jr., (Eds.), *Handbook of Research on Instructional Systems and Educational Technology* (pp. 104–115). Hershey, PA: IGI Global. doi:10.4018/978-1-5225-2399-4.ch010

Roberts, C. (2017). Advancing Women Leaders in Academe: Creating a Culture of Inclusion. In S. Mukerji & P. Tripathi (Eds.), *Handbook of Research on Administration, Policy, and Leadership in Higher Education* (pp. 256–273). Hershey, PA: IGI Global. doi:10.4018/978-1-5225-0672-0.ch012

Rodgers, W. J., Kennedy, M. J., Alves, K. D., & Romig, J. E. (2017). A Multimedia Tool for Teacher Education and Professional Development. In C. Martin & D. Polly (Eds.), *Handbook of Research on Teacher Education and Professional Development* (pp. 285–296). Hershey, PA: IGI Global. doi:10.4018/978-1-5225-1067-3.ch015

Romanowski, M. H. (2017). Qatar's Educational Reform: Critical Issues Facing Principals. In I. Management Association (Ed.), Educational Leadership and Administration: Concepts, Methodologies, Tools, and Applications (pp. 1758-1773). Hershey, PA: IGI Global. doi:10.4018/978-1-5225-1624-8.ch080

Ruffin, T. R., Hawkins, D. P., & Lee, D. I. (2018). Increasing Student Engagement and Participation Through Course Methodology. In M. Khosrow-Pour, D.B.A. (Ed.), Encyclopedia of Information Science and Technology, Fourth Edition (pp. 1463-1473). Hershey, PA: IGI Global. doi:10.4018/978-1-5225-2255-3.ch126

Rutaisire, J. (2011). Innovations in Technology for Educational Marketing: Stakeholder Perceptions and Implications for Examinations System in Rwanda. In P. Tripathi & S. Mukerji (Eds.), *Cases on Innovations in Educational Marketing: Transnational and Technological Strategies* (pp. 214–233). Hershey, PA: IGI Global. doi:10.4018/978-1-60960-599-5.ch013

Related References

Sabina, L. L., Curry, K. A., Harris, E. L., Krumm, B. L., & Vencill, V. (2017). Assessing the Performance of a Cohort-Based Model Using Domestic and International Practices. In I. Management Association (Ed.), Educational Leadership and Administration: Concepts, Methodologies, Tools, and Applications(pp. 913-929). Hershey, PA: IGI Global. doi:10.4018/978-1-5225-1624-8.ch044

Santamaría, A. P., Webber, M., & Santamaría, L. J. (2017). Effective School Leadership for Māori Achievement: Building Capacity through Indigenous, National, and International Cross-Cultural Collaboration. In I. Management Association (Ed.), Educational Leadership and Administration: Concepts, Methodologies, Tools, and Applications (pp. 1547-1567). Hershey, PA: IGI Global. doi:10.4018/978-1-5225-1624-8.ch071

Santamaría, L. J. (2017). Culturally Responsive Educational Leadership in Cross-Cultural International Contexts. In I. Management Association (Ed.), Educational Leadership and Administration: Concepts, Methodologies, Tools, and Applications (pp. 1380-1400). Hershey, PA: IGI Global. doi:10.4018/978-1-5225-1624-8.ch064

Sarafidou, J., & Xafakos, E. (2015). Transformational Leadership and Principals' Innovativeness: Are They the "Keys" for the Research and Innovation Oriented School? In K. Beycioglu & P. Pashiardis (Eds.), *Multidimensional Perspectives on Principal Leadership Effectiveness* (pp. 324–348). Hershey, PA: IGI Global. doi:10.4018/978-1-4666-6591-0.ch015

Segredo, M. R., Cistone, P. J., & Reio, T. G. (2017). Relationships Between Emotional Intelligence, Leadership Style, and School Culture. *International Journal of Adult Vocational Education and Technology, 8*(3), 25–43. doi:10.4018/IJAVET.2017070103

Shaik, N., & Ritter, S. (2012). Social Media Based Relationship Marketing. In I. Management Association (Ed.), E-Marketing: Concepts, Methodologies, Tools, and Applications (pp. 88-110). Hershey, PA: IGI Global. doi:10.4018/978-1-4666-1598-4.ch006

Shalev, N. (2017). Empathy and Leadership From the Organizational Perspective. In Z. Nedelko & M. Brzozowski (Eds.), *Exploring the Influence of Personal Values and Cultures in the Workplace* (pp. 348–363). Hershey, PA: IGI Global. doi:10.4018/978-1-5225-2480-9.ch018

Siamak, M., Fathi, S., & Isfandyari-Moghaddam, A. (2018). Assessment and Measurement of Education Programs of Information Literacy. In R. Bhardwaj (Ed.), *Digitizing the Modern Library and the Transition From Print to Electronic* (pp. 164–192). Hershey, PA: IGI Global. doi:10.4018/978-1-5225-2119-8.ch007

Siozos, P. D., & Palaigeorgiou, G. E. (2008). Educational Technologies and the Emergence of E-Learning 2.0. In D. Politis (Ed.), *E-Learning Methodologies and Computer Applications in Archaeology* (pp. 1–17). Hershey, PA: IGI Global. doi:10.4018/978-1-59904-759-1.ch001

Siu, K. W., & García, G. J. (2017). Disruptive Technologies and Education: Is There Any Disruption After All? In I. Management Association (Ed.), Educational Leadership and Administration: Concepts, Methodologies, Tools, and Applications (pp. 757-778). Hershey, PA: IGI Global. doi:10.4018/978-1-5225-1624-8.ch037

Skibba, K., Moore, D., & Herman, J. H. (2013). Pedagogical and Technological Considerations Designing Collaborative Learning Using Educational Technologies. In J. Keengwe (Ed.), *Research Perspectives and Best Practices in Educational Technology Integration* (pp. 1–27). Hershey, PA: IGI Global. doi:10.4018/978-1-4666-2988-2.ch001

Slagter van Tryon, P. J. (2017). The Nurse Educator's Role in Designing Instruction and Instructional Strategies for Academic and Clinical Settings. In J. Stefaniak (Ed.), *Advancing Medical Education Through Strategic Instructional Design* (pp. 133–149). Hershey, PA: IGI Global. doi:10.4018/978-1-5225-2098-6.ch006

Slattery, C. A. (2018). Literacy Intervention and the Differentiated Plan of Instruction. In *Developing Effective Literacy Intervention Strategies: Emerging Research and Opportunities* (pp. 41–62). Hershey, PA: IGI Global. doi:10.4018/978-1-5225-5007-5.ch003

Smith, A. R. (2017). Ensuring Quality: The Faculty Role in Online Higher Education. In K. Shelton & K. Pedersen (Eds.), *Handbook of Research on Building, Growing, and Sustaining Quality E-Learning Programs* (pp. 210–231). Hershey, PA: IGI Global. doi:10.4018/978-1-5225-0877-9.ch011

Souders, T. M. (2017). Understanding Your Learner: Conducting a Learner Analysis. In J. Stefaniak (Ed.), *Advancing Medical Education Through Strategic Instructional Design* (pp. 1–29). Hershey, PA: IGI Global. doi:10.4018/978-1-5225-2098-6.ch001

Spring, K. J., Graham, C. R., & Ikahihifo, T. B. (2018). Learner Engagement in Blended Learning. In M. Khosrow-Pour, D.B.A. (Ed.), Encyclopedia of Information Science and Technology, Fourth Edition (pp. 1487-1498). Hershey, PA: IGI Global. doi:10.4018/978-1-5225-2255-3.ch128

Stocklin, S. (2015). Building Capacity by Managing a Mission. In J. Feng, S. Stocklin, & W. Wang (Eds.), *Educational Strategies for the Next Generation Leaders in Hotel Management* (pp. 115–139). Hershey, PA: IGI Global. doi:10.4018/978-1-4666-8565-9.ch005

Related References

Storey, V. A., Anthony, A. K., & Wahid, P. (2017). Gender-Based Leadership Barriers: Advancement of Female Faculty to Leadership Positions in Higher Education. In V. Wang (Ed.), *Encyclopedia of Strategic Leadership and Management* (pp. 244–258). Hershey, PA: IGI Global. doi:10.4018/978-1-5225-1049-9.ch018

Stottlemyer, D. (2018). Develop a Teaching Model Plan for a Differentiated Learning Approach. In *Differentiated Instructional Design for Multicultural Environments: Emerging Research and Opportunities* (pp. 106–130). Hershey, PA: IGI Global. doi:10.4018/978-1-5225-5106-5.ch005

Stottlemyer, D. (2018). Developing a Multicultural Environment. In *Differentiated Instructional Design for Multicultural Environments: Emerging Research and Opportunities* (pp. 1–27). Hershey, PA: IGI Global. doi:10.4018/978-1-5225-5106-5.ch001

Swami, B. N., Gobona, T., & Tsimako, J. J. (2017). Academic Leadership: A Case Study of the University of Botswana. In N. Baporikar (Ed.), *Innovation and Shifting Perspectives in Management Education* (pp. 1–32). Hershey, PA: IGI Global. doi:10.4018/978-1-5225-1019-2.ch001

Swanson, K. W., & Collins, G. (2018). Designing Engaging Instruction for the Adult Learners. In M. Khosrow-Pour, D.B.A. (Ed.), Encyclopedia of Information Science and Technology, Fourth Edition (pp. 1432-1440). Hershey, PA: IGI Global. doi:10.4018/978-1-5225-2255-3.ch123

Swartz, B. A., Lynch, J. M., & Lynch, S. D. (2018). Embedding Elementary Teacher Education Coursework in Local Classrooms: Examples in Mathematics and Special Education. In D. Polly, M. Putman, T. Petty, & A. Good (Eds.), *Innovative Practices in Teacher Preparation and Graduate-Level Teacher Education Programs* (pp. 262–292). Hershey, PA: IGI Global. doi:10.4018/978-1-5225-3068-8.ch015

Taliadorou, N., & Pashiardis, P. (2015). Emotional Intelligence and Political Skill Really Matter in Educational Leadership. In K. Beycioglu & P. Pashiardis (Eds.), *Multidimensional Perspectives on Principal Leadership Effectiveness* (pp. 228–256). Hershey, PA: IGI Global. doi:10.4018/978-1-4666-6591-0.ch011

Taliadorou, N., & Pashiardis, P. (2017). Emotional Intelligence and Political Skill Really Matter in Educational Leadership. In I. Management Association (Ed.), Educational Leadership and Administration: Concepts, Methodologies, Tools, and Applications (pp. 1274-1303). Hershey, PA: IGI Global. doi:10.4018/978-1-5225-1624-8.ch060

Tam, F. W., & Kwan, P. Y. (2011). School Images, School Identity, and How Parents Select Schools for Their Children: The Case of Hong Kong. In P. Tripathi & S. Mukerji (Eds.), *Cases on Innovations in Educational Marketing: Transnational and Technological Strategies* (pp. 87–103). Hershey, PA: IGI Global. doi:10.4018/978-1-60960-599-5.ch005

Tandoh, K. A., & Ebe-Arthur, J. E. (2018). Effective Educational Leadership in the Digital Age: An Examination of Professional Qualities and Best Practices. In J. Keengwe (Ed.), *Handbook of Research on Digital Content, Mobile Learning, and Technology Integration Models in Teacher Education* (pp. 244–265). Hershey, PA: IGI Global. doi:10.4018/978-1-5225-2953-8.ch013

Tinoca, L., Pereira, A., & Oliveira, I. (2014). A Conceptual Framework for E-Assessment in Higher Education: Authenticity, Consistency, Transparency, and Practicability. In S. Mukerji & P. Tripathi (Eds.), *Handbook of Research on Transnational Higher Education* (pp. 652–673). Hershey, PA: IGI Global. doi:10.4018/978-1-4666-4458-8.ch033

Tobin, M. T. (2018). Multimodal Literacy. In M. Khosrow-Pour, D.B.A. (Ed.), Encyclopedia of Information Science and Technology, Fourth Edition (pp. 1508-1516). Hershey, PA: IGI Global. doi:10.4018/978-1-5225-2255-3.ch130

Torres, M. L., & Ramos, V. J. (2018). Music Therapy: A Pedagogical Alternative for ASD and ID Students in Regular Classrooms. In P. Epler (Ed.), *Instructional Strategies in General Education and Putting the Individuals With Disabilities Act (IDEA) Into Practice* (pp. 222–244). Hershey, PA: IGI Global. doi:10.4018/978-1-5225-3111-1.ch008

Toulassi, B. (2017). Educational Administration and Leadership in Francophone Africa: 5 Dynamics to Change Education. In S. Mukerji & P. Tripathi (Eds.), *Handbook of Research on Administration, Policy, and Leadership in Higher Education* (pp. 20–45). Hershey, PA: IGI Global. doi:10.4018/978-1-5225-0672-0.ch002

Umair, S., & Sharif, M. M. (2018). Predicting Students Grades Using Artificial Neural Networks and Support Vector Machine. In M. Khosrow-Pour, D.B.A. (Ed.), Encyclopedia of Information Science and Technology, Fourth Edition (pp. 5169-5182). Hershey, PA: IGI Global. doi:10.4018/978-1-5225-2255-3.ch449

Usman, L. M. (2011). Adult Education and Sustainable Learning Outcome of Rural Widows of Central Northern Nigeria. *International Journal of Adult Vocational Education and Technology*, 2(2), 25–41. doi:10.4018/javet.2011040103

Vettraino, L., Castello, V., Guspini, M., & Guglielman, E. (2018). Self-Awareness and Motivation Contrasting ESL and NEET Using the SAVE System. In M. Khosrow-Pour, D.B.A. (Ed.), Encyclopedia of Information Science and Technology, Fourth Edition (pp. 1559-1568). Hershey, PA: IGI Global. doi:10.4018/978-1-5225-2255-3.ch135

Wang, V. C. (2013). Marketing Educational Programs through Technology and the Right Philosophies. In P. Tripathi & S. Mukerji (Eds.), *Marketing Strategies for Higher Education Institutions: Technological Considerations and Practices* (pp. 15–24). Hershey, PA: IGI Global. doi:10.4018/978-1-4666-4014-6.ch002

Wiemelt, J. (2017). Critical Bilingual Leadership for Emergent Bilingual Students. In I. Management Association (Ed.), Educational Leadership and Administration: Concepts, Methodologies, Tools, and Applications (pp. 1606-1631). Hershey, PA: IGI Global. doi:10.4018/978-1-5225-1624-8.ch074

Williams, D. D. (2006). Measurement and Assessment Supporting Evaluation in Online Settings. In D. Williams, M. Hricko, & S. Howell (Eds.), *Online Assessment, Measurement and Evaluation: Emerging Practices* (pp. 1–9). Hershey, PA: IGI Global. doi:10.4018/978-1-59140-747-8.ch001

Wolf, F., Seyfarth, F. C., & Pflaum, E. (2018). Scalable Capacity-Building for Geographically Dispersed Learners: Designing the MOOC "Sustainable Energy in Small Island Developing States (SIDS)". In U. Pandey & V. Indrakanti (Eds.), *Open and Distance Learning Initiatives for Sustainable Development* (pp. 58–83). Hershey, PA: IGI Global. doi:10.4018/978-1-5225-2621-6.ch003

Woodley, X. M., Mucundanyi, G., & Lockard, M. (2017). Designing Counter-Narratives: Constructing Culturally Responsive Curriculum Online. *International Journal of Online Pedagogy and Course Design*, *7*(1), 43–56. doi:10.4018/IJOPCD.2017010104

Woods, P. A., & Woods, G. J. (2011). Lighting the Fires of Entrepreneurialism?: Constructions of Meaning in an English Inner City Academy. *International Journal of Technology and Educational Marketing*, *1*(1), 1–24. doi:10.4018/ijtem.2011010101

Yell, M. L., & Christle, C. A. (2017). The Foundation of Inclusion in Federal Legislation and Litigation. In C. Curran & A. Petersen (Eds.), *Handbook of Research on Classroom Diversity and Inclusive Education Practice* (pp. 27–52). Hershey, PA: IGI Global. doi:10.4018/978-1-5225-2520-2.ch002

Zhao, J. (2011). China Special Education: The Perspective of Information Technologies. In P. Ordóñez de Pablos, J. Zhao, & R. Tennyson (Eds.), *Technology Enhanced Learning for People with Disabilities: Approaches and Applications* (pp. 34–43). Hershey, PA: IGI Global. doi:10.4018/978-1-61520-923-1.ch003

Zinger, D. (2016). Developing Instructional Leadership and Communication Skills through Online Professional Development: Focusing on Rural and Urban Principals. In A. Normore, L. Long, & M. Javidi (Eds.), *Handbook of Research on Effective Communication, Leadership, and Conflict Resolution* (pp. 354–370). Hershey, PA: IGI Global. doi:10.4018/978-1-4666-9970-0.ch019

Zutshi, A., Pogrebnaya, M., & Fermelis, J. (2014). Wellness Programs in Higher Education: An Australian Case. In N. Baporikar (Ed.), *Handbook of Research on Higher Education in the MENA Region: Policy and Practice* (pp. 391–419). Hershey, PA: IGI Global. doi:10.4018/978-1-4666-6198-1.ch017

About the Contributors

Fatoş Silman was born in London in 1971. She did her BA and MA studies in English Language and Literature at Eastern Mediterranean University, North Cyprus. She completed her PhD in Educational Administration and Planning at Middle East Technical University, Turkey. She did one year academic research as an Honorary Fellow, at the University of Wisconsin-Madison, US between the years 2003-2004. Her research interests are gender issues in higher education, educational administration and educational sociology.

Zehra Altınay Gazi is teaching doctorate, graduate and undergraduate degree courses in Ataturk Education Faculty at Near East University. Zehra Altınay Gazi is the Vice Director of Institute of Educational Sciences. She is also board member of Distance Education Center. Further to this, Assoc. Prof. Dr. Zehra Altınay Gazi is the Director of Societal Research and Development Center. She is the section editor in education and science journal which is SSCI journal. Zehra Altınay Gazi has two national academic content books published by reputable publishing houses. Further to this, she has international academic content books. In addition, she has international book chapters published by reputable publishing housees. Zehra Altınay Gazi has articles which were indexed at Social Sciences Index (SSCI), international book chapters and international articles that were indexed at the Educational field indexes (British Education Index, ERIC, Science Direct, Scopus, etc.). She also presented scientific papers and reports at international conferences.

Fahriye Altınay is a Director of Graduate School of Educational Sciences at Near East University. Her research interest is educational management and technology. She is active on research projects on disability and technology for societal development. She is vice chair of societal research and development center.

* * *

Mehmet Altinay is the professor of Economics and Tourism management at Kyrenia University. He has more than 40 years of experience in industry and academia.

Amna Hashim Hamdan Alzadjali was born in the Sultanate of Oman. Amna studied their masters in Muutar University in Jordan, where Amna studied curriculum and methods of teaching mathematics. Amna works in Educational and Vocational college Oman for eleven years. Amna is presently undergoing their PhD in the department of Education administration control economy and planning.

Mustafa Cirakli completed his doctoral studies in Politics at Lancaster University (UK). During this time, he taught on various undergraduate and postgraduate courses at Lancaster University and the University of Manchester on comparative politics, IR theory and European studies. His primary areas of interest lie in the fields of identity, immigration and citizenship. On identity and immigration, his work focuses on unrecognized states and kin-states in international relations which has grown out of his work on local responses toward patron-states and their role in constructing counter-hegemonic/hybrid identities. On citizenship, he is interested in the linkages between competing notions of citizenship, globalization and the nation-state in the developing world.

Gokmen Dagli's research interest is educational management.

Aylin Goztas, Head of Public Relations Department of Faculty of Communications, Ege University. She has more than 20 books published in the field and plenty of publications. Her work mostly consists of risk and crisis management, total quality systems, business communications, project management, social movements, global trends.

Şerife Gündüz is an Assistant Professor in the Institute of Educational Sciences at Near East University. Since 2005 Şerife Gündüz has been tutoring Masters and PhD courses related to the field of Environmental Education. My research areas are environmental education and nature protection. Now Şerife Gündüz wors on the environmental education curriculum for primary schools in North Cyprus. Şerife Gündüz is the head of environmental education and management masters & pHD programmes of my University. Şerife Gündüz published various articles on environmental issues in international and national journals. One of Şerife Gündüz's research interests is "Migrant Adaptation - A Cross-Cultural Problem". Related with my studies, Şerife Gündüz is currently working on a Review of Research project about Migration, Minority Groups and Cultural Differences, with Special Regard to Children and Women.

Ainur Seitbattalovna Kenebayeva received her MIB in Hotel and Tourism Management from International College of Hospitality Administration Cesar Ritz (Switzerland) in 2011 and PhD in Tourism from Eurasian National University (Astana, Kazakhstan) in 2015. In 2015 she was hired by University of International Business (Almaty, Kazakhstan) and is currently Associate Professor for Management and Business Department. She writes and presents widely on issues of business and entrepreneurship, rural tourism, hospitality industry and marketing.

Umut Koldas is the director of the Near East Institute and Lifelong Education Center at the Near East University in Lefkosa, North Cyprus. He is an Associate Professor at the Department of International Relations at he same university. He received his two master degrees on International Relations from the Middle East Technical University and on Media and Communications from the London School of Economics respectively. He earned his PhD in International Relations at the Middle East Technical University. His research interests and publications include: new multi-dimensional and inter-disciplinary studies of security, issues of democratization, state-minority relations and citizenship in the Middle East and the Mediterranean region (with particular emphasis on Turkey and Israel) and representation of minorities in the media.

Keith John Lay is a Lecturer in Language Education at Cyprus International University in Nicosia, Cyprus. Lay takes a multidisciplinary approach to research due to a background in Criminology, Language Teaching, and Education. Lay has presented research studies on education technology in three countries as well as having a special interest in nonverbal communication in education.

Behcet Öznacar's research interest is educational management and risk management.

Emel Kusku Ozdemir was born in 1988 in Bulgaria. She is a doctoral student of Communication Research Program in the Department of Public Relations and Publicity in Ege University. She graduated from Ege University with her B.S. in Public Relations and Publicity in 2012. She is interested in doing research in the area of marketing communication and consumer behaviors.

M. Rajesh is Regional Director of Indira Gandhi National Open University, India.

Ramesh Sharma holds a Ph.D. in Education in the area of Educational Technology and is currently working as an Associate Professor of Educational Technology and Learning Resources in the Educational Technology and Publishing (ETP) Unit at Wawasan Open University, Malaysia. He has served as a Visiting Professor at University of Fiji, Fiji; Commonwealth of Learning as Director of the Commonwealth Educational Media Centre for Asia, New Delhi; Indira Gandhi National Open University, India; and University of Guyana, Guyana, South America. He is the co-Editor of the 'Asian Journal of Distance Education'. In addition, he has been associated with several peer reviewed journals as Reviewer, Editor and Editorial Advisory Board member in the field of Open and Distance Learning such as "Distance Education", "International Review of Research in Open and Distributed Learning (IRRODL)", "International Journal of Distance Education Technologies (IJDET)", and "Indian Journal of Open Learning (IJOL)". He is also on the Editorial Advisory Board and an author for the "Encyclopedia of Distance Learning (4 volumes), 2005" (https:// www.igi-global.com/book/encyclopedia-distance-learning/351).

Belal Shneikat is Assistant Professor of Business Administration at The University of Kyrenia. He has more than 5 years of experience in recruiting international students for some universities in North Cyprus. He got his B.Sc. degree in Regional Planning and Master of Business Administration from Al-Balqa' Applied University in Jordan in 2005 and 2008 respectively. PhD in Business Administration from Eastern Mediterranean University in 2016.

Fusun Topsumer is a Professor in the Department of Public Relations and Publicity at the Faculty of Communication, at Ege University, and is also the Chair of the Department of Research Methods. In addition to the author's books and book chapters, she has numerous international and national articles, papers and publications.

Index

Recommended Reference Books

ISBN: 978-1-5225-2145-7
© 2017; 408 pp.
List Price: $210

ISBN: 978-1-5225-2334-5
© 2017 ; 375 pp.
List Price: $195

ISBN: 978-1-5225-1718-4
© 2017; 457 pp.
List Price: $270

ISBN: 978-1-5225-0672-0
© 2017; 678 pp.
List Price: $295

ISBN: 978-1-5225-2630-8
© 2018; 209 pp.
List Price: $145

ISBN: 978-1-5225-1621-7
© 2017; 173 pp.
List Price: $135

Looking for free content, product updates, news, and special offers?
Join IGI Global's mailing list today and start enjoying exclusive perks sent only to IGI Global members.
Add your name to the list at **www.igi-global.com/newsletters.**

Publisher of Peer-Reviewed, Timely, and Innovative Academic Research

www.igi-global.com   ✉ Sign up at www.igi-global.com/newsletters   f facebook.com/igiglobal   t twitter.com/igiglobal

Ensure Quality Research is Introduced to the Academic Community

Become an IGI Global Reviewer for Authored Book Projects

The overall success of an authored book project is dependent on quality and timely reviews.

In this competitive age of scholarly publishing, constructive and timely feedback significantly expedites the turnaround time of manuscripts from submission to acceptance, allowing the publication and discovery of forward-thinking research at a much more expeditious rate. Several IGI Global authored book projects are currently seeking highly qualified experts in the field to fill vacancies on their respective editorial review boards:

Applications may be sent to:
development@igi-global.com

Applicants must have a doctorate (or an equivalent degree) as well as publishing and reviewing experience. Reviewers are asked to write reviews in a timely, collegial, and constructive manner. All reviewers will begin their role on an ad-hoc basis for a period of one year, and upon successful completion of this term can be considered for full editorial review board status, with the potential for a subsequent promotion to Associate Editor.

If you have a colleague that may be interested in this opportunity,
we encourage you to share this information with them.

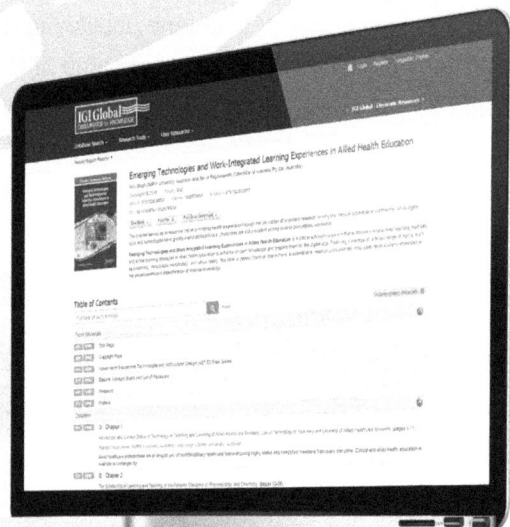

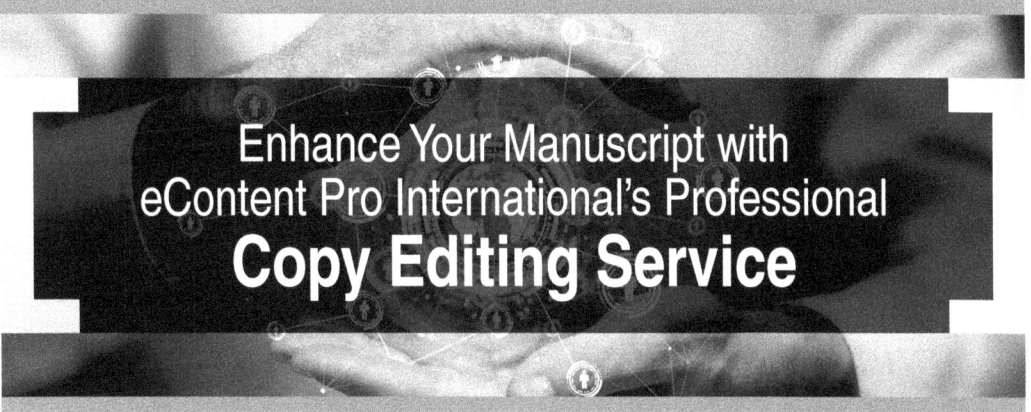

Information Resources Management Association

Advancing the Concepts & Practices of Information Resources Management in Modern Organizations

Become an IRMA Member

Members of the **Information Resources Management Association (IRMA)** understand the importance of community within their field of study. The Information Resources Management Association is an ideal venue through which professionals, students, and academicians can convene and share the latest industry innovations and scholarly research that is changing the field of information science and technology. Become a member today and enjoy the benefits of membership as well as the opportunity to collaborate and network with fellow experts in the field.

IRMA Membership Benefits:

- **One FREE Journal Subscription**

- **30% Off Additional Journal Subscriptions**

- **20% Off Book Purchases**

- Updates on the latest events and research on Information Resources Management through the IRMA-L listserv.

- Updates on new open access and downloadable content added to Research IRM.

- A copy of the Information Technology Management Newsletter twice a year.

- A certificate of membership.

IRMA Membership $195

Scan code or visit **irma-international.org** and begin by selecting your free journal subscription.

Membership is good for one full year.

Lightning Source UK Ltd.
Milton Keynes UK
UKHW051003051118
331795UK00013B/1627/P